GOD's MAN
in Babylon

The Visions and Prophecies
of Daniel

GOD's MAN in Babylon

The Visions and Prophecies of Daniel

HAROLD A. SEVENER

CHOSEN PEOPLE MINISTRIES
241 East 51st Street
New York, NY 10022
www.chosenpeople.com

Dedication

This book is first dedicated to my wife, Grace, without whose help, encouragement, and assistance it would never have been finished.

Second, it is dedicated to the members of the Board of Directors of Chosen People Ministries, who gave to me the opportunity to put into written form the understanding of God's Word that He has placed upon my heart.

Finally, it is dedicated to my mother, and in memory of my father, whose lives served as role models of the faith, and of the godly living that so exemplifies Daniel the Prophet.

Table of Contents

Introduction

This unusual volume by a leader in the Messianic Jewish movement has a number of factors that make it an outstanding exposition. The author comes from a studied background of the faith of Israel, and through the exposition frequently brings in sidelights of insight which would largely have been missed by a Gentile reader.

The work is not intended to be a critical commentary, and no effort is made to survey existing current literature on the Book of Daniel. The treatment intends to explain in practical, understandable terms what the Book of Daniel means.

The author approaches his study from what is commonly known as the premillennial and pretribulational position. This has as a part of its theology the teaching that Israel has a future, that the Messiah is coming back to restore Israel to their land, and that He will reign over them for the thousand years of the millennial kingdom on the throne of David in Jerusalem. Simultaneously, He will rule over the entire world as King of kings and Lord of lords.

The work is characterized by frequent quotation from Scriptures and an occasional quotation from authorities on different subjects.

An unusual feature of the book is its practical application of spiritual truth. Many have not fully realized that Daniel is so full of practical application to believers today. This is contained not only in the biographical or historical sections but also in the prophetic sections, where God's treatment of Israel in the past, present, and future has many important lessons which should be learned.

An outstanding feature of the work is attention to the historical background, particularly in chapter 8 and chapter 11, where this exposition goes far beyond normal treatments in tracing out the historical background of Antiochus Epiphanes and the detailed prophecies of Daniel 11:1–35. These detailed prophecies do much to establish prophecy as legitimate prediction of the future, with many of its predictions now literally fulfilled.

The exposition does not necessarily debate optional expositions and tends to expound the author's point of view. In the nature of a complicated book like Daniel, not every decision will be accepted by the reader, but, on the whole, the book follows the time-honored and traditional interpretation that takes prophecy literally and attempts to make sense out of what God predicts. Many new insights are provided in this treatment which are not found in most books on Daniel.

As the Book of Daniel is one of the most important prophetic books of the Old Testament, its understanding is absolutely essential to comprehending prophecy as a whole and understanding such important books in the New Testament as the Book of Revelation. This work will find its place in the libraries of earnest Christians who want to know what the Bible teaches, how it applies to our lives, and how it affects our present and our future.

John F. Walvoord
Chancellor
Dallas Theological Seminary

◆

CHAPTER ONE

A Captive in a Foreign Land

In the third year of the reign of Jehoiakim king of Judah, Nebuchadnezzar king of Babylon came to Jerusalem and besieged it. And the LORD delivered Jehoiakim king of Judah into his hand,...

Among these were some from Judah: Daniel, Hananiah, Mishael and Azariah....

But Daniel resolved not to defile himself with the royal food and wine,...

To these four young men God gave knowledge and understanding of all kinds of literature and learning. And Daniel could understand visions and dreams of all kinds.

In every matter of wisdom and understanding about which the king questioned them, he found them ten times better than all the magicians and enchanters in his whole kingdom.

— Daniel 1:1, 2a, 6, 8a, 17, 20 (NIV)

A PROPHET, NOT AN HISTORIAN

Hundreds of years ago, God outlined His prophetic program for Israel and the nations, and He told it to the prophet Daniel.

The book of Daniel is not listed among the prophets in the *Tenach* (the Jewish Bible). Instead, it is placed in the *Ketuvim* (the writings).

Why this happened remains a mystery, since Daniel was certainly recognized as a prophet. Yeshua,[1] our Messiah, called Daniel a prophet (see Matthew 24:15). Josephus also referred to Daniel in this way. In his history of the Jews, Josephus recorded that the priests of Israel showed the scroll of the prophet Daniel to Alexander the Great, telling him that he was the fulfillment of the prophecy. Josephus wrote, "...And when the book of Daniel was showed him (Alexander the Great), wherein Daniel declared that one of the Greeks should destroy the empire of the Persians, he supposed that himself was the person intended; and as he was then glad he dismissed the multitude for the present,...."[2]

Thus, while the book of Daniel was not placed among the prophets within the Jewish Scriptures, he was certainly recognized as a prophet and his writings and visions are recognized as prophecies relating to Israel and the nations.

Under the direction of the Holy Spirit, Daniel divided his writing into two major sections. One section is written in Hebrew; the other part is written in Aramaic (the language of the Chaldeans, Babylonians, etc.). The Hebrew portion deals with the Jewish people and with the city of Jerusalem under Jewish control, while the chapters written in Aramaic deal with the Gentile nations' domination over Jerusalem and the Jewish people.

Very few portions of Scripture are written in Aramaic. However, like Daniel's writing, those portions which are written in Aramaic emphasize the domination of the Gentile nations over Israel. Ezra, chapters 4:8 through 6:19 and 7:12–27, as well as Jeremiah 10:11, are written in Aramaic. Each of these passages contain a message to the Gentiles.

The Aramaic section of Daniel begins in chapter two, verse 4, and continues through the end of the seventh chapter. The remainder of the book is written in Hebrew. Within the Aramaic sections we see power in the hands of the Gentile nations presented in its character, course, and consummation. The Hebrew section of the book presents the same power localized in connection with the Jews and Jerusalem.

GOD SQUARES THE ACCOUNT

Daniel, like the prophet Ezekiel, was one of the Jewish captives who lived in Babylon around the year 606 B.C.

God had long before told the prophet Jeremiah that He would bring Nebuchadnezzar, king of Babylon, against Israel if the nation refused to repent. God further told Jeremiah the length of the captivity — seventy years (see Jeremiah 25:8–10). When the people of Israel entered the promised land, God told them that every seventh year was to be His. However, the people of Israel had not kept one sabbatic year for 490 years.

Throughout the 490 year span God sent prophets to speak to the people, to plead with them to repent, but they refused to do so. Through the prophet Jeremiah, God warned the nation that He would hold them accountable for their sin of failing to keep His sabbatic year; His judgment would come. Like men today, perhaps they felt God would overlook their omission.

God is patient and long-suffering, but He does have a fixed program of redemption and judgment — the dates of which have been sovereignly fixed. God began squaring the account by raising up Nebuchadnezzar, king of Babylon, to bring judgment against Israel for their continued sin and disobedience. The nation of Israel had cheated Him out of seventy years; God therefore gave the nation into the hands of Nebuchadnezzar for seventy years of judgment.

Nebuchadnezzar's earlier attacks on Israel, and his ultimate destruction of Jerusalem in 586 B.C., began what the Scripture calls the "times of the Gentiles" or, the times when the Gentile nations would dominate the land of Israel. (The date 586 B.C. is usually given as the beginning date for the start of the "Times of the Gentiles" as this uses the date of the destruction of the Temple.)

It was during the early series of invasions, beginning in 606 B.C., that Daniel, along with thousands of others, was taken captive and carried away to Babylon. Thus, the events recorded in Daniel's prophecy happened during the years of his captivity in Babylon — under the prophetic period of time called the "times of the Gentiles." This fact becomes important to the understanding of Daniel's prophecy, as well as to the understanding of the visions of Nebuchadnezzar.

GOD KEEPS HIS COVENANT

God's promises to the people of Israel, as given through Daniel and recorded in his writings, were made while the nation was in captivity — outside their land. His promises were a reminder to the Jewish people of the fact that God is a covenant-keeping God. He fulfills His word despite the disobedience of his children, and despite their location.

Even today, two major Jewish holidays continue as reminders of God's faithfulness: the Feast of Purim (cf. Esther) and the Feast of Hanukkah (cf. John 10:22). Both holidays occurred when the Jewish people were under the domination of the Gentile powers: Purim, under the Persian leaders; Hanukkah, under the Roman leaders while a remnant of the Jewish people were back in the land.

Daniel, himself, was another reminder that God keeps His covenants. He was born of royal, or princely, descent. We read, "Then the king ordered Ashpenaz, chief of his court officials to bring in some of the Israelites from the royal family and the nobility" (Daniel 1:3). Had the nation of Israel not been taken into captivity, Daniel might have been a ruler in Israel. But because of the sin of Jehoiakim and Jehoiachin, God told the prophet, Jeremiah, no seed of the royal line would again sit upon the throne of David (see Jeremiah 22). When God's judgment fell upon Jehoiakim, it ended the reign of the Davidic Throne until the Messiah, Yeshua, came.

In 2 Chronicles 36:5–7 we read, "Jehoiakim was twenty-five years old when he became king, and he reigned in Jerusalem eleven years. He did evil in the eyes of the LORD his God. Nebuchadnezzar king of Babylon attacked him and bound him with bronze shackles to take him to Babylon. Nebuchadnezzar also took to Babylon articles from the temple of the LORD and put them in his temple there." Daniel 1:2 records, "And the LORD delivered Jehoiakim king of Judah into his hand, along with some of the articles from the temple of God. These he carried off to the temple of his god in Babylonia and put in the treasure house of his god." The 70 year captivity literally brought about the end of the kingdom of Judah, and the end of the throne for Israel, until Messiah would come.

IN A PLACE OF PROMINENCE

We are not told the age of Daniel when he was taken captive. We do know, however, that because of his royal lineage, he was given a place of prominence in the kingdom of Babylon. We know, too, that this custom

4

was practiced as a way of assimilating the captives into Babylonian society. It is known that Daniel's life extended from the period of Nebuchadnezzar to the time of King Cyrus of Persia — a time span covering events of history over a period of 73 years. Most scholars believe that Daniel lived to be well over 90 years of age, making him a contemporary of Jeremiah, Ezekiel, and of Joshua the high priest, mentioned by the prophet Zechariah. He was a contemporary of Ezra and Zerubbabel.

FAITH TESTED

Daniel's life chronicles the story of God's faithfulness to individuals who choose obedience to Him — despite all circumstances. Taken captive as a young man, probably in his late teens or early twenties, Daniel was exposed to the degraded atmosphere of the Babylonian court — to the licentious, blasphemous and pagan behavior of the kings, princes, and nobles of Babylon.

From what is known historically, many of the Jewish people assimilated into the cultic worship and practices of the Babylonian mystic religion. But Daniel refused to be corrupted. Instead, he chose to worship God despite all obstacles. God always rewards such faith and obedience.

Soon after being taken captive, Daniel and his three friends, Hananiah, Mishael, and Azariah, were faced with a test of their faith. According to Daniel 1:4, 5 captives who were of royal descent were to be taught the language and literature of Babylon, and assigned food and wine from the king's table. Their training was to cover a period of three years, after which they were to enter the king's service. We might say they were to attend the "university of paganism" — three long years under the tutelage of idolatrous teachers and instructors. The Scriptures tell us that Daniel complied with the mandatory attendance — he listened and he learned — but he did not allow himself to be corrupted by their teaching. Instead, he evaluated the teaching in the light of the knowledge and experience he had with Almighty God.

CHANGING NAMES, NOT CHARACTER

The names Daniel, Hananiah, Mishael, and Azariah are most interesting. Each one of them has a special meaning. The name Daniel means

5

"God is my judge." Hananiah means "My Lᴏʀᴅ is gracious." Mishael means "Who is what God is?" or some would translate it "He that is the strong God." And Azariah means "The Lᴏʀᴅ is my help." By their names, and by the testimony of their lives, these four Israelite young people demonstrated that God is exactly who He said He is; He is gracious; He is our strength and help; He is the judge over all the earth.

When Daniel and his friends arrived in Babylon they were immediately given Babylonian names. In Daniel 1:7 we read, "The chief official gave them new names: to Daniel, the name Belteshazzar; to Hananiah, Shadrach; to Mishael, Meshach; and to Azariah, Abednego." Evidently the Babylonian names were an attempt to translate the characteristics of the Hebrew names into the Chaldean dialect.

Belteshazzar means, "Bell's price (Bell being a Babylonian god), keeper of the treasure of Bell." Shadrach means "the illumination or the light of Wok who was the sun god." Meshach literally means "who is what Aku is?" And Abednego means, "the servant of Nebo" the one who was the god of fire. The names reveal that Daniel and his three friends were being groomed to carry out priestly duties and functions relating to the Babylonian deities.

Daniel was cognizant of this, and in verse 8 of chapter One we read, "But Daniel resolved not to defile himself with the royal food and wine, and he asked the chief official for permission not to defile himself this way."

Stripped of everything, living in a foreign country, in the court of a pagan king, with his name changed to a name representing the treasurer of a pagan deity, Daniel resolved — he purposed in his heart — not to defile himself in any way. Daniel was a man of principle; he was a man of conviction. Not only did he possess faith, he *lived* faith. His relationship with his Lᴏʀᴅ was demonstrated in his life's actions. He knew what was right and he set his mind to that course of action.

Verse 9 of Daniel chapter one continues, "Now God had caused the official to show favor and sympathy to Daniel, but the official told Daniel, 'I am afraid of the Lᴏʀᴅ my king, who has assigned your food and drink. Why should he see you looking worse than the other young men your age? The king would then have my head because of you.'"

It is wonderful to see the way God works! When individuals purpose in their hearts to do what is right, God works behind the scenes to prepare for the accomplishment of His will. The book of James states, "He that knoweth to do good and does not do it, to him it is sin" (James 4:17 KJV). God wants His children to live by the convictions of their faith, and when they do, He prepares others to respond to their righteous actions.

Having found favor with the individuals in authority over him, Daniel asked the chief official to put him and his friends, Hananiah, Mishael, and Azariah to a test. He asked that they be given nothing but vegetables to eat, and water to drink, for a period of ten days. Their appearance was then to be compared with that of the young men who were eating the royal food. Although he was taking a great risk to himself in doing so, the official agreed.

Faith and Character Rewarded

Verse 15 of chapter one states: "At the end of the ten days they looked healthier and better nourished than any of the young men who ate the royal food."

The diet of vegetables and water, blessed by God, proved to be more nourishing than all the rich food and wine lavished upon their peers. This is a beautiful spiritual lesson. The world offers every type of food — every type of enticement and enjoyment — but it's allurements produce only brief satisfaction; they do not produce the fruits of righteousness; they do not quench the thirsting of our souls. That which appeals to our senses is often an illusion — as the English poet and dramatist, William Shakespeare, recognized and wrote, "...all that glistens is not gold."

In contrast to the enticements of the world, we see the "vegetables and water" of God's Word. Those who are willing to feast upon the Word of God will receive spiritual nourishment. They will grow in wisdom and understanding of God. Their souls will be satisfied. They will find His peace — which passes all understanding! When we are willing to feast on God's Word, and to trust Him completely, He will use every circumstance of our lives to perfect His purpose.

So it was with Daniel, Hananiah, Mishael, and Azariah. Verse 17 states, "To these four young men God gave knowledge and understanding of all kinds of literature and learning. And Daniel could understand visions and dreams of all kinds." Although they had been removed to a foreign country — to a different culture — and were in servitude to a pagan king, these young Jewish men faithfully served their God. Hence, God blessed them.

As a part of that blessing, God gave them knowledge and understanding of all kinds of literature and learning. He did not censor their reading, nor their exposure to the pagan culture in which they were living. Rather, He gave them the ability to discern His truths in spite of the pagan secular teaching they were receiving. He enabled them to exercise godly wisdom. They were therefore able to put everything into proper perspective.

This is a spiritual principle which is still applicable today. As believers, we need to study the Word of God and be sensitive to the leading of the Holy Spirit. With the Holy Spirit as our teacher, we can then view the political arena, the economic arena, and other theaters of learning with a balanced perspective. This is what Daniel and his friends did. They applied godly wisdom to their lives, and in so doing, separated truth from error — based upon God's Word and on a living relationship with God the Father.

When it came time for the king to talk with Daniel, Hananiah, Mishael, and Azariah, he found there were none equal to them in all of Babylon. "In every matter of wisdom and understanding about which the king questioned them, he found them ten times better than all the magicians and enchanters in his whole kingdom" (v. 20).

GOD'S PURPOSE FOR DANIEL

Having met Daniel and his three friends, let us now see how God used Daniel and the gift of understanding of visions and dreams which He had given to him.

The book of Daniel falls into a natural division based upon the Hebrew and the Aramaic parts of the prophecy. There is also a natural division based upon the visions that Daniel interprets, and the visions that Daniel sees.

We could call chapters 1–6 "Daniel, the Interpreter of Visions," and chapters 7–12, "Daniel, the Seer of Visions." The first half of the book deals primarily with the visions seen by the Gentile kings. These were interpreted by the prophet Daniel, revealing God's great program of judgment and redemption in reference to the Gentile nations of the world. In the last half of the book God reveals His truth to Daniel in vision form. Daniel's vision basically gives us an understanding of how God will perfect His will and purpose for the nation of Israel.

Chapters 1–6 give a Gentile view of history, while chapters 7–12 a Jewish view of history. This great book ties together both the Jew and the Gentile in God's program of redemption. It gives a preview of the great truth taught in the book of Galatians that in the Messiah, Yeshua, there is "neither Jew nor Greek, slave nor free, male nor female; for you are all one in Christ Jesus" (Galatians 3:28).

It further reveals that within a small segment of the "times of the Gentiles," God chose to raise up a Jewish prophet to interpret and to preach His truth to the Gentile kings He had chosen as instruments of chastisement on Israel for her sins and disobedience. Daniel was that prophet, interpreting the visions and dreams of Nebuchadnezzar in chapters 1–4, interpreting the message on the wall for Belshazzar in chapter 5, and recording his own visions while serving king Darius in chapter 6.

Scripture reveals that a few centuries after Daniel, but still during the times of the Gentiles, the Church was born at Pentecost. Once again, God raised up Jewish men, filled them with His Holy Spirit, and sent them forth to Gentile kings to preach the Good News of salvation. They preached the Gospel, "the power of God unto salvation to everyone who believes, to the Jew first and also to the Greek" (Romans 1:16). The Scriptures indicate further that when the Church is complete, and is raptured (or caught away) — before that great period of time called the Tribulation — God will again raise up Jewish evangelists who will proclaim the Gospel to Gentile leaders throughout the world. In the Tribulation period He will raise up 144,000 from all the tribes of Israel to proclaim God's coming judgment in the person of the LORD Yeshua, the Messiah (see Revelation 7, 14).

Throughout history God has made provision for the Gentile kings to hear His program of redemption through the Jewish people. It is a sad, but true, commentary on Christendom and the Church that so few Gentile Christians recognize the need for sharing the Gospel with Jewish people. Great concern has been shown by the Church for world missions — for world evangelism (and this is biblical) — yet organized Christianity has shown little concern for the evangelization of the Jews. This author believes that God has a special blessing for Gentile believers, in this age, who faithfully carry the truth of His Word back to the Jewish people.

NOTES

Chapter 1. A Captive in a Foreign Land

1   Yeshua (meaning "salvation") is the Hebrew word for the name "Jesus." The name "Yeshua" will be used throughout this commentary except in direct quotes from Scripture.

2   *The Works of Flavius Josephus*, translated by William Whiston, (Grand Rapids, MI: Associated Publishers and Authors, Inc., n.d.) book 11, chapter 8, p 244.

♦

Chapter Two
A Revealer of Dreams

In the second year of his reign, Nebuchadnezzar had dreams; his mind was troubled and he could not sleep.

So the king summoned the magicians, enchanters, sorcerers and astrologers to tell him what he had dreamed,...

The king replied to the astrologers, 'This is what I have firmly decided: if you do not tell me what my dream was and interpret it, I will have you cut into pieces and your houses turned into piles of rubble.'...

The king asked Daniel...'Are you able to tell me what I saw in my dream and interpret it?'

Daniel replied, 'No wise man, enchanter, magician or diviner can explain to the king the mystery he has asked about, but there is a God in heaven who reveals mysteries. He has shown King Nebuchadnezzar what will happen in days to come.'

— Daniel 2:1–2, 5, 26–28

Nebuchadnezzar inherited the throne of Babylon from his father, Nabopolassar. It is known from history, as well as from Scripture, that Nebuchadnezzar was used of God to capture the city of Jerusalem (see

Jeremiah 25, 27), and that by the second year of his reign, he had already brought numerous Jewish people, including Daniel, back to Babylon.

THE KING'S DREAM

Nebuchadnezzar was troubled in his sleep — he was dreaming dreams — so he summoned his magicians, his enchanters, his sorcerers, and his astrologers. He asked each one of them to tell him his dream, and then to interpret it.

Whether Nebuchadnezzar had forgotten his dream, and wanted the wise men to recall it for him, or whether he was simply putting them to the test, is unclear. The weight of evidence seems to indicate that he knew exactly what his dream was — he recalled it vividly — but he could not interpret it. He evidently lacked confidence in the advice of his wise men and in their abilities to interpret his dreams.

God had chosen Nebuchadnezzar to be used as His rod of chastisement against Jerusalem and Judah. Perhaps He had given the king insight into the shallow and fickle advice which his advisors so freely dispensed, resulting in Nebuchadnezzar's desire to test their skills. Whatever the reason, Nebuchadnezzar demanded that his advisors first recite his dream, and then give the interpretation of it (see Daniel 2:2–5).

Although Daniel, Hananiah, Mishael and Azariah had been placed in the elite core of wise men, they were separated from the other wise men and astrologers because they were Jews. They were therefore not present when the other wise men of Babylon appeared before Nebuchadnezzar.

The wise men and astrologers of Babylon had often been called upon to interpret dreams, visions, and symbols. But never before had they been called upon to *recite* a dream before giving its interpretation. The astonished response of the wise men of Babylon is seen in verses 10 and 11: "The astrologers answered the king, 'There is not a man on earth who can do what the king asks! No king, however great and mighty, has ever asked such a thing of any magician or enchanter or astrologer. What the king asks is too difficult. No one can reveal it to the king except the gods, and they do not live among men.'"

In reality, the wise men of Babylon were not wise at all. Perhaps they were knowledgeable in the things of the world, and in the traditions of pagan Babylon, but they knew nothing of Almighty God. They had no concept or understanding of the God of Israel who was dwelling among them in the persons of Daniel, Hananiah, Mishael, and Azariah. God's representatives had not been included in the company of wise men who appeared before the king. It was an omission which ultimately brought all of the wise men of the land face to face with certain death.

THE KING'S ANGER

When the wise men could not give a recitation of the dream, or the interpretation of it, the king became so angry that he issued a decree calling for the death of all of the wise men of Babylon (see Daniel 2:12).

Although Daniel and his friends had been segregated from the "elitist" core and ignored (because they were Jews) when the wise men of Babylon were summoned to appear before the king, it is clear that they were certainly to be included in the king's death decree. We read that Arioch, the commander of Nebuchadnezzar's guard, wasted no time in carrying out the king's command. Men were sent to look for Daniel and his friends as Arioch made preparations to put the other wise men of Babylon to death.

Daniel could have cowered in fear but, instead, we read that with wisdom and tact he calmly asked Arioch why the king had issued such a harsh decree (see Daniel 2:14, 15). In the eye of the storm, God had given His servant, Daniel, peace and presence of mind. While Arioch revealed the story behind the decree, Daniel must have been praying, for Scriptures reveal that Daniel, a man slated for death, went to the king to appeal for a stay of time — time in which to interpret the king's dream.

DANIEL'S RESPONSE

We do not find Daniel lifted up in pride, boasting to the king that he would recite the king's dream and give its interpretation right there on the spot. Daniel understood his need for the power of God in his life. We read that he left the king's court and returned to his own house, whereupon he laid the matter before his friends Hananiah, Mishael, and Azariah, and asked them to pray with him. Notice the urgency of verse 18: "He urged them to plead for mercy from the God of heaven concerning this mystery, so that he and his friends might not be executed with the rest of the wise men of Babylon."

Scriptures state, "The prayer of a righteous man is powerful and effective" (James 5:16b). Prayer *does* change things! It is the oil which lubricates the wheels of mercy and justice. God's promise to us is, "The LORD is far from the wicked but he hears the prayer of the righteous" (Proverbs 15:29). This promise of God was fulfilled to Daniel, for we read, "During the night the mystery was revealed to Daniel in a vision..." (Daniel 2:19).

Daniel's response to answered prayer was praise to the God of heaven. His response is one Christians should read and meditate upon often. He praises God's sovereignty (see Daniel 2:20–23). He recognizes that it is God who controls time; He has determined its length, its breadth, its conditions. Blessed, indeed, are the Christians who understand that God controls time. He controls the times of happiness and joy, as well as the times of sadness and loss. Too often we fail to wait upon the LORD. We want to do things in our own time. We want to hurry God's program. But God tells us that He is the One who controls the times and the seasons of our lives. His promise is, if we will trust Him, we will know His perfect peace.

Daniel not only recognized God's sovereignty over time, he also recognized His sovereignty over the reign and over the deposition of kings. It is God who controls the governments of the world. In His Sovereignty, God works out His program of redemption and judgment through the rise and the fall of the nations. This is one of the reasons we are told to pray for those in authority over us.

Daniel continued to praise God by affirming that He is the One who gives wisdom to the wise and knowledge to the discerning. He is the One who reveals deep and hidden things to those who ask. How fresh this truth was in Daniel's mind! He and his three friends were in great need of wisdom. They needed knowledge of the king's dream, and insight into its meaning. They knew that God alone, the One who reveals deep and hidden things, could supply for that need. In faith, they asked God to reveal the mystery of the dream and its meaning, and He answered their prayers.

Note how Daniel closes his prayer: "...You have given me wisdom and power, you have made known to me what we asked of you, you have made known to *us* the dream of the king" (Daniel 2:23). There is a change from the singular to the plural. Daniel acknowledged that God had given him wisdom and power, and had made known to him the dream and its interpretation. But Daniel continued his praise, acknowledging that God had responded to the prayers of all four men who had been praying. Daniel was not lifted up in pride because God's answer had come to him, personally, in a vision. He knew God had answered the prayers of each man through the vision which was revealed to him.

Daniel's willingness to include his friends in God's blessing of answered prayer is seen again when he appeared before the king. He said to the king: "This was the dream, and now *we* will interpret it to the king" (Daniel 2:36). There is no indication that Daniel's three friends were with him as he appeared before the king. However, his usage of the plural "we" is not to be understood as the usual editorial "we." Daniel's friends may not have been with him "in the flesh," but they were with him in spirit. They had been very much involved in discovering the interpretation of the dream as they had prayed through the night with him. And they continued to be involved as Daniel made the dream and its interpretation known to the king, as they continued to uphold Daniel in prayer while he was in the king's court.

Daniel exemplified a marvelous characteristic of humility. He could have stood before the king, taking full credit for reciting the dream and its interpretation. He could have been puffed up with pride for his great accomplishment, looking for honors to be bestowed upon him. But Daniel was a man who walked with God — a man who knew God — a man who had purposed in his heart that his life would bring honor to God. Daniel was a man who exemplified God's character. Instead of taking full credit, he gave the glory for answered prayer to God.

Daniel was not seeking rewards from the king, but we read that the king paid him honor by giving him a high position and by lavishing many gifts upon him. The king placed Daniel in charge of all the wise men, and made him a ruler over the entire province of Babylon. But Daniel's ego was not affected by the king's praise and rewards. He remembered his faithful prayer partners — his friends. We read, "Moreover, at Daniel's request the king appointed Shadrach, Meshach, and Abednego [or their Hebrew names, Hananiah, Mishael, and Azariah] administrators over the province of Babylon, while Daniel himself remained at the royal court" (Daniel 2:49).

We all need friends who will pray with us and for us! Empowered by prayer, individuals on the front-line, as well as those behind the scenes, share equally in God's blessings. Those who are witnessing, as well as those who are praying, receive God's blessings; they share equally in God's grace. This principle is seen within Scriptures in stories of the warriors of Israel who were rewarded equally. Some went into battle. Some remained behind. All were blessed equally because of their obedience to God (see 1 Samuel 30:22–25). Christians need to be sensitive to how God is using their brothers and sisters in Yeshua to witness to His redemptive grace, and then to be willing to uphold those brothers and sisters in prayer.

Notice the sensitivity of Daniel. Before appearing before the king, he went to Arioch and said, "...Do not execute the wise men of Babylon. Take me to the king, and I will interpret his dream for him" (Daniel 2:24). How remarkable that he would specifically request that the wise men of Babylon be spared certain death, when the failure of those same men to include Daniel and his friends in their audience before the king had brought them all to the very brink of death. How unique the program of God is! The wise men of Babylon were saved by the very Jews they had excluded. And, today, we are saved by a Jew who was excluded by the rulers and wise men of his own people. Our Messiah, Yeshua, was rejected by the leaders of Jerusalem, turned over to the Romans, crucified. But by His death and resurrection, He provided salvation for Jew and Gentile alike. God's mercy, compassion, and redemptive grace is more than we can ever fathom!

DANIEL CONFRONTS THE KING

The king asked Daniel (also called Belteshazzar), 'Are you able to tell me what I saw in my dream and interpret it?' Daniel replied, 'No wise man, enchanter, magician, or diviner can explain to the king the mystery he has asked about, but there is a God in heaven who reveals mysteries. He has shown King Nebuchadnezzar what will happen in the days to come (Dan. 2:26, 27).

King Nebuchadnezzar's question to Daniel would have been asked in the Aramaic tongue, hence the parenthetical statement concerning Daniel's name "who was also called Belteshazzar." The king had ascribed to Daniel the name, 'Belteshazzar.' The name literally meant, "the keeper of the treasures of Bel." According to Babylonian theology, Bel was the supreme ruler — the life-giver, the god of justice, the god who held society together and who controlled the elements, particularly fire. Knowing nothing of the God of Israel, Nebuchadnezzar had translated Daniel's Hebrew name ("God is my judge") to a name which ascribed to his pagan theological understanding.

Daniel's response is given in verse 27. He states, "No wise man, enchanter, magician, or diviner can explain to the king the mystery he has asked about." But Daniel does not stop there. He goes on, stating that there is a God in heaven who reveals mysteries. He tells Nebuchadnezzar that it was this God who revealed the king's future through his dream. With holy boldness, Daniel removed himself from the company of the pagan magicians, soothsayers, and religious leaders of Babylon. He stated outright that there is only one God who is worthy of worship — the God of Abraham, Isaac, and Jacob.

The words of Daniel are awesome. He was speaking to a king who thought himself to be deity; he had the power of life and death. But before the king could say anything, Daniel squelched all references to the pagan deities, telling the king about the One Supreme God who, alone, can reveal truth. Daniel exhibited as much courage before the king that day as he later demonstrated when he was placed in a den of lions. This holy boldness came as a result of prayer and of his walk with the LORD. It came as the result of his personal experience and knowledge of who God is. It is this type of holy boldness that set Daniel and his three friends apart.

We also see the humility of Daniel. In verse 30 of Daniel, chapter two. It states, "As for me, this mystery has been revealed to me, not because I have greater wisdom than other living men, but so that you, O king, may know the interpretation and that you may understand what went through your mind." Daniel evidently understood why the Jewish people had been taken into Babylon; he understood why Jerusalem had fallen. He understood that God, in His sovereignty, had placed

Nebuchadnezzar over the Jewish people during their captivity. But he also knew that God would faithfully keep His promises to Israel, and that in His time, God would restore the nation of Israel back to their land. In his humble way, Daniel told the king that the knowledge and wisdom he had received from the LORD had been given to him for one purpose — so he could give a message of peace to king Nebuchadnezzar.

Daniel was experiencing what every believer can experience. God has committed to each believer the wisdom and knowledge of the ages. Believers who know the Word of God, and who have hidden it away in their hearts, understand that God has a glorious future in store for His children and for the Church. They know He has a glorious future in store for Israel. Students of the Word of God also know there is a time of agonizing testing coming to those who are living during the time of the Tribulation. The Word of God speaks clearly of the reality of hell and of eternal separation from God; this will be the fate of those who refuse to accept God's grace through the shed blood of Yeshua.

God has revealed His truth so that His children can be the bearers of Good News. He has committed the ministry of reconciliation to every believer (see 2 Corinthians 5:17–20). Christians are God's ambassadors of Good News, bringing the tidings of peace to the Jew first and also to Gentiles. In His sovereignty, God has placed believers in different spheres of authority, activity, employment, and family situations. Within each unique set of circumstances He expects His children to share the Good News that He is real, that He is alive, that He is working in history. He is the one who came in the person of Yeshua, our Messiah. He is the One who is coming again! We need to be sensitive to the places in which God has placed us, and to use those spheres of influence to witness for Yeshua. Daniel used his position, his sphere of influence, to tell the king about the Lord of lords, the God of gods — and his actions were consistent with his words. In popular terminology, "Daniel walked his talk."

THE DREAM REVEALED

Having boldly proclaimed to Nebuchadnezzar that it was God who had revealed the truth to him, Daniel proceeded to describe and relate the king's dream. He said, "You looked, O king, and there before you stood a large statue — an enormous, dazzling statue, awesome in appearance. The head of the statue was made of pure gold, its chest and arms of silver, its belly and thighs of bronze, its legs of iron, its feet partly of iron and partly of baked clay. While you were watching, a rock was cut out, but not by human hands. It struck the statue on its feet of iron and clay and smashed them. Then the iron, the clay, the bronze, the silver and the gold were broken to pieces at the same time and became like chaff on a threshing floor in the summer. The wind swept them away without leaving a trace. But the rock that stuck the statue became a huge mountain and filled the whole earth" (Daniel 2:31–35).

Daniel described to the king an enormous statue. Its size may have been reflected in the statue that the king erected some seventeen years later — a statue that stood ninety feet high and nine feet wide (see Daniel 3:1).

Remember, Nebuchadnezzar was a Gentile king to whom God was revealing truth regarding the Gentile nations; this truth takes on the form and the shape of an enormous man. Perhaps this, in itself, is a clue to the meaning of the dream. Man, apart from God, always views himself as being larger than he actually is.

In the Scriptures "Gentilism" is equated with paganism. Gentilism (paganism) is in direct opposition to the revealed truth of God. It is out of paganism that an attempt to deify man comes.

THE DREAM INTERPRETED

Nebuchadnezzar was the pagan king whom God chose to represent the beginning of this pagan domination of Israel, and the beginning of the "times of the Gentiles." Daniel tells the king. "This was the dream, and now we will interpret it to the king. You, O king, are the king of kings. The God of heaven has given you dominion and power and might and glory; in your hands He has placed mankind and the beasts of the field and the birds of the air. Wherever they live, he has made you ruler over them all. You are the head of gold" (Daniel 2:36–38).

Notice the scope of authority which God has extended to the Gentile nations through Nebuchadnezzar. Their authority would spread over the beasts of the field and the birds of the air, and over mankind itself, taking in every individual where they lived upon the face of the earth. God had told Jeremiah concerning Nebuchadnezzar, "With my great power and outstretched arm I made the earth and its people and the animals that are on it, and I give it to anyone I please. Now I will hand all your countries over to my servant Nebuchadnezzar king of Babylon; I will make even the wild animals subject to him" (Jeremiah 27:5, 6).

God, in His sovereignty, is the one who created the earth, the animals, and the nations. He is the one who established them, and who gives them power and authority. He is also the one who judges them. The very nations themselves are in the hand of God. He establishes them in His time, and He will judge them in His time. To these nations, as well, God has committed the responsibility of human government. Within their spheres of power and authority, and within their own sovereignty, they are to do what is right. They are to act righteously in accordance with God's will. Failure to do so will result in chastisement.

During this great span of time called the "times of the Gentiles" God, in effect, has extended to the Gentile nations the same privilege of blessing, prosperity, autonomy, and authority that He had extended to Israel when they occupied their land. It was Israel's failure to properly govern, control, and follow the commands and the laws of God which resulted in their chastisement and judgment. Now, through Daniel, God was telling the Gentile nations (beginning with Nebuchadnezzar) that they, too, would have an opportunity for blessing if they would be willing to be obedient to Him. Their failure to be obedient would result in certain judgment, just as Israel's failure to be obedient resulted in their judgment.

The Head of Gold

Daniel told King Nebuchadnezzar that he, Nebuchadnezzar, was the head of gold, and that his empire symbolically represented the beginning of the "times of the Gentiles." Daniel forewarned Nebuchadnezzar that his actions and his treatment of the Jewish people within his empire would determine God's blessings upon his empire. Daniel told Nebuchadnezzar that his failure to respond to the truth of God would result in judgment upon his nation.

In this, God foretold the failure of the nations. The head of gold only represented Babylon. The four types of metal in the dream symbolized four world empires which would come upon the scene of history. Each empire would be different from the others. Historically, these empires are known as Babylon, Medo-Persia, Greece, and Rome. Looking at history, one can see the progression of degeneration in the four kingdoms as their histories unfold. At the same time, there is a progression of sin in the nations as they rebel against God. As history records, the nations removed themselves further and further away from God. The Gentile nations became just as sinful and rebellious as ancient Israel. Mankind continually attempts to eradicate belief in God. God's judgment is inevitable. He holds the Gentile nations accountable, just as He held Israel accountable.

God placed Daniel and his three friends, Hananiah, Mishael, and Azariah within the very highest echelon of leadership in the court of Babylon to reveal His truth. He placed Daniel in a place of strategic leadership so that Daniel could reveal God's program of judgment and redemption to the king of Babylon.

In interpreting the dream to the king, Daniel used a title which was commonly borne by kings of Persia and by the princes of Armenia. He says, "You, O king, are the king of kings," (Daniel 2:37), and that is exactly what Nebuchadnezzar was (see Jeremiah 27:6, 7). In every sense of the word, Nebuchadnezzar represented God's sovereign authority over the nations of the world and over the beasts of the field. "Why would God entrust such power and authority to a pagan Gentile king?" The reason becomes obvious when we begin to understand the total program of God.

God chose Israel to be a light unto the nations of the world but, instead, they wanted to be like the other nations. Rather than to reflect the light of God and His righteousness, His power, and His authority, Israel chose to reflect their own religious traditions. God's grace was to be revealed through the sacrificial systems and through the holy days He had given to Israel. However, Israel soon substituted man-made traditions and superstition in their place. Through contamination with the nations, the true worship of God was diluted into a likeness of Gentile (pagan) systems of worship in the world. Israel failed to fulfill God's purpose for them. By exiling Israel to Babylon and dispersing Israel among the nations of the world, God was, in effect, allowing them to become like the other nations. God placed in the hand of a pagan — a Gentile king — the authority to chastise Israel and to rule over the nations of the world until His Messiah would come.

Daniel is very careful to point out that it was the God of heaven who had made Nebuchadnezzar king of kings. Nebuchadnezzar was brought face-to-face with the fact that his authority was limited by the sovereignty of the God of Israel. He could only do what God allowed him to do. Nebuchadnezzar had to abide by the restrictions which God placed on him, or he, like Israel, would be judged. When Nebuchadnezzar abused his authority, God removed His hand of blessing from him, and He turned Nebuchadnezzar into a wolf-man. The king was reduced to eating the grass of the field for a period of seven years (see Daniel 4:28–37).

One of the factors that led to the fall of Jerusalem and to Israel's captivity in Babylon was the utter refusal of the leaders and of the priests to accept the fact that God could, and would, use an unrighteous Gentile king to bring judgment upon Israel. This was the burden of the prophet Habakkuk. He writes, "Your eyes are too pure to look on evil; you cannot tolerate wrong. Why then do you tolerate the treacherous? Why are you silent while the wicked swallow up those more righteous than themselves?" (Habakkuk 1:13). God had told the prophet Habakkuk, "Look at the nations and watch — and be utterly amazed. For I am going to do something in your days that you would not believe, even if you were told. I am raising up the Babylonians, that ruthless and impetuous people, who sweep across the whole earth to seize dwelling places not their own. They are a feared and dreaded people; they are a law to themselves and promote their own honor" (Habakkuk 1:5–7).

The problem is the age-old question. Why do the wicked seemingly prosper and the righteous suffer? Why do bad things happen to good people? The prophet Habakkuk, like the prophet Daniel, recognized the sovereignty of God. He recognized that all that God does is good; He does bless the righteous. They may suffer in this life, but theirs is an eternal reward. Habakkuk expressed his faith in the LORD in this way, "Though the fig tree does not bud and there are no grapes on the vines, though the olive crop fails and the fields produce no food, though there are no sheep in the pen and no cattle in the stalls, yet I will rejoice in the LORD. I will be joyful in God my Savior. The Sovereign LORD is my strength; he makes my feet like the feet of a deer, he enables me to go on the heights" (Habakkuk 3:17–19).

This is the lesson of faith. This is the path of righteousness. This is being obedient to God's revealed will. God, in His grace, and for His purpose, chose Nebuchadnezzar to be His king of kings over the empires of the world, over the beasts of the field, over Israel herself. By doing this, God demonstrated to Israel that He could take a wicked and unrighteous king and, through His grace and mercy, change him into a man of faith. This was the lesson that Israel had forgotten. It is a lesson many of us forget. God is gracious and merciful. He gives each one of us the freedom to act in accordance with His revealed will. Failure to be obedient results in chastisement, and continued disobedience results in God's judgment.

FUTURE EMPIRES

Daniel pointed out to King Nebuchadnezzar that following his reign, a second empire would arise; it would be inferior to Babylon. This nation was Medo-Persia. Daniel then told the king that after the second empire, a third kingdom of bronze would arise. Historically, we know this to be the kingdom of Alexander the Great, or the Grecian Empire. A fourth kingdom would then arise, represented by iron. This kingdom would be able to break everything into pieces; it was symbolically represented by the Roman Empire. Finally, in the image, there are the feet and toes which are made up of baked clay, partly of iron and partly of clay. The feet and toes represented future empires as they arise on the scene of history until the "times of the Gentiles" comes to completion.

We have already pointed out that each of these four kingdoms was inferior to the other. The specific gravity of the metals used in the image lessened as they went downward on the image, so that the lightest was at the bottom (the feet) and the heaviest was at the top, therefore destroying all hope of stability.

The image is a picture of the continuing deterioration of the Gentile nations within history. Nebuchadnezzar ruled as the result of the divine appointment of God. The kings of Persia who followed him ruled on the lower basis of their nobility of birth. The Greeks ruled on the basis of their individual influence. And, finally, Rome ruled on the lowest level of all — on the basis of popular choice. Their emperors came into power as the result of military elections. Such has been the progression, or perhaps we should say the regression, of world government.

Greater detail is given to the last empire, symbolically and historically represented by Rome. However, the description of this last empire is truly unique; it does not altogether fit historic Rome. The two legs find a counterpart in history in the division of the eastern and western empires under Valens and Valentinian in 364 C.E., yet there has never been any condition resembling a ten-fold division of nations as suggested by the ten toes of the image. It would appear that the ten toes represent nations that are yet to come.

The prophet John, writing in the book of Revelation, described such a world empire. He used the symbolism of horns to describe a ten nation confederacy, rather than the symbolism of the ten toes. But the vision represents the same truth. John writes, "The ten horns you saw are ten kings who have not yet received a kingdom, but who for one hour will receive authority as kings along with the beast" (Revelation 17:12). During the last days God will bring together the nations of the world existing during the Tribulation Period — nations that are an outgrowth of the old Roman Empire. This will be the final fulfillment of the vision seen by Nebuchadnezzar.

Interestingly, since the re-establishment of the nation of Israel in 1948 and the capture of the city of Jerusalem in June 1967, we are beginning to see the formation of what has been called the "United States of Europe," or the European Common Market. Europe has been moving toward economic and political stability. Some see this as the first stage in the setting up of the last kingdoms of the world before our LORD returns.

DESTRUCTION OF WORLD EMPIRES

God placed Daniel in this strategic place in the Babylonian court to be a witness to His truth, even as He has placed each one of us in a crucial era of history to be His faithful witnesses to a world standing on the edge of eternity, nearing God's coming day of judgment.

The vision of the image seen by Nebuchadnezzar seemingly ignores the long period of time between the destruction of the Roman Empire and the establishment of the ten-toed empire in the Tribulation. Yet upon further examination of the passage in Daniel, one realizes that it has not been ignored at all, but is symbolized in the use of the material that was used. "The head of the statue was made of pure gold, its chest and arms of silver, its belly and thighs of bronze, its legs of iron, its feet partly of iron and partly of baked clay" (Daniel 2:32).

When Daniel gave the king the interpretation of the vision concerning the feet and the toes he said, "Just as you saw that the feet and toes were partly of baked clay and partly of iron, so this will be a divided kingdom; yet, it will have some of the strength of iron in it, even as you saw iron mixed with clay. As the toes were partly iron and partly clay, so this kingdom will be partly strong and partly brittle. And, just as you saw the iron mixed with baked clay, so the people will be a mixture and will not remain united, any more than iron mixes with clay" (Daniel 2:41, 42).

The mixture of iron and clay symbolize the growth of western civilization. Western civilization grew out of the continuing expansion of the Babylonian Empire from the east to the west. The mixture of the iron with the clay symbolizes the composite mixture of the societies represented by these various empires — including superstitions, customs, and pagan religious practices of the western nations.

The western world is still represented by a political and religious system inherited from Rome, extending back in time to Babylon. Until the time of the end, there can be no one-world government; its diversity will keep it from being unified.

According to Nebuchadnezzar's vision, at the time of the end, God will take from these western nations ten nations and unify them into a single empire. The book of the Revelation reveals that this will be the Tribulation Empire — an empire which will ultimately be headed by the Beast, or the antichrist (See Revelation 13). This Beast will seek to destroy the testimony of God on earth. He will attempt to destroy all those who believe in Yeshua as their Messiah and Savior. He will turn his wrath against Israel, seeking to destroy the Jewish people. But God will not allow this to happen. The Beast, or antichrist, will not be successful. According to the vision that Nebuchadnezzar had, and that Daniel interpreted, a great rock cut without hands will smash the image on the feet and destroy it. The reason the image was struck on the feet, rather than on the head, is because of the progressive inferiority of the metals used. Its weakest point was its feet. By striking the image on the feet, the total image collapses.

The rock cut without hands which strikes the feet of this image is most interesting. Archaeologists and historians tell us that the soil of Babylon produces no stones. All of the buildings in Babylon, with the exception of a few important ones, were built of brick made of clay. However, in northern Assyria, there were limestone quarries. Assyrians often lined their mud-built walls with limestone and erected great stone statues at the palaces or temple entrances. Thus, a stone kingdom, or a kingdom established out of stone, would intimate to Nebuchadnezzar that this would either be an enemy kingdom or it would signify to him a sacred or divine kingdom. Babylon's main procession street, or sacred way, was paved with great slabs of limestone. Another peculiarity of Babylonian society was the use of so-called foundry stone. These stones were used to identify individual property lines. Curses were placed upon anyone who would dare to remove one. References to such boundary stones are prevalent in Scripture (see Joshua 15:6). Thus, for the Babylonian king, Nebuchadnezzar, this stone cut without hands held great significance. It was divine. It was foreign to Babylon. And it would determine and set the limits of society.

These are the very characteristics of the Messiah himself — the one who is referred to in Scripture as the Stone. In Genesis 49:24 we read, "But his bow remained steady, his strong arms stayed limber, because of the hand of the Mighty One of Jacob, because of the Shepherd, the Rock of Israel." In Isaiah 28:16 we read, "So this is what the sovereign LORD says, 'See I lay a stone in Zion, a tested stone, a precious cornerstone for a sure foundation; the one who trusts will never be dismayed.'" In the New Testament, in Matthew 21:42, Yeshua applies Psalm 118:22, 23 to Himself. "Jesus said to them, 'Have you never read in the Scriptures: "The stone the builders rejected has become the capstone; the LORD has done this, and it is marvelous in our eyes"? Therefore I tell you that the kingdom of God will be taken away from you and given to a people who will produce its fruit. He who falls on this stone will be broken to pieces, but he on whom it falls will be crushed.'" This stone, then, represents none other than Yeshua, the Messiah of Israel, the Son of God. In His birth He was virgin born (see Isaiah 7:14). He was the son given (see Isaiah 9:6). He is the rock cut without human hands. It will be God's Messiah, Himself, who will bring an end to the Gentile domination of Israel. He will establish His kingdom in Jerusalem. God will certainly fulfill His Word.

Daniel told Nebuchadnezzar, "The great God has shown the king what will take place in the future. The dream is true and the interpretation is trustworthy" (Daniel 2:45). The word, "trustworthy," means "to be made sure, it will literally come to pass." History has already recorded the rise and fall of the first four empires. In our days we are seeing the demise of the kingdom of iron and clay. As we see the events of history unfold let us cry out with the apostle John, "Even so come LORD Jesus" (Revelation 22:20).

Having heard the interpretation of his dream and vision, and recognizing its truth, this great Gentile king, Nebuchadnezzar, unto whom God committed the kingdoms of the world, bowed down and fell prostrate at the feet of Daniel (see Daniel 2:46). The king paid Daniel honor and ordered that an offering of incense be presented to him. In chapter two, verse 47 we read that the king said to Daniel, "...Surely your God is the God of gods and the Lord of kings and a revealer of mysteries, for you were able to reveal this mystery." What a unique picture this is! Here we see the head of the Gentile kings, the head of the nations that would begin this great period of time called the "times of the Gentiles," bowing down before a lowly Jew who had been taken captive and brought into Babylon. This, in itself, is significant. This is the outworking of God's promise to Abraham, to Isaac, and to Jacob. Scripture tells us that in the Kingdom when the Messiah, Himself, will rule and reign, Israel will once again be established as the head of the nations, and the Gentile nations, now represented by Nebuchadnezzar, will recognize Israel's place of sovereignty in God's program. They will seek to worship the Lord of lords and King of kings through the nation of Israel.

But not only did the king honor Daniel but he also, at Daniel's request, appointed Shadrach, Meshach, and Abednego as administrators over the Province of Babylon while Daniel, himself, remained in the royal court (see Daniel 2:49).

◆

CHAPTER THREE

Comrades Who Were More Than Conquerors

King Nebuchadnezzar made an image of gold, ninety feet high and nine feet wide, and set it up on the plain of Dura in the province of Babylon....

Then the herald loudly proclaimed, 'This is what you are commanded to do, O peoples, nations and men of every language: As soon as you hear the sound of the horn, flute, zither, lyre, harp, pipes and all kinds of music, you must fall down and worship the image of gold that King Nebuchadnezzar has set up. Whoever does not fall down and worship will immediately be thrown into a blazing furnace.'

— Daniel 3:1, 4–6

THE KING'S PRIDE

A period of time has elapsed, and the scene in Babylon has dramatically changed. Nebuchadnezzar is no longer humbled by the vision that was revealed to him. He is no longer looking to Daniel, or to Daniel's God. Instead, he is lifted up in pride. He is on an ego trip.

Dr. Harry Ironside has pointed out, "...we are reminded that even divine truth, if not held in fellowship with God, may actually be used to puff one up. Mere knowledge, apart from divine love, puffs up."[1] This happened to King Nebuchadnezzar. The prophet Daniel had revealed to Nebuchadnezzar that God had a unique place in history for him, but the king was no longer giving praise to God. He was no longer acting in humility and in love. He no longer recognized God's sovereignty. Instead, he used his position and power to glorify himself. Nebuchadnezzar wanted to be remembered in history. He reasoned that the best way to be remembered was to build a great image — a memorial. Perhaps he used the image from his dream as a model for this great image of gold. After all, Daniel had told him that god had made him the head of gold!

Whatever his reasoning, Scripture states that it was Nebuchadnezzar's pride that caused him to set up the great image of gold. The image was ninety feet high and nine feet wide. It was set up on the plain of Dura in the province of Babylon. The precise location of Dura cannot be determined with any degree of certainty. Excavations have, however, uncovered a mound near a small tributary of the Euphrates called Dura. In the excavations archaeologists discovered a hugh rectangular brick structure forty-five feet square and twenty feet high which they have suggested may have been the base, or the platform, for some colossal image — perhaps for the great image Nebuchadnezzar constructed.

Recognition, or an ego boost, is something men and women from every age, and every nation, have sought. Many, like Nebuchadnezzar, have gone to great lengths, and to great expense, to ensure that their names are permanently inscribed or memorialized in some way. The names of well-known TV evangelists, writers, gospel singers, etc., are known and revered. But what of the countless thousands of individuals who faithfully pray and witness? These faithful children of God receive no recognition or acclaim in this world, yet God knows each one. In heaven, when God rewards His servants for faithfulness in service, our Savior will recognize their faithfulness, and say to them, "Well done good and faithful servant" (Matthew 25:23).

Once Nebuchadnezzar had completed his image, he summoned all of the principal officers of the state. They are named for us in Daniel 3:2. Keil and Delitzsch, in their commentary on Daniel, describe the different classes as follows:

(1) The administrators of the Khshatra, the chief representatives of the king in the provinces.

(2) The military chiefs of the provinces.

(3) The presidents of the civil government.

(4) The chief judges.

(5) The superintendent of the public treasury.

(6) The lawyers.

(7) The judges.

(8) All the governors of the provinces and the prefects who were subordinate to the chief governor.[2]

Anyone who held an office of importance was assembled before the image. They were instructed that upon hearing the first chords of the great orchestra, they were to fall down and worship the image of gold. The punishment for disobedience was harsh: "Whoever does not fall down and worship will immediately be thrown into a blazing furnace" (Daniel 3:6).

It is puzzling that the listing of the official positions does not include the one man who should have been there — Daniel. Nor does the listing include Daniel's three friends, Hananiah, Mishael, and Azariah — or, as they were known in Babylon, Shadrach, Meshach, and Abednego. No reason is given within Scripture for the omission of the names of these four men from this great assembly. Some scholars have suggested that Daniel was on an important mission, but this does not explain the absence of Hananiah, Mishael, and Azariah. Clearly, Daniel and his three friends knew what the king had proposed, and they deliberately chose to stay away. They made a conscious choice to be obedient to God rather than to submit to the idol worship of Babylon. They knew full well the consequences of their actions. In contrast to Nebuchadnezzar, who was lifted up in pride as a result of his place in history, Daniel was humbled by the place God had given him. He was not looking to be memorialized in history. He was looking to be memorialized in God's book of remembrances.

The life of Daniel the prophet stands as an example to all believers. He was a man of humility, combined with boldness. He had strong convictions, and openly confessed his faith in God. God is looking for believers who will follow Daniel's example!

THE KING'S DECREE

Obedience to the king's decrees was not a matter of choice. Individuals who failed to obey the king's command were not given opportunity for explanation, or for appeal. There was no postponement of judgment. The sentence was carried out immediately. Cruelty in punishment was typical of the Assyrians and Babylonians. Cremation was a common practice among the Akkadians; it was later adopted by the Babylonians. Most likely, the burning fiery furnace into which offenders were to be cast was the very furnace normally used for the cremation of the dead. It would appear that the king had already had prepared the crematorium furnaces for all who failed to worship the image of gold.

God also demands obedience. He has declared that a day is coming when people will be forced to make a choice between life and death. In the time of the Tribulation, all who choose to receive the mark of the beast will live, but to refuse his mark will bring the judgment of death. Believers are called upon to take a stand for their faith, and to be obedient to God. As society moves ever closer to the period of time called the Tribulation, even greater demands will be placed upon the actions and attitudes of believers. Many who follow Yeshua will be persecuted; some may even suffer martyrdom.

The king's command for his subjects to fall down and worship the idol created an atmosphere for the ugly head of anti-Semitism. We read that some of the astrologers went to the king to denounce the Jews. Who could have foreseen that this web of political intrigue would become a trap to destroy the Jews. Years later, Haman used a similar ploy in his attempt to destroy the Jewish people (see the book of Esther).

Nebuchadnezzar's decree, as recorded in chapter two, to have all of the wise men of Babylon killed, nearly claimed the lives of Daniel and his three friends. Only by Divine intervention were their lives preserved. Once again, the lives of these four Jewish men were in jeopardy because they had refused to become involved in the pagan, idolatrous worship of Babylon.

As they stood before king Nebuchadnezzar, the astrologers reminded him of his decree of death to anyone who would not fall down and worship the image of gold. Then they said, "But there are some Jews whom you have set over the affairs of the province of Babylon — Shadrach, Meshach, and Abednego — who pay no attention to you, O king. They neither serve your gods nor worship the image of gold you have set up" (Daniel 3:12). How diabolically clever these astrologers were!

They implied that Shadrach, Meshach, and Abednego paid no attention to the king. In reality, they had followed the king's orders precisely in administering the affairs of the provinces in Babylon. They were doing an excellent job. The implication of the accusation was that they were totally rebellious against the king. The fact is, their decision not to worship the image of gold was not an act of rebellion. They were following a practice permitted by the king as a result of their interpretation of his dream.

THE KING'S FURY

How quickly Nebuchadnezzar had forgotten his promises to Daniel and his friends. How quick he was to heed the words of the astrologers. Nebuchadnezzar was furious when he heard of the Jews who would not worship the image of gold! He immediately summoned Shadrach, Meshach, and Abednego, repeating his command, and offering them a second chance to obey, saying, "If you are ready to fall down and worship the image I made, very good. But if you do not worship it, you will be thrown immediately into a blazing furnace. Then what god will be able to rescue you from my hand?" (verse 15b).

In the heat of the moment, Nebuchadnezzar changed the emphasis from a contest between Shadrach, Meshach, Abednego and himself, to a challenge between himself and God. The king seems to have forgotten that it was God who had entrusted him with the power and authority he enjoyed. His ego seems to have deluded him into believing that his power and authority were equal to that of Almighty God. In his arrogance, he no longer recognizes God's power to strip him of his position.

The response of Shadrach, Meshach, and Abednego is beautiful! Their response is one of confidence in the presence and power of Almighty God. They state, "O Nebuchadnezzar, we do not need to defend ourselves before you in this matter. If we are thrown into the blazing furnace, the God we serve is able to save us from it, and he will rescue us from your hand, O king. But even if he does not, we want you to know, O king, that we will not serve your gods or worship the image of gold you have set up" (Daniel 3:16–18).

What fantastic words of faith! These men knew God's power and authority. They knew His sovereignty. They knew His love. They knew God would keep His word. And most important, they knew that eternal life was more important than physical life. Yeshua said, "Do not be afraid of those who kill the body but cannot kill the soul. Rather, be afraid of the one who can destroy both soul and body in hell" (Matthew 10:28). Shadrach, Meshach, and Abednego made it clear to the king that their lives were in God's hands. They were determined to be obedient to Him, regardless of the outcome.

Nebuchadnezzar was furious! His total attitude changed. Selfishness, greed and pride can blind the hearts and eyes of men to the truth of God. Self righteousness results in a religious pride that will not allow one to back down. Yeshua was confronted with this religious pride when He came to the religious leaders of Israel. They could not recognize their own sin. In their self righteousness and pride they rejected Him. Nebuchadnezzar also rejected God and the testimony of Shadrach, Meshach, and Abednego.

The king ordered that the furnace be heated seven times hotter than usual. He then commanded that the strongest of the soldiers tie up Shadrach, Meshach, and Abednego and cast them alive into the blazing furnace. Still clothed in their royal robes — in their trousers and turbans — the three Jewish men were bound and tossed alive into the fiery furnace.

The Scriptures state that the flames were so hot they killed the men who cast Shadrach, Meshach, and Abednego into the furnace (see Daniel 3:22). Evidently Nebuchadnezzar wanted to make an example of these infidels. He wanted all of Babylon to know what would happen to subjects who would not fall down and worship his great idol. He must have made a great procession, for we find that he, himself, was present at the furnace. He went down below to look into the opening where bodies could be viewed during the cremation process.

THE KING'S ASTONISHMENT

Looking into the furnace, King Nebuchadnezzar leaped to his feet in amazement, and asked his advisors, "Wasn't it three men that we tied up and threw into the fire?" Their response was, "Certainly, O king." The astonished king shouted, "Look! I see four men walking in the fire, unbound and unharmed and the fourth looks like a son of the gods" (verse 25).

What god would be able to rescue Shadrach, Meshach, and Abednego from the hand of Nebuchadnezzar? The God who has promised that He will never leave us nor forsake us! The God who would become a Man so that He might redeem us. Although Nebuchadnezzar, in his pagan way, stated that he saw one as the son of the gods, we know that he saw the Son of God, a theophany.

Nebuchadnezzar had challenged the King of kings and Lord of lords. He lost the challenge. God revealed Himself in a way that Nebuchadnezzar could not challenge. The king had ordered that the three men be bound and thrown into the fiery furnace, and now he saw four men unbound and unharmed walking about among the flames. The presence of the fourth man was not only there as a challenge to Nebuchadnezzar, He (God) was there as a comfort to Shadrach, Meshach, and Abednego.

God did not remove Daniel's friends from the fire, nor did He put the fire out. He was *with them* through the experience. His presence was manifested to them. He unshackled them, releasing them from bondage, while allowing them to go unharmed through the searing heat of the fiery furnace. God often deals with His children in this same way. He does not always remove them from times of affliction, but He gives them freedom, by His grace, to go through the afflictions. Faith is strengthened and refined in difficult experiences. But in the midst of the fire, God verifies to us over and over again that His promise is true — He will never leave us nor forsake us (see Hebrews 13:5). He is a faithful friend who sticks closer than a brother. He is faithful to the end.

The picture of Shadrach, Meshach, and Abednego in the fiery furnace, along with the presence of the Son of God, is a beautiful picture of God's faithfulness to all who have placed their faith in Him. But the picture also symbolizes the nation of Israel as they are scattered among the nations of the world. Long years before the Babylonian captivity, God told the nation of Israel, through His servant Moses, that sin and disobedience would lead to dispersion from the promised land (see Deuteronomy 28–30). He warned the people that in the diaspora they would find no rest for the soles of their feet; their very lives would hang in doubt. But He also promised that Israel would never be completely destroyed. Through the prophet Jeremiah, God declared that as long as the sun, the moon, and the stars exist, the nation of Israel will exist before Him forever (see Jeremiah 31:31–37). All attempts to eradicate the Jewish people will fail. All attempts to destroy the nation of Israel will come to naught. Just as He preserved Shadrach, Meshach and Abednego in the fiery furnace, He will also preserve the nation of Israel as they pass through the fiery furnace of judgment — during the diaspora while they are dwelling among the nations of the world, or during the time of the Great Tribulation. God will not allow Israel to cease from being a nation!

Because God has preserved Israel, despite sin and disobedience, and has not allowed the nation to be completely destroyed, believers today can have confidence that He will keep every promise He has given within His Word. Like Shadrach, Meshach, and Abednego, a fourth person (the Son of the living God) walks with us. He unshackles our hands and our feet, giving us freedom to go through the fires of affliction in God's protection and in His grace. We have the promise of God that "in all things God works for the good of those who love him, who have been called according to his purpose" (Romans 8:28).

One can almost see King Nebuchadnezzar rubbing his eyes in disbelief at what he was seeing, muttering under his breath that this just wasn't possible. We read: "Nebuchadnezzar then approached the opening of the blazing furnace and shouted, 'Shadrach, Meshach, and Abednego, servants of the Most High God, come out! Come here'" (verse 26). What an about face! Only a short time before, while sentencing Shadrach, Meshach, and Abednego, Nebuchadnezzar had sarcastically asked them what god could possibly rescue them from his hand. Now he shouts, "Servants of the Most High God, come out! Come here."

THE KING'S CHANGED ATTITUDE

Pride had clouded Nebuchadnezzar's memory of the God Daniel had revealed to him — the God of heaven and earth who is the revealer of secrets and mysteries. The miracle of the fourth man walking in the fiery furnace with Shadrach, Meshach and Abednego had dissipated the cloud of pride, and Nebuchadnezzar's memory of the God of Daniel was restored. We read, "Then Nebuchadnezzar said, 'Praise be to the God of Shadrach, Meshach, and Abednego, who has sent his angel and rescued his servants! They trusted in him and defied the king's command and were willing to give up their lives rather than to serve or worship any god except their own God'" (verse 28).

The word translated "angel" is the word normally translated "messenger." In other words, Nebuchadnezzar recognized that the God of heaven had sent His messenger to protect and to rescue the three Jewish men.

Witnessing the startling events of the fiery furnace led to another change in the attitude of the king. Nebuchadnezzar's words are recorded in Daniel 3:25: "He said, 'Look! I see four men walking around in the fire, unbound and unharmed, and the fourth looks like a son of the gods.'" This is plural. He did not say the "Son of God" but "the son of the gods." However, after the miracle has happened, Nebuchadnezzar says *the* God of Shadrach, Meshach and Abednego sent His messenger, His angel, to deliver His servants. Through this miracle, Nebuchadnezzar was once again brought face-to-face with the sovereignty of Almighty God, and he recognized that, indeed, He is the King of kings and Lord of lords. Nebuchadnezzar learned that the piety and obedience of Shadrach, Meshach, and Abednego was honored by their God, and He rewarded them with victory!

Nebuchadnezzar then did a most amazing thing. He declared that anyone who spoke against the God of Shadrach, Meshach and Abednego would be cut into pieces and their houses turned into piles of rubble. The king recognized, and stated for the record, "No other god can save in this way" (Daniel 3:29). As the curtain on the drama of the fiery furnace falls, we read, "Then the king promoted Shadrach, Meshach and Abednego in the province of Babylon" (Daniel 3:30).

NOTES

Chapter 3. Comrades Who Were More Than Conquerors

[1]   Harry Ironside, *Daniel*, (Neptune, NJ: Loizeaux Brothers, Inc., 2nd ed, March 1920), p 46.

[2]   C.F. Keil and F. Delitzsch, *Commentaries on the Old Testament — Daniel*, (Grand Rapids, MI: Wm. B. Eerdmans Publishing Co., 1955), p 290.

♦

CHAPTER FOUR

Telling the King Bad News

King Nebuchadnezzar, To the peoples, nations, and men of every language, who live in all the world: May you prosper greatly! It is my pleasure to tell you about the miraculous signs and wonders that the Most High God has performed for me.

How great are his signs, how mighty his wonders! His kingdom is an eternal kingdom; his dominion endures from generation to generation.

I, Nebuchadnezzar, was at home in my palace, contented and prosperous. I had a dream that made me afraid. As I was lying in my bed the images and visions that passed through my mind terrified me.

— Daniel 4:1–5

Daniel now rehearses the events which indicate that Nebuchadnezzar ultimately became a believer in the God of Abraham, Isaac, and Jacob — the God of Daniel, Hananiah, Mishael, and Azariah. Nebuchadnezzar had witnessed the miracles of Almighty God; he had listened to the prophet, Daniel; he had observed the lives of Daniel and his friends. Nebuchadnezzar had even, at one time, declared God's sovereignty, and had openly proclaimed that no subject within his kingdom was to speak against the God of Israel.

Nebuchadnezzar also published a decree concerning God to the then-known world in which he said, "It is my pleasure to tell you about the miraculous signs and wonders that the Most High God has performed for me. How great are His signs, how mighty His wonders! His kingdom is an eternal kingdom; his dominion endures from generation to generation" (Daniel 4:2, 3).

In the Masoretic text, Jewish scholars have placed the words of chapter four, verses 2 through 3, at the conclusion of chapter three. This appears to be correct; it also demonstrates that through testimony of miracles and the faithful witness of Daniel and his three friends, Nebuchadnezzar's hardened heart was ultimately opened to faith in the Most High God.

Notice verses two and three of chapter four, along with verse 37. In verse 37 king Nebuchadnezzar says, "Now I, Nebuchadnezzar, praise and exalt and glorify the King of heaven, because everything he does is right and all his ways are just. And those who walk in pride he is able to humble." No longer is the God of Daniel (and the God of Meshach, Shadrach and Abednego) just a god above other gods. Nebuchadnezzar now states that He alone is God; He alone does righteously. Nebuchadnezzar has finally learned, and states, that His Kingdom (that is, God's Kingdom) is an eternal kingdom; His dominion is from generation to generation. These are no longer words of unbelief. They are the words of a believer in Almighty God. What caused the change? In Job 33:14–17 we read how God may speak once or twice; He may speak in a dream or in a vision; He will work with man to change his heart from sin to righteousness.

Three Warnings Unheeded

God spoke to Nebuchadnezzar not just once but three times. Within Scripture the number three is often used as a symbol of God's righteousness. Isaiah records that the seraphim proclaimed three times, "Holy, Holy, Holy is the Lord Almighty; the whole earth is full of His glory" (Isaiah 6:3).

The book of Revelation declares a three-fold pronouncement of woe upon the inhabitants of earth between the sounding of the trumpet of the fourth angel and the sounding of the trumpet of the fifth angel during the Tribulation. John wrote, "Woe! Woe! Woe to the inhabitants of the earth, because of the trumpet blasts about to be sounded by the other three angels!" (Revelation 8:13). The number three is symbolically used of God, and of His unique unity as Father, Son, and Holy Spirit. Nebuchadnezzar, a Gentile king, the head of gold, who was chosen of God to be the first leader of the Gentiles' rule over Israel during the "times of the Gentiles," was about to receive a fuller revelation of the very unique God of Israel.

God spoke to him the first time in his dream of the great image. Through Daniel's interpretation of his dream, Nebuchadnezzar understood that he had been divinely appointed to rule over nations and over beasts. He was the head of gold!

God spoke to Nebuchadnezzar a second time through the theophany of the heavenly messenger who was walking in the midst of the flames in the fiery furnace, protecting and saving His three faithful servants. Nebuchadnezzar knew that this "heavenly messenger" was the divine intervention of Daniel's God.

In Daniel, chapter four, God speaks to Nebuchadnezzar a third time. Once again, God spoke to him in a dream. Perhaps Nebuchadnezzar would have called his dream a "nightmare," for he states, "... visions that passed through my mind terrified me" (Daniel 4:5). Life had become too comfortable for Nebuchadnezzar. He writes that he was contented and prosperous. Contentment and prosperity often lead to complacency, and the king had pushed thoughts of the Sovereign God far into the background of his thoughts. His pride had returned. He felt good about himself, his position, about his possessions. In this dream, God startled Nebuchadnezzar into a recognition of His supremacy. Through this dream, God reminded the king of the fact that everything he possessed, and all he was, came from the hand of Almighty God. His was a position of privilege, and thus of responsibility.

In his dream, Nebuchadnezzar saw a great tree with its limbs and branches touching one end of the earth to the other. The top of the tree was touching heaven itself. The tree was available for food, and from its abundance all animals and creatures were fed. Nebuchadnezzar watched as a heavenly messenger, or a watchman, gave a command that the great tree should be cut down — only its stump was to remain. He saw that the tree's stump and roots were to be bound with iron and bronze; they were to remain in the ground so that the stump was totally subjected to the rain from heaven, and to all of the elements of nature — to the animals as well as to the plants. Then the angelic watchman turned and addressed king Nebuchadnezzar, telling him he would live among the animals and among the plants. Nebuchadnezzar was further told that his mind would be changed from that of a man to that of an animal until seven periods of time, or a period of seven years, had passed over him.

Any one seeing such a dream or vision would be deeply troubled. Nebuchadnezzar was especially so because he had an inkling that the vision referred to him. The words of the angelic messengers must have brought back memories of past experiences with the God of Daniel when they declared, "The holy ones declare the verdict, so that the living may know that the Most High is sovereign over the kingdoms of men and gives them to anyone He wishes and sets over them the lowliest of men" (Daniel 4:17).

What a drastic change this message was from Nebuchadnezzar's earlier vision, when he was told that the Most High God had chosen him to be the head over the nations (see Jeremiah 25:8–14; Jeremiah 27:4–11).

One would think that after his earlier experiences with the God of Daniel, Nebuchadnezzar would have wasted no time in calling Daniel. But old habits are hard to break, and his immediate response was to call for his magicians and diviners to interpret his dream (perhaps Nebuchadnezzar, still terrified, did not want to know the meaning of the dream). They, of course, were unable to make its interpretation known to Nebuchadnezzar, so as a last resort he summoned Daniel.

Nebuchadnezzar knew that Daniel was different from the other magicians and diviners. He knew that Daniel would tell him the truth! Nebuchadnezzar told Daniel, "...I know that the spirit of the holy gods is in you, and no mystery is too difficult for you" (Daniel 4:9). But Nebuchadnezzar still looked upon Daniel's God as one among many. He still did not understand that Daniel's God was the One True God, who alone is omnipotent, omniscient, and omnipresent: Beside Him there are no others!

As the king rehearsed his dream to Daniel, and as God revealed its interpretation to him, Daniel understood the gravity of the lesson represented in the dream and he became greatly perplexed and alarmed. Evidently his concern showed on his face, for the king said, "... Belteshazzar, do not let the dream or its meaning alarm you" (Daniel 4:19). But Daniel *was* alarmed. He knew the seriousness of the dream and its interpretation. He knew God was going to judge the king, as He had promised to do, if the king failed to be accountable to the revelation of God previously given to him.

God does hold us accountable. Privilege always brings responsibility. God had spoken to Nebuchadnezzar on two previous occasions; he was thus accountable for the revelation he had received. Daniel, too, had received special revelation from God. He, too, had been placed in a position of privilege and responsibility.

No one likes to be the bearer of bad news. This was especially true in the kingdom of Persia where the king was sovereign and an equal with his gods. The king held Daniel's life in his hands! It was common practice for magicians and soothsayers to interpret dreams to please the kings. But Daniel knew he could not do this. He had a responsibility before God to tell the truth. He realized, as well, that once he revealed the interpretation of the dream to the king, his own life would be in jeopardy.

An Unpleasant Task

Not fearing the consequences, Daniel spoke the truth, telling Nebuchadnezzar what his dream meant. "You, O king, are that tree. You have become great and strong. Your greatness has grown until it reaches the sky and your dominion extends to the distant parts of the earth" (Daniel 4:22).

The tree was a beautiful picture of Nebuchadnezzar's sovereignty and of the empire God had given him. The prosperity he enjoyed, and the expansion of his kingdom — all had been given to him by the hand of Almighty God. But Nebuchadnezzar had failed to recognize God's hand upon his life. He failed to give thanks to God. In his pride he had refused to believe that the God of Daniel was the LORD of the universe.

In the story of Nebuchadnezzar's failure, we see the seemingly innocent sin which so easily besets us all. Pride, and our desire to be self-sufficient can cause us to ignore God. As we enjoy our positions, and the material blessings God grants, it is easy to begin taking the credit for our successes. Believers need to reflect upon the account of Nebuchadnezzar's failure, and guard against following the same path through daily prayer and recognition of God's love and His grace in their lives.

Without hesitation, and without regard to the danger to his own life, Daniel completed the interpretation of the dream to king Nebuchadnezzar, saying, "...O king, this is the decree the Most High has issued against my LORD the king: You will be driven away from people and will live with the wild animals; you will eat grass like cattle and be drenched with the dew of heaven. Seven times will pass by for you until you acknowledge that the Most High is sovereign over the kingdoms of men and gives them to anyone He wishes. The command to leave the stump of the tree with its roots means that your kingdom will be restored to you when you acknowledge that Heaven rules" (Daniel 4:24). Through the interpretation of this Nebuchadnezzar's dream, God reveals to this great Gentile king that he will be reduced to an animal. He is told that God's sentence upon him will drive him to live in the fields for a period of seven years.

Out of concern and compassion for the king, Daniel continued by giving a word of personal witness to Nebuchadnezzar, stating: "...O king, be pleased to accept my advice: Renounce your sins by doing what is right, and your wickedness by being king to the oppressed. It may be that then your prosperity will continue" (Daniel 4:27). Daniel certainly was a unique individual! He knew that the king held his life in his hands, yet he spoke authoritatively and honestly to the king, telling him to repent of his sins, to renounce his sin, and to do what was right.

THE PROUD KING HUMBLED

Daniel was able to speak with authority because he lived a righteous life. He had not compromised his spiritual or moral principles. He lived his life to bring glory to God. King Nebuchadnezzar had observed Daniel's life. He knew Daniel's advice was true, but he refused to heed it. He refused to repent and to change his ways. He refused to acknowledge God. He did not punish Daniel for telling him the truth, but he did not accept the interpretation of the dream either. His pride would not allow him to think of his own mortality or vulnerability. He was king of Babylon — undefeated in battle — sovereign over the kingdoms of the world.

One short year later, while Nebuchadnezzar was out admiring all that he possessed, and while he was considering how great he was, he heard a voice decreeing that God's judgment was about to come upon him. He was immediately cast out into the field and away from people. There, he ate grass like cattle. His body was drenched with the dew of heaven and his hair grew like the feathers of an eagle and his nails like the claws of a bird (see Daniel 4:28–33).

Medical science tells us there is a disease called Lycanthropy. It is a psychosis where one actually believes he has become a wolf. Perhaps it was this or a similar type of disease that God used to judge Nebuchadnezzar. Interestingly, the annals of the Babylonian kings also record the disappearance of Nebuchadnezzar. There even seems to be some reference to the madness that befell him. During this seven-year period no other Babylonian king arose to take over the empire from Nebuchadnezzar. After the seven years had expired, king Nebuchadnezzar raised his eyes toward heaven — his sanity restored — and said, "...I praised the Most High; I honored and glorified him who lives forever. His dominion is an eternal dominion; his kingdom endures from generation to generation. All the peoples of the earth are regarded as nothing. He does as he pleases with the powers of heaven and the peoples of the earth. No one can hold back his hand or say to him: 'What have you done?'" (Daniel 4:34, 35).

Through his third encounter with the God of Israel, Nebuchadnezzar finally became a believer. He finally acknowledged God in faith. He stated, "Now I, Nebuchadnezzar, praise and exalt and glorify the King of heaven, because everything he does is right and all His ways are just. And those who walk in pride he is able to humble" (Daniel 4:37).

These are the words of one who fully trusts in God. It is not easy to say, "God, everything you do is right and all of your ways are just." This is especially true when the pathway of life becomes rocky and when we find ourselves in the pit of despair — when there's not enough money, when illness strikes, or when death sends its cold chill through a family. Yet, when we are able to come to this stage of surrender, we find true contentment. It is in coming to this point of surrender that we are able to live at complete peace with ourselves and with one another. This is what Nebuchadnezzar experienced. He was now at peace with God.

This vision and experience of Nebuchadnezzar is truly unique within Scripture. We need to remember that Nebuchadnezzar was the head of the Gentile nations — nations God was using to bring judgment upon Israel —judgment that was to last for a period of 70 years.

Instead, the extent of the Babylonian captivity for the Jewish people and for the nation of Israel has continued to the present day. A small remnant of Jewish people returned from Babylon at the end of the 70 year period of captivity. However, in fulfillment of the prophecies and visions given to Daniel, God continued to disperse and scatter Israel among the nations of the world because of their sin and disobedience. During this time the other empires which God told Daniel about came upon the scene of history bringing continued judgment and chastisement upon Israel. Ultimately, God will bring judgment upon the Gentile nations for a period of seven years — a period of time the Scriptures call the Tribulation. After the seven years, God will establish His Kingdom upon the earth.

What God allowed Nebuchadnezzar to go through typifies and symbolizes what actually happens during the times of the Gentiles. First, the pride of the Gentile nations will lift them up, causing them to place their trust and confidence in their own power. In their positions of privilege and power, they will do exactly as they please, without regard for God or His Word, and without regard for the people of Israel (see Romans 9–11). Second, during the period called the Tribulation, God will pour out His wrath upon the Gentile nations. Interestingly, God will not completely destroy the nations. Just as the stump in Nebuchadnezzar's dream remained in the ground, reminding him that his kingdom would be restored, so some from the Gentile nations will survive and will go into the Millennial Kingdom of our LORD.

Even as God has preserved a remnant in Israel, unto whom the King will return, so it also appears that God will reserved unto Himself a remnant from the Gentile nations who will profess faith in Him. In the Kingdom Age, Jew and Gentile alike, will worship the LORD, the God of heaven.

CHAPTER FIVE

Reading Divine Graffiti

King Belshazzar gave a great banquet for a thousand of his nobles and drank wine with them....

As they drank the wine, they praised the gods of gold and silver, of bronze, iron, wood, and stone.

Suddenly the fingers of a human hand appeared and wrote on the plaster of the wall, near the lampstand in the royal palace. The king watched the hand as it wrote. His face turned pale and he was so frightened that his knees knocked together and his legs gave way....

Then all the king's wise men came in, but they could not read the writing or tell the king what it meant. . . .

So Daniel was brought in before the king,...

— Daniel 5:1,4–6, 8, 13a

The light of God which had begun to shine in the life of king Nebuchadnezzar gradually dimmed following his death. He was succeeded by his son, Evil-Merodach, during the thirty-seventh year of the exile of Jehoiachin, king of Judah (see 2 Kings 25:27; Jeremiah 52:31). Evil-Merodach reigned for only two years before he was murdered by his brother-in-law, Neriglissar, who then seized the throne. Neriglissar, too, was succeeded by his son, Labashi-Marduk, who reigned for less than a year before he was violently put to death by a group of conspirators, led by a native Babylonian named Nabonidus. Violence begets violence. Terror begets terror.

Nabonidus then established a co-regency with his son, Belshazzar, whom we meet in Daniel, chapter five. Nabonidus tried, though unsuccessfully, to convince the Babylonians to replace their pantheon of gods with worship of the moon god. Thus, the light which had been revealed in Nebuchadnezzar's court through the prophet Daniel, and then through the king himself after he had come to recognize the sovereignty of God, grew dimmer with each successive king, and was finally extinguished during the reign of Belshazzar. Each and every king who succeeded Nebuchadnezzar did what was right in his own eyes. Each one failed to heed the word of God as it had been revealed through Daniel and his friends, as well as through Nebuchadnezzar himself.

THE KING'S PARTY

Daniel, chapter five, tells about a great banquet which king Belshazzar held for one thousand of his nobles. In the midst of this feast and drunken fracas the king issued a command to have the gold and silver goblets (which his grandfather, Nebuchadnezzar, had taken from the temple in Jerusalem) brought to him so that he and his nobles, his wife, and his concubines could drink from them. Daniel says, "As they drank the wine, they praised the gods of gold and silver, of bronze, iron, wood and stone" (Daniel 5:4).

This was no ordinary feast. It was an idolatrous, pagan festival. King Belshazzar was a worshiper of the pantheon of Babylonian deities which his father, Nabonidus, had established. The king's decision to call for the holy vessels was a deliberate, conscious decision, through which he could act out his disdain for the One True God, the God of Abraham, Isaac, and Jacob — the God who had revealed Himself and His truth to his grandfather, Nebuchadnezzar. As Belshazzar drank from the holy vessels which had been taken from the temple in Jerusalem, he used them to praise his pagan deities. He was not only treating the holy things of God with indifference, he was making a mockery of them, and of God. He was desecrating them in pagan ritual worship.

God will not be mocked! What God has declared holy is holy. God is indeed long suffering, but He is also holy and righteous. He does not deal lightly with the sins of pride, arrogance, and deliberate disobedience. Nebuchadnezzar learned this! No one can take the things of God and use them to profane the very name and person of our Creator.

WRITING ON THE WALL

The wrath of God was about to be revealed to Belshazzar! Suddenly, in the midst of his pagan ceremony, the fingers of a human hand appeared near the lampstand in the royal palace, and began to write a message on the plaster of the wall. The king's face turned pale, and he was so frightened that his knees knocked together and his legs gave way (see Daniel 5:5, 6).

Just as we hear stories of our fathers and our grandfathers as we are growing up, Belshazzar must surely have heard stories about his grandfather, Nebuchadnezzar. He must have heard stories about Nebuchadnezzar's dreams and the interpretations of those dreams. Certainly he had heard about the Jewish captives — Daniel and his three friends — and of their God. The stories of God's dealings with Nebuchadnezzar were a part of Belshazzar's family lineage. Surely Belshazzar had read in the royal court of Babylon the decree that Nebuchadnezzar had made:

His dominion is an eternal dominion; his kingdom endures from generation to generation. All the peoples of the earth are regarded as nothing. He does as He pleases with the powers of heaven and the peoples of the earth. No one can hold back his hand or say to him, "What have you done?" (Daniel 4:34, 35).

When the hand began to write on the plastered wall of his palace, Belshazzar must have felt a rush of fear and dread flow through him — the fear and dread of one who has been caught in his sin. Belshazzar knew he was guilty before the God of the whole earth. As creatures made in the image of God, we all know when we have sinned against Him. One's conscience bears record — unless it has been seared by deliberate, unrepentant thoughts or actions.

Yet, in spite of his fear, nothing is said about Belshazzar having a change of heart. He never repented. Instead, he called for his enchanters, his astrologers, and his diviners. He called for the wise men of Babylon, and asked them to read and interpret the message on the wall. A handsome reward was offered: "Whoever reads this writing and tells me what it means will be clothed in purple and have a gold chain placed around his neck, and he will be made the third highest ruler in the kingdom" (Daniel 5:7). But like the wise men and astrologers in the days of King Nebuchadnezzar, none of the pagan wise men could read the writing on the wall, or tell what it meant.

In his heart Belshazzar must have known his day of judgment had come. He was cognizant of his sinfulness, and he feared the consequences. There was no one in all of his court, among all of his friends, who knew how to help him; no one could tell him what the message on the wall meant. We read, "So King Belshazzar became even more terrified and his face grew more pale. His nobles were baffled" (Daniel 5:9).

Yeshua once asked, "What good is it for a man to gain the whole world yet forfeit his soul? Or what can a man give in exchange for his soul?" (Mark 8:36). Belshazzar had gained the whole world but he had lost his soul in the process. In the frightening moments of waiting for the interpretation of the writing on the wall, Belshazzar knew and feared the consequences of his sinful life. Throughout his reign, he had surrounded himself with ungodly people, and in his moment of crisis there was no one who could offer help. There were no godly people to give him godly counsel in his time of need. Such are the consequences of surrounding oneself with friends and advisors who do not know the living God.

At this point in Daniel's narrative we are told that the queen (this would actually mean the queen mother) heard the commotion in the banquet hall and went to see what was taking place. The queen mother, Nitocris, was the widow of Nebuchadnezzar. Apparently she, like Nebuchadnezzar, had remained faithful to the God of Daniel. She had not been present at the feast, but, hearing the terrible commotion in the banquet room, she went to see what was happening. Her absence from the banquet may indicate that she did not condone the actions of her grandson, King Belshazzar.

Nitocris told Belshazzar that she knew about a man in the kingdom who had proven that he had insight and intelligence. She went on to tell Belshazzar that the spirit of the Holy God dwelled within this person. She also reminded Belshazzar that his grandfather, Nebuchadnezzar, had appointed this man to be the chief of all the magicians, enchanters, astrologers, and diviners. Evidently, through the succession of evil kings who had come after Nebuchadnezzar, Daniel had lost his high place of authority and, like other Jewish men in captivity, had been relegated to a lesser position within the kingdom. But the queen mother knew where he could be located.

It is not known how or why Nitocris knew where Daniel lived. Perhaps she remained in touch with him because she was concerned over what was happening within the empire. Her grandson, Belshazzar's, ungodly lifestyle and friends were in stark contrast to the faith in God exhibited by Nebuchadnezzar during the last years of his reign.

We are reminded of the importance of the role of parents. Perhaps Nebuchadnezzar's faith in God came too late in his life for him to establish himself as a righteous role model for his children and grandchildren. It is clear that the light he received was not passed on to the next generation. What we instill in our children *is* passed on from generation to generation.

Belshazzar had refused to heed God's revelation. He had heard about the One True God, for Daniel 5:22–23 says, "But you his son, O Belshazzar, [speaking of the king's relationship to Nebuchadnezzar, his grandfather] have not humbled yourself, though you knew all this. Instead, you have set yourself up against the LORD of heaven."

King Belshazzar failed to heed the warning and testimony given by Nebuchadnezzar. He may also have received warnings from Daniel and from Daniel's three friends, Shadrach, Meshach, and Abednego. Perhaps there were even warnings from his grandmother, the queen mother. But Belshazzar had hardened his heart to the warnings, and to the Word of the LORD. He apparently did not want to change his lifestyle. In his sinful pride, perhaps he believed judgment would never fall on him.

The Bible tells us that the wages of sin is death. One may continue in sin for a season, believing there will be no consequences, but God does not forget or overlook sin. Unless we turn to the LORD, forsaking our sins and asking His forgiveness, we will be held accountable for our sin. The judgment of God will ultimately fall. Belshazzar had turned his back on this basic spiritual principle. He chose to worship the pagan gods of Babylon and to enjoy the fruits of sin.

DANIEL SUMMONED

Perhaps it was fear of the unknown that ultimately prompted Belshazzar to listen to the queen mother. Evidently, he called for Daniel and offered the same reward for a correct interpretation that he had made to the other wise men of Babylon — the position as the third highest ruler in the kingdom. Ironically, Daniel had occupied this same position under the rule of King Nebuchadnezzar, and he was not impressed with the king's offer. Scripture says, "Then Daniel answered the king, 'You may keep your gifts for yourself and give your rewards to someone else. Nevertheless, I will read the writing for the king and tell him what it means'" (Daniel 5:17).

Once again, we see Daniel's holy boldness in those amazing, powerful words! Over the years, Daniel had seen the power of God at work in the Babylonian empire; he had also experienced the presence and power of God in his own life. He was a man of faith, a man who boldly spoke forth God's truth. In effect, Daniel told the king, "You can't give me anything because you are finished. Whatever you have to give is meaningless." Belshazzar could give Daniel nothing; he had nothing to give. Daniel, on the other hand, had much to give Belshazzar, including the interpretation of the handwriting.

When the great tempter, Satan, offers to give us the pleasures of this world, our response should be like that of Daniel — "You can't give me anything because you're a defeated foe. Whatever you have to give is empty and meaningless." Those who succumb to Satan's temptations find that his gifts are empty and hollow.

Additionally, this contrast distinguishes a believer in the LORD Yeshua from an unbeliever. A believer has everything to give — the message of God's gift of eternal life made possible through the death, burial, and resurrection of His Son, Yeshua. The unbeliever needs to receive the LORD before he has anything to give. Thus, believers are commanded to share the Good News of salvation with those who are lost.

The world's voices are loud and enticing, and Belshazzar was quick to listen to them. But while Belshazzar was living his sinful, idolatrous life, Daniel was communing with God. Daniel's hearing was sensitive to the still small voice of the living God, who spoke through His Word and in prayer.

In chapter seven of Daniel we read, "In the first year of Belshazzar king of Babylon, Daniel had a dream, and visions passed through his mind as he was lying on his bed. He wrote down the substance of his dream" (verse 1). The din of the world's voices will always drown out the still small voice of God if we allow them to. But God desires our fellowship. His voice can be heard when we are willing to listen.

In Daniel's dream, God had revealed His plan for the Gentile nations, as well as for the Jewish nation. He had revealed that the Babylonian empire was coming to an end. Daniel's boldness in refusing the king's offer was based upon his knowledge of (and faith in) the revealed Word of God.

Daniel told the king he would read the writing on the wall and give its interpretation. He began by reciting highlights from the life of Belshazzar's grandfather, Nebuchadnezzar. However, Daniel did not tell Belshazzar about the vision and the dream Nebuchadnezzar had had about the Gentile nations, nor did he give Belshazzar a course in eschatology. Instead, Daniel told Belshazzar how his grandfather, Nebuchadnezzar, had been lifted up in pride, and how, because of his sin of arrogance and pride, God had brought judgment upon him. Daniel rehearsed the account of Nebuchadnezzar's position of world leadership, his pride, his judgment, and his final recognition of the sovereignty of God. Daniel concluded his testimony with awesome words of condemnation: "But you his son, O Belshazzar, have not humbled yourself, though you knew all this" (Daniel 5:22). Belshazzar had known the history of his grandfather; he could not plead innocence or ignorance. His sinfulness was deliberate. He would therefore be held responsible and accountable for his actions. His sin would not go unpunished!

DECIPHERING THE MESSAGE

Daniel then read the mysterious inscription that had appeared upon the wall of the palace: "Me'ne, Me'ne, Te'kel, Uphar'sin." There has been much speculation on why the wise men of Babylon could not read these words, since they were rather common words in the Chaldean vocabulary. Some commentators have suggested that they could only be read by divine inspiration. Others have suggested that the senses of the king and the wise men had been blunted, due to the great amount of alcohol they had consumed during their drunken orgy. Still others have suggested that the words were written in the Samaritan language, or in the Aramaic language, and were thus strange to the king and to the wise men of Babylon. Medieval rabbis suggested that the characters of the writing were arranged in a vertical pattern, rather than in the normal horizontal arrangement, thus making it difficult to read — or that perhaps they were written in an abbreviated form.

Most likely, however, God simply blinded the hearts and minds of the king and his wise men so that they were unable to read or to understand the message on the wall. Centuries earlier God had hardened the heart of Pharaoh so that he was unable to understand the miracles which Moses performed. Paul wrote about the period of time called the "Tribulation," when God's wrath will be poured out upon mankind, saying, "For this reason God sends them a powerful delusion so that they will believe the lie and so that all will be condemned who have not believed the truth and have delighted in wickedness" (2 Thessalonians 2:11, 12).

Belshazzar's time of judgment had come. God's time of judgment upon Babylon had come. It was inevitable; there would be no escape. The understanding of the message on the wall belonged to one who understood the holiness and the sovereignty of God, to one who was in touch with God, to one such as Daniel. So it is with all miracles. They are for the believers — to strengthen their faith, or to bring about repentance. They are not given to produce faith; they are given to show the power of God. Miracles often serve to produce further hardening of the hearts of unbelievers and skeptics. This was the reason Yeshua pronounced such final judgment upon the cities of Chorazin, Bethsaida, and Capernaum (see Matthew 11:20–24; Luke 10:13–15). Belshazzar had experienced a miracle but he failed to recognize it. Shackled in sin, his heart could no longer be reached by God's grace.

We find that each of the words, "Me'ne, Me'ne, Te'kel, Uphar'sin," relate to the monetary system used in Babylon. Me'ne, Te'kel, and phar'sin (which is the singular form of Uphar'sin) were shekels, or forms of currency. Their value was determined by weight. Thus, the literal meaning of the words when translated was, "numbered, numbered, weighed, divided." Daniel then gave Belshazzar the interpretation of the words. He said, "This is what these words mean: *Me'ne*: God has numbered the days of your reign and brought it to an end. *Te'kel*: You have been weighed on the scales and found wanting. *Pe'res*: Your kingdom is divided and given to the Medes and Persians" (Daniel 5:26–28).

By taking each word separately, Daniel emphasized God's total judgment upon the king and upon the Babylonian empire. Me'ne, he declared, signified that God had numbered the days of Belshazzar's kingdom and that it was finished. God knows the end from the beginning. He is the one who is in control of the nations. In his permissive will He allows them to rise and to fall. Since nations are made up of individuals, individuals are responsible for doing God's will. They are responsible for the light God has revealed to them — both in natural revelation and in special revelation. Nations and kingdoms are then judged accordingly.

Te'kel, Daniel said, indicated that Belshazzar had been weighed in the balance of Divine justice, and he had been found wanting. According to Egyptian mythology, Osiris was said to have weighed the actions of the dead in a balance. Other religions have expressed this idea as well, and it is quite possible that this expression was familiar to the Babylonians. That God weighs the actions of men is not a concept unfamiliar to Scripture. The Bible tells us that God weighs both the actions and the spirit of man (see 1 Samuel 2:3; Proverbs 16:2). Belshazzar had misused his position. He had dishonored the Almighty. He had ignored God's rule. His stewardship was a failure. As a leader he had been a miserable failure. He had been weighed, and found wanting.

The final word, "Uphar'sin," was changed by Daniel to "Pe'res." In using this Aramaic word, Daniel makes an interesting play on words. The word, Uphar'sin, which was inscribed on the wall literally meant, "and a phar'sin" or, "and half a shekel." In his interpretation of the message, Daniel substituted the word "Perez," telling the king that the kingdom would be divided by the Medes and the Persians — the word "Persians" being taken from the word "Pe'res." In other words, Daniel literally told king Belshazzar that the Persians would take over the kingdom of Babylon. This is significant because Babylon was considered impregnable. The city was intensely fortified. In fact, the findings of archaeology show that the city's double walls, made of earth and brick, were over 300 feet high and 85 feet broad. It is hard to imagine, but these walls were as high as a thirty story building. The walls were further strengthened by over 250 towers and over 100 gateways with gates of polished brass. In building the city and in recognizing the need for water during time of siege, the Babylonians had actually taken the river Euphrates and channeled it through their city for a perpetual water supply. The city itself was literally an armed fortress.

Historians tell us how the Babylonians would sit in their city and laugh at the thought of an invading force trying to capture Babylon. They rested in the security of their empire. But at the very same time when Belshazzar was feeling so secure behind the great walls of his fortified city, hosting his great banquet — at the very same time he was boasting over defiling the vessels taken from the temple, doing whatever his evil imagine desired — the Persians were advancing up the dry river bed of the Euphrates to conquer the city. In fulfillment of Jeremiah's prophecy in Jeremiah 50:38, Babylon would be destroyed. Jeremiah stated, "A drought on her waters! They will dry up. For it is a land of idols, idols that will go mad with terror."

JUDGMENT FALLS

Just how did the Persians accomplish the feat of conquering the mighty city of Babylon? The annals of history tell us that Cyrus, the Persian king, with the assistance of two Babylonian deserters whom the historian, Xenophon, named as Gadatus and Gobryras, diverted the course of the Euphrates river into a new channel. Knowing this great feast was to take place, they waited patiently until they knew Belshazzar and his friends would be drunk. Cyrus then led his Persian troops through the dry river bed, through the two-leafed gates of brass which opened upon it, and into the city itself. The words of the prophet Isaiah (see Isaiah 44:27–45:2) and the prophecies of Jeremiah (see Jeremiah 51:28–32) were precisely fulfilled!

Chapter five closes with the words: "That very night Belshazzar, king of the Babylonians, was slain, and Darius the Mede took over the kingdom at the age of sixty-two" (Daniel 5:31). Historic records verify that the rivers of Babylon were diverted to allow the Persians into the city; that Belshazzar, king of the Babylonians, was slain; and that Darius, the Mede, took over the kingdom.

How precise the Word of God is. His timing is always perfect! The sin of Belshazzar had run its course and God had prepared new leadership. Nearly twenty years before the fall of Babylon an Asiatic conqueror named Cyrus became the military leader and king of Persia. His advent was foretold a century and a half earlier by the prophet Isaiah who wrote, "who says of Cyrus, 'He is my shepherd and will accomplish all that I please; he will say of Jerusalem, 'Let it be rebuilt,' and of the temple, 'Let its foundation be laid'" (Isaiah 44:28). Isaiah wrote further, "This is what the Lord says to his anointed, to Cyrus, whose right hand I take hold of to subdue nations before him and to strip kings of their armor, to open doors before him so that gates will not be shut…" (Isaiah 45:1).

God knew the follies and the foibles of Nebuchadnezzar. He knew his shortcomings and his failures. Even while Nebuchadnezzar was in charge of the kingdoms of the world, God told the prophet Isaiah that He would raise up a man by the name of Cyrus to replace Nebuchadnezzar. God further revealed to Isaiah that it would be through his servant Cyrus that the Jewish people would be allowed to return from their captivity in Babylon.

How patient and loving our God is, working behind the scenes of history to perfect His program. If God does this for unbelievers, how much more we, as believers, should trust Him for every circumstance of life! God's faithfulness, as shown through His Word, should spur believers on to claim His promise that "…all things God works for the good of those who love him, who have been called according to his purpose" (Romans 8:28). Knowing that God is the author of history, the One who controls history, should give us confidence and boldness in our daily lives. Regardless of our circumstances, we should encourage ourselves with the truth that God is with us. He has promised that He will never forsake us. We can trust Him wholly!

Thus in God's time, at His *precise time*, the kingdom of Babylon was taken over by the Medes and Persians and placed in the hand of Darius the Mede.

♦

CHAPTER SIX

Defying the King's Decree

It pleased Darius to appoint 120 satraps to rule throughout the kingdom,…

So the administrators and the satraps went as a group to the king and said: 'O King Darius, live forever! The royal administrators, prefects, satraps, advisers and governors have all agreed that the king should issue an edict and enforce the decree that anyone who prays to any god or man during the next thirty days, except to you, O king, shall be thrown into the lions' den.'…

So King Darius put the decree in writing.

— *Daniel 6:1, 6–7, 9*

Historians have had difficulty trying to identify Darius. The name itself is not a proper name, but is an appellative which was borne by many different men and simply means, "the one who subdues."

Scholars have made many attempts to identify exactly who Darius was. The most able attempt was done by Dr. James G. Whitcomb in his book, "Darius the Mede."[1] He argues that Darius was another name for Gubaru, the governor of Babylon, who was referred to in various sixth century B.C. cuneiform texts. If this is so, it would be in keeping with the way the Medes and the Persians governed the empires which they conquered, and it would certainly fit into the context of history.

We find that Darius wasted no time in finding men who could help him rule. He appointed 120 satraps (governors of the provinces in ancient Persia) to rule throughout the kingdom (Daniel 6:1). He also appointed three administrators over the 120 satraps, and one of the administrators was Daniel (6:2)

The apostle Paul said, "I know what it is to be in need, and I know what it is to have plenty..." (Philippians 4:12). Daniel, too, had learned that contentment comes from experiencing God's peace, not from the promotions or from the adulation of men. During the years of his captivity, Daniel had been promoted to high positions of authority by King Nebuchadnezzar, by King Belshazzar, and by Darius. He had experienced the mercurial attitudes of the kings of Babylon and he knew that the praise of man is temporal. Daniel therefore purposed in his heart to do all to the glory of God.

DANIEL'S FAITHFULNESS

In his position as a commissioner, Daniel continued to maintain his righteous lifestyle. He was not corrupted by the king's court or by the ungodly men whom Darius had appointed to help him rule the kingdom. He distinguished himself among the commissioners and satraps by his exceptional qualities — so much so that the king made plans to set Daniel over the entire kingdom (see Daniel 6:3). Jealousy and outrage filled the hearts of the other administrators and satraps! An account of their behavior is given in Daniel 6:4, 5: "At this, the administrators and the satraps tried to find grounds for charges against Daniel in his conduct of government affairs, but they were unable to do so. They could find no corruption in him, because he was trustworthy and neither corrupt nor negligent. Finally these men said, 'We will never find any basis for charges against this man Daniel unless it has something to do with the law of his God.'"

What a fantastic testimony to the character and life of Daniel! His actions were perfectly consistent with his words; he was righteous in both word and deed. Since the politicians and pagan religious leaders could find nothing wrong with the way Daniel ruled over the kingdom, and since they could not find any corruption in his civil life, they attacked him where they knew he would be vulnerable — in the area of his faith and worship.

These men evidently had their own C.I.A! They watched Daniel for many months until they became thoroughly familiar with his habits. According to Dan. 6:10, Daniel went up to his room three times each day. Facing Jerusalem, he got down on his knees and he prayed, giving thanks to his God, just as he had always done.

The practice of praying three times each day is still carried on by the Jewish people. They have morning, afternoon, and evening prayers. Synagogues today are built so that worshipers face Jerusalem. It is a practice based on the longing of the Jewish people to return to Jerusalem; it is based on the longing of the Jewish people to have the temple rebuilt. Many of the customs and traditions kept by Jewish people today originated during the Babylonian captivity, perhaps modeled after Daniel's lifestyle and godly habits.

Daniel did not worship God, or maintain a consistent prayer life, because he *had* to. His worship, praise and prayers were the spontaneous response of his love for God. He *wanted* to worship God.

The Deadly Plot

Knowing of Daniel's disciplined life, the pagan administrators and satraps drew up a decree, which they asked King Darius to issue. It was designed to bring the king's judgment upon anyone who worshiped anything or anyone other than the king himself. They knew Daniel would not obey such a decree. We read, "So the administrators and the satraps went as a group to the king and said: 'O king Darius, live forever! The royal administrators, prefects, satraps, advisers, and governors have all agreed that the king should issue an edict and enforce the decree that anyone who prays to any god or man during the next thirty days, except to you, O king, shall be thrown into the lions' den. Now, O king, issue the decree and put it in writing so that it cannot be altered — in accordance with the laws of the Medes and Persians which cannot be annulled.' So King Darius put the decree in writing" (Daniel 6:6–9).

The administrators and satraps began their proposal to the king with a lie. They said, "The royal administrators, prefects, satraps, advisers, and governors have *all agreed...*" (verse 7). Daniel was one of the administrators, but he had not even been asked for his opinion about such a decree, or consulted in any way. In fact, it appears that these men scheduled an audience with the king without even informing Daniel.

Secondly, the administrators and satraps went before the king as a group (there is strength in numbers), and they appealed to the greed and to the pride of the king. First they assured the king that the decree would be temporary in nature — thirty days — just long enough to reinforce the king's image before the people (just long enough to entrap Daniel!). The king must have been flattered to think that his advisers were so concerned about promoting his image. Their arguments appealed to the king's ego, and convinced him that no one in the kingdom would mind worshiping him for so short a time; certainly the gods of Persia wouldn't mind. "So king Darius put the decree in writing" (verse 9).

Satan's attacks are always cleverly disguised. He uses lies and deceit to appeal to the pride and to the ego of mankind. Men do not see that the enemy of our souls has our destruction in mind. Satan used his wily tactics when he attacked Adam and Eve; he used them when he attacked the kings of Israel; he used them when he attacked the LORD, Yeshua. He uses the same tactics when he attacks individuals today.

The Scriptures tell us that Satan will wage an attack on Israel and the Jewish people during the Tribulation. In that time his lies and deceit will discredit the Jewish people, and the nation of Israel, bringing the nations of the world in conflict against them. His ultimate goal has always been to destroy Israel, and thereby to discredit God's Word.

The fact that the administrators and satraps suggested a thirty-day time limit on the king's decree was a wonderful testimony to Daniel's consistency in worship. These men knew that thirty days would be more than adequate time to trap Daniel. And they were right. As soon as Daniel learned of the king's decree, he went home to his prayer closet — an upstairs room where the windows opened toward Jerusalem. Daniel got down on his knees, just as he had done every day for years, and he prayed to the God of Israel. This is genuine faith! He knew what he was doing could result in his death. He knew that, according to the rule of the Medes and the Persians, once the king's decree was put into writing, it could not be altered — not even by the king himself. Daniel knew if he was caught praying to the God of Israel, there could be no reprieve. Yet, as always, his trust was in God, not in man.

FAITH VERSUS THE KING'S LAW

Knowing that Daniel would not deviate from his consistent pattern of prayer and worship, the administrators and satraps again went as a group to look for Daniel — 122 men driven by hate, who were determined to excise Daniel from among their ranks. As they knew they would, they found him on his knees, praising God and asking Him for help (see Daniel 6:10, 11).

Scripture reminds us that we are to pray for those who persecute us; we are to pray for those who have authority over us. This runs contrary to human nature, but it is the will of God. God works through the prayers of His people. Through intercessory prayer, God bestows His blessings, or His hand of judgment can be stayed. Daniel was in intercessory prayer for the king, for his enemies, for the people of Israel.

Seeing Daniel on his knees in prayer, 122 men hurried back to the king's palace to report on Daniel's infraction! Can't you picture it in your mind's eye? While Daniel was still praying, these men brought their accusation before the king. Both historical records and the Scriptures indicate that Darius was a good king — but he was human. In a moment of pride, a moment of weakness, he had passed a law which he now learned was going to cost him a friend, a trusted ally, an able administrator in his kingdom. Describing the king's reaction to the accusation of the administrators, Daniel wrote: "When the king heard this, he was greatly distressed; he was determined to rescue Daniel and made every effort until sundown to save him" (Daniel 6:14).

Throughout the book of Daniel we are taught that God places men and women in strategic locations, in strategic positions of power and authority. He does this so they can act as instruments of His righteousness, so they can fulfill His will and purpose in the society where He has placed them. But, we are also taught a sad lesson: the sins of rebellion, pride, greed and envy render people totally incapable of accomplishing glory for God's Name.

Darius did everything in his power to try to save Daniel. All day and all evening he tried to rescue him, but the consequences of his sin had to be paid.

God forgives sin, He forgives the sinner, but the consequences of sinful actions cannot be wiped away. This is why sin is so devastating. The Pandora's Box which sin opens cannot be closed, any more than the ripples in a pool of water can be stopped once a pebble has been tossed into it. The ripples continue until they spread across the pond. So it is with sin. This is why the Bible emphasizes God's holiness over and over, and emphasizes the need for God's children to demonstrate His character in word and in deed.

In the evening, when the king's advisors came to him, they reminded him that Daniel must be put in the lions' den. At last, they thought, they would be rid of Daniel! At last, they would be rid of the God Daniel so ably represented!

A Remorseful King

"So the king gave the order, and they brought Daniel and threw him into the lions' den. The king said to Daniel, 'May your God, whom you serve continually, rescue you'" (Daniel 6:16). Apparently Darius, too, had heard the stories of Daniel and of Daniel's faithful God. It is likely that he had been impressed by the truth and righteousness which characterized Daniel's actions. Realizing that he was powerless to help Daniel, the king expressed his hope that Daniel's God would be able to rescue him.

"King Darius carried out the details of his edict with sorrow and inner turmoil. He ordered that a great stone be placed over the mouth of the den. He then sealed the den of lions with his own signet ring, and with the rings of his nobles (the very accusers of Daniel), so there would be no way for Daniel to escape, or for anyone to assist in his escape without first breaking the seal. But Darius took no pleasure from his actions. We read, "Then the king returned to his palace and spent the night without eating and without any entertainment being brought to him. And he could not sleep" (Daniel 6:18).

This is not the behavior of an uncaring, self-worshiping ruler. They are the actions of a conscience-stricken man, a sorrowful man who greatly regretted issuing the decree which was about to cause the loss of a friend and an able administrator. Darius recognized that he had been lifted up in pride when he issued his decree. Because of one prideful moment — a moment in which he'd been overcome by his desire to gratify the lust of the flesh and pride —he was paying the horrible price of condemning a friend to death.

If king Darius agonized over the physical life of his friend, Daniel, how much more we, as believers, should agonize over the spiritual destiny of our family members, of our friends, of those around us who are doomed to a Christ-less eternity because no one has taken the time, or cared enough, to share the Gospel — the Good News of salvation. Yeshua wept over the city of Jerusalem. He knew full well that these very same leaders over whom He wept would reject Him and turn Him over to the Romans for crucifixion. Nevertheless, in His love and concern for them, He wept. As He hung upon the cross, He cried out, "Father forgive them, for they do not know what they are doing" (Luke 23:34). Such concern and compassion should characterize every follower of Yeshua!

Filled with remorse and concern, the king lost his appetite for food and for entertainment. Sleep would not come, and all night long Darius paced the floors of his palace. He could not get Daniel off his mind! At the first light of dawn, Darius hurriedly made his way to the lions' den (See Daniel 6:19).

Place yourself in Babylon in your mind's eye. You see Darius, the king of the most powerful empire in the world almost running in the early morning dawn as he makes his way to a den of lions where a "law breaker" had been tossed for deliberately breaking the king's law. You see the king slow down as he approaches the den and, although he is out of breath, he calls out in a voice which expresses both grave concern and hope, "Daniel, servant of the living God, has your God, whom you serve continually, been able to rescue you from the lions?" (Daniel 6:20).

Did you catch the tone of voice? Darius was *expecting* Daniel to respond. He was *expecting* Daniel to be alive. He was expecting the impossible! This is faith. The Bible tells us, "Now faith is being sure of what we hope for and certain of what we do not see" (Hebrews 11:1).

A HEDGE OF PROTECTION AND VICTORY

Daniel's response was immediate. He harbored no anger toward the king for carrying out the punishment connected with ignoring his decree.

He did not, out of spite, make the king call time and time again. Daniel responded immediately, affirming God's protection of him. "O king, live forever! My God sent his angel, and he shut the mouths of the lions. They have not hurt me, because I was found innocent in his sight. Nor have I ever done any wrong before you, O king" (Daniel 6:21, 22). What remarkable words! God had sent His messenger. God had shut the mouths of the lions. Once again, God's protection had surrounded His servant!

God is the same yesterday, today, and forever! What He did for Daniel, He will do for every individual who trusts Him. He sends His messengers, His angels, to protect His children — the inheritors of salvation (see Hebrews 1:14). By placing faith in God's Son, the Messiah, Yeshua, we become the inheritors of salvation.

God honored the faith of Daniel. Indeed, Daniel's God, whom he served continually, had rescued him and King Darius was overjoyed! After a night spent agonizing over the loss of Daniel, one can almost feel the flood of emotion felt by Darius as Daniel's response to his call echoed through the rocks of the lions' den. Darius immediately gave the order to lift Daniel out of the lions' den, and the king, himself, examined Daniel. The words of Scripture could not be more poignant, "...no wound was found on him, because he had trusted in his God" (verse 23).

We find that Darius wasted little time rounding up the men who thought they had been so clever in their false accusations against Daniel. Imagine their surprise when they learned that Daniel had been lifted from the lions' den — unharmed. Imagine their horror when they realized that the king had issued a new command that they, along with members of their families, be thrown into the lions' den. Those who had been the perpetrators of evil were destroyed. Scripture records that before they reached the floor of the den, the lions overpowered them and crushed all of their bones (see Daniel 6:24).

Where there is trust in self, there is failure. Where there is trust in the pagan idols of society, in manmade plots and schemes, there is death. But where there is faith, there is victory! Where there is trust in the King of kings and Lord of lords, there is life!

The king then issued a new proclamation — a proclamation which gave honor and glory to the God of Daniel. He wrote: I issue a decree that in every part of my kingdom people must fear and reverence the

God of Daniel. For he is the living God and he endures forever; his kingdom will not be destroyed, his dominion will never end. He rescues and he saves; he performs signs and wonders in the heavens and on the earth. He has rescued Daniel from the power of the lions (Daniel 6:26, 27).

Darius must have *heard* about the God of Daniel through the stories and gossip in the palace; he *saw* the God of Daniel through Daniel's righteous life, but he *experienced* the power and sovereignty of the God of Daniel when he witnessed that Daniel's God had been able to rescue him. Like Nebuchadnezzar, Darius came to recognize that it is Almighty God who sets up kingdoms; it is Almighty God who sets up kings; it is Almighty God who has an everlasting kingdom and who is intimately involved with His creation.

In a very real way, Daniel's experience in the lions' den illustrates God's faithfulness in preserving Israel. God preserved Daniel in spite of malicious lies and unalterable laws. Likewise, through the ages, God has preserved the nation of Israel. He keeps His promises! A remnant of Israel will always survive. Israel and the Jewish people validate the Word of God to be true!

Even as the Gentile kings Nebuchadnezzar and Darius came to faith through Daniel's testimony, so also will the Gentile nations come to faith through the nation of Israel. The Gospel began with the Jewish people; during the Tribulation the Gospel will continue to go forth through the Jewish people; and during the Kingdom Age it will be the Jewish people, restored and redeemed, whom God will use as a testimony to the nations.

Daniel's God — our God — is able to save us in every circumstance of life. He is able to rescue His children from every lions' den and from every fiery furnace of life. Daniel's faith in the God of Israel never wavered. God honored that faith. The closing words of chapter six state, "So Daniel prospered during the reign of Darius and the reign of Cyrus the Persian" (Daniel 6:28).

NOTES
Chapter 6. Defying The King's Decree
[1] James G. Whitcomb, *Darius the Mede*, (Grand Rapids, MI: Wm. B. Eerdmans Publishing Co., 1959).

◆

CHAPTER SEVEN

Revealing Visions of World Events

In the first year of Belshazzar king of Babylon, Daniel had a dream, and visions passed through his mind as he was lying on his bed. He wrote down the substance of his dream.

Daniel said: "In my vision at night I looked, and there before me were the four winds of heaven churning up the great sea. Four great beasts, each different from the others, came up out of the sea...."

I approached one of those standing there and asked him the true meaning of all this.

So he told me and gave me the interpretation of these things: "The four great beasts are four kingdoms that will rise from the earth....

...The fourth beast is a fourth kingdom that will appear on earth. It will be different from all the other kingdoms and will devour the whole earth, trampling it down and crushing it. The ten horns are different from the earlier ones; he will subdue three kings. He will speak against the Most High and oppress his saints...

Then the sovereignty, power and greatness of the kingdoms under the whole heaven will be handed over to the saints, the people of the Most High. His kingdom will be an everlasting kingdom, and all rulers will worship and obey him."

— *Daniel 7:1–3, 16–17, 23–25a, 27*

Chapters one through six saw Daniel presented as (1) a young Jewish captive who made up his mind that he would not defile himself, (2) a man who was faithful in his worship of God, (3) a man around whom God placed a hedge of protection, (4) a man unto whom God revealed wisdom to interpret the visions of Gentile kings — visions depicting the empires of the world from the perspective of these kings, and (5) a man who was trusted, and who (through God) was given a place near the top of the hierarchy of those who had conquered him and his people.

The first six chapters of Daniel could be entitled: "Daniel, the Interpreter of Visions." In chapters 7 and 8, we see that Daniel was not just an interpreter of visions. God also gave visions to Daniel — visions which speak of the great Gentile kingdoms of the world *from God's perspective.* Chapters 7 and 8 could therefore be entitled: "Daniel, the Seer of Visions."

The first of these visions came during the first year of Belshazzar, king of Babylon, the grandson of Nebuchadnezzar — the same Belshazzar who refused to follow Nebuchadnezzar's edict to worship the God of Daniel. Instead of worshiping the God of gods, Belshazzar followed the example of his father, Nabonidus, who worshiped the pantheon of Babylonian gods.

During the early reign of Belshazzar, Daniel had been dismissed from the position of leadership which he had held under Nebuchadnezzar. He was demoted to a place of low esteem, along with other exiled Jews from Jerusalem.

Daniel's visions covered the same span of time as the visions of King Nebuchadnezzar, but with a different emphasis. Nebuchadnezzar saw a great image of a man made of gold, silver, and other precious metals. The head of gold represented Babylon and king Nebuchadnezzar, while the various other metals that comprised the image represented the succeeding empires that would follow Babylon — Medo-Persia, Greece, and Rome. In King Nebuchadnezzar's dream, this huge man with the head of gold was seen from the viewpoint of the Gentile nations, and represented their power, their success, and their control over Israel. Daniel, in his vision, saw these very same nations from the viewpoint of the Jewish people.

Nebuchadnezzar's vision of the great image was seen from the perspective of man's evaluation of the great empires of the world. Man sees them as precious metals, as strong, valuable, and able to conquer. The metals were molded together to form the image of a gigantic man, suggesting that man will mold and shape the world to suit himself.

When God gave the same vision to Daniel from *His* perspective (Daniel 7), the kingdoms were no longer valuable metals. Instead, they were vicious beasts. They were no longer molded together to form a society, but they were different animals — each fierce and wild, each able to destroy the other. God never looks on the outward appearance of man. He is totally concerned with the heart of man. The Bible tells us that the heart of man is desperately wicked, yet God says that He can, and He will, regenerate the heart by His spirit through faith in the LORD, Yeshua.

THE FOUR WINDS

As Daniel begins to describe his vision of the great Gentile nations, he states: "In my vision at night I looked, and there before me were the four winds of heaven churning up the great sea. Four great beasts, each different from the others, came up out of the sea" (Daniel 7:2, 3).

The word translated "wind" in this verse is the same Hebrew or Aramaic word that is translated "Spirit." The rabbis have interpreted these four winds to be the cardinal winds — those which are directly controlled by God. In their commentary on Daniel, C.F. Keil & Delitzsch state that the four winds are the heavenly forces by which God sets the nations of the world in motion. These four winds represent the movement of God upon the nations of the world. It is a picture of God's sovereignty in setting up and putting down nations, and their kings and rulers. The four winds depict the way in which God works with nations as they respond to His righteous rule, or to sin, iniquity, and to Satanic influence on society.

The four winds in Daniel's vision serve as potent reminders that no influence or power may exert itself within God's creation except by His directive or by His permissive will. Nothing can happen by chance or coincidence. Nothing happens without God's knowledge. He is omniscient, omnipotent, and omnipresent. These winds symbolize His Holy Spirit as God strives with human beings, convincing them of sin, of judgment, and of righteousness.

We must recall that Daniel was in exile when he received the visions of the Gentile kingdoms. He was far away from the land of Israel — from Jerusalem and from the ruined temple where God's presence had dwelt. Babylon was in power. Medo-Persia was already beginning to rise as a threat to the Babylonian rule. In these visions, God was reminding the prophet Daniel that even though nations may rise and fall, He takes care of His own. He is ever-present. He has promised to preserve a remnant of Jews. He will preserve all who believed on Him. His truth will prevail and His Chosen People will survive!

THE GREAT SEA

In Daniel's vision the four winds were said to be "churning upon the great sea" (Daniel 7:2). The sea referred to here is not the Mediterranean Sea. Daniel was in Babylon, an area which is now in the modern country of Iraq. He was hundreds of miles removed from the coast line and from the Mediterranean Sea. It is conceivable, in fact, that Daniel may never have seen the Mediterranean Sea, since he was taken captive as a young man from the Province of Judah and Jerusalem.

The word "sea" in the prophetic Scriptures refers to the Gentile nations. In Revelation 17:15, the angel interprets the prophecy concerning "mystery Babylon" which God gave to the prophet John. (Mystery Babylon is a great Gentile system of worship and of economic and political power that will arise in the latter days of the Tribulation Period.) John wrote, "Then the angel said to me, 'The waters you saw, where the prostitute sits, are peoples, multitudes, nations and languages.'" The angel told John that the word "sea" or "waters," in the prophetic sense, refers to the nations of the world. God told the prophet Daniel that it is His Holy Spirit who "churns the great sea," who brings judgment on the Gentile nations. God, in His sovereignty, allows the nations to rise and to fall. Although the Gentile kings may appear to be in control, it is God who is in control of the Gentile kings!

The promises God made to Daniel, and to Israel, have also been made to each individual who has placed his or her faith in the LORD, Yeshua. What is true of the nations, is true of His children. It may appear that life's circumstances are in control, but God says to His own, "I am the

One who is controlling all circumstances." He then encourages His children with the truth that no temptation or test has confronted them, or ever will confront them, that will be greater than their ability to endure, through His grace. God comforts His children with His promise that all things — yes, even the hard things of life — work together for their good and for His glory.

God is sovereign. These truths are indeed comforting. They brought comfort to the heart of Daniel, and they bring comfort and hope to the hearts of believers today. God encourages His children to look beyond the ever-present threat of war in the Middle East; look beyond the fact that the economic conditions of the nations are in shambles; look beyond the seeming lack of solutions for the problems facing mankind and they will find that He is present; He is in control. God's children need not fear.

THE FOUR BEASTS

Let us look again at the vision described in Daniel 7:2–14. Daniel saw four great beasts coming up out of the sea (verse 3). The four beasts represent the four major Western empires of the world.

BABYLON. The first empire was the Babylonian Empire. Daniel wrote, "The first was like a lion, and it had the wings of an eagle. I watched until its wings were torn off and it was lifted from the ground so that it stood on two feet like a man, and the heart of a man was given to it" (Daniel 7:4).

The winged lion is an apt symbol of the Babylonian Empire. In fact, Scripture refers to Babylon, and to Nebuchadnezzar, as both a lion and as an eagle. The prophet Jeremiah wrote, "A lion has come out of his lair; a destroyer of nations has set out. He has left his place to lay waste your land. Your towns will lie in ruins without inhabitant" (Jeremiah 4:7). He later prophesied, "Israel is a scattered flock that lions chased away. The first to devour him was the king of Assyria; The last to crush his bones was Nebuchadnezzar, king of Babylon" (Jeremiah 50:17). Warning the nation further, he said, "This is what the LORD says: 'Look! An eagle is swooping down, spreading its wings over Moab'" (Jeremiah 48:40). And, "Look! an eagle will soar and swoop down, spreading its wings over Bozrah. In that day the hearts of Edom's warriors will be like the heart of a woman in labor" (Jeremiah 49:22).

As sculptures have been unearthed from Ninevah and from Persepolis, historians and archaeologist have discovered that the winged lion was used as a symbol of Babylon's might and power. Historians tell us that the winged lion represented Nebuchadnezzar's superiority and might; it also represented the rapidity with which Nebuchadnezzar made his conquests and established his empire throughout the then-known world.

Daniel watched as the wings of the lion were suddenly plucked off, and the lion was lifted into the erect position of a man standing on his two feet. At the same time, the heart of a man was given to the lion.

This vision beautifully describes what happened to Nebuchadnezzar as a result of the witness of God through the prophet Daniel. The reader will recall that shortly after Nebuchadnezzar came into power, he was given a vision of a great tree that would be cut down; only its stump would remain (see Daniel 4). He then saw himself as an animal in the field, eating grass and straw for a period of seven years. The fulfillment of his vision soon came to pass. He met the God of Daniel, and the great and powerful Babylonian Empire which had moved so swiftly to conquer the then-known world, suddenly came to a halt. Because Nebuchadnezzar had allowed his heart to be lifted up in pride, the empire was stripped from him. For seven long years he suffered the consequences of his sin.

Interestingly, historians tell us that during this time the sudden and swift conquests by the Babylonians stopped. They also point out that after Nebuchadnezzar's humbling experience living with the wild animals, the ferocity and the cruelty that had formerly characterized Babylon was changed.

The accuracy of the details found in God's Word is amazing and thrilling! The perfect fulfillment of prophecy gives us the assurance that just as God fulfilled his prophetic Word in the days of Daniel, He will so fulfill His prophetic Word in our day. There is a direct correlation between repentance, righteousness, and the survival of a nation. God always honors righteousness and repentance. He stays His hand of judgment when people are willing to humble themselves, repent and turn away from sin, and recognize Him as the Sovereign Lord.

Daniel continues the description of his vision: "And there before me was a second beast, which looked like a bear. It was raised up on one of its sides, and it had three ribs in its mouth between its teeth. It was told, 'Get up and eat your fill of flesh!'" (Daniel 7:5).

MEDO-PERSIA. Next to the lion, the bear is the most feared animal in the Middle East. Although the bear is not as powerful and courageous as the lion, it is still strong. It is also cruel and cunning. But the bear is a slothful, slow-moving animal. It only attacks when it is threatened, or when it needs food.

The bear in Daniel's vision was pictured as having eaten; its appetite had been satiated. Also, it was standing on its hind legs with greater height on one side than the other, and it had three ribs between its teeth.

The portrait of this bear symbolized with incredible accuracy the combined empire of the Medes and the Persians. (Recall Nebuchadnezzar's vision — recorded in Daniel 2 —of the Medo-Persian Empire, which was represented by the two arms of the great image. True to that vision, the Medes and the Persians coalesced to form a supra-empire. They borrowed, each from the other, the strength and the military might they needed to conquer the world.)

The three ribs seen in the mouth of the bear symbolized Babylon, Libya, and Egypt and their imminent fall to the gluttonous appetite of Medo-Persia. The Medo-Persian bear moved with God-given authority. Daniel 7:5 concludes with the command, "Get up and eat your fill of flesh." It appears that limits had been set by God as to how much of the world this bear could devour. It could go no further than Babylon, Libya, and Egypt — but in its conquest it would totally consume these nations.

Historically, the scenario from Daniel's vision is what actually happened. The Medo-Persian Empire ruled supreme over the conquered territories. But this new empire, like Babylon, was not to last for ever. Its rulers also forgot that they ruled and reigned by the grace and the permissive will of Almighty God. Refusing to repent and to recognize the prophet of God in their midst, the kings and leaders of the empire continued in their sin. Because of their rebellion against God, their days were numbered and God's judgment soon fell.

As it is with the nations of the world, so it is with individuals — since nations are made up of individuals. Just as someone must be on the throne over a nation, so "something" or "someone" must be on the throne of an individual's heart — either sin, or the Spirit of God —one or the other will consume the human heart.

Those who allow God to rule on the throne of their hearts experience His peace; they experience victory over fear and the trials of life. But those who allow sin to rule experience strife and turmoil in life, and they will ultimately experience God's judgment. The rulers of Medo-Persia refused to heed God's warnings. The bear, too, would come to his end.

GREECE. The third beast described by Daniel was a leopard or panther. It represented the Empire of Greece. Daniel wrote, "After that, I looked, and there before me was another beast, one that looked like a leopard. And on its back it had four wings like those of a bird. This beast had four heads, and it was given authority to rule" (Daniel 7:6).

A leopard or panther is not as kingly as a lion, nor as strong as a bear. It is similar, however, in its fierceness, and it is superior in its swiftness and in its ability to single out and catch its prey.

The leopard in Daniel's vision was even faster than a normal leopard because it had the addition of four wings on its body. Wings throughout the Scriptures symbolize rapid motion and speed. Notice, though, that the beast also had four heads. One would expect that an animal with four heads would have two wings for each head, or eight wings. But this creature only had four wings. Thus, it would appear that the beast's ability to move rapidly was ultimately hindered by the fact that, as a four-headed beast, it only had four wings.

Daniel's vision of the third beast is an accurate and amazing portrait of the rise and fall of the Grecian Empire. At the age of twenty, Alexander the Great ascended the throne of his father, Philip of Macedon. Under Alexander, the countries of Greece were united with lightening-like speed. In a few short years he conquered the then-known world.

Alexander led the Greek armies across Hellespont into Asia Minor in 334 B.C. He defeated the Persian forces at the river Granicus. He moved with amazing speed and met and defeated the Persians at Issus. He then turned south and moved down the Syrian coast, advancing to Egypt, which literally fell to him without a fight. Then, heading east, he met the armies of Darius for the last time, defeating them in the Battle of Arbella, east of the Tigris River. Babylon, Susa, and Persepolis, the capital of

Persia were rapidly occupied.

Alexander then began to consolidate his empire. He took Persians into his army, encouraged his soldiers to intermarry, and began a policy to Hellenize Asia and to establish Greek cities in the eastern part of the empire. He then marched eastward toward India and won a great battle at the Hydastas River. His armies, exhausted and far away from home, refused to go any further. Historians tell us that Alexander sat down and wept because he had no more empires to conquer. Allowing his own passions to rule over him, and not recognizing that it was God who had given him his power and authority, Alexander began to live carelessly. His life became dissipated with sin. At the age of thirty-two he died in Babylon. In twelve short years, Alexander the Great, described and symbolized in Scriptures as the leopard, had conquered the world.

In his writings, Josephus, the Jewish historian, offered an interesting account of Alexander the Great's attempt to conquer Jerusalem. A small contingent of Jews who had remained in Jerusalem during the captivity were maintaining what was left of the temple and its worship. When they heard that Alexander the Great intended to conquer Jerusalem, they went to meet him and his army. According to Josephus, the high priest went out clothed in his priestly robes and with the miter on his head. He told Alexander that he'd had a vision from God in which he saw that Alexander would conquer the Persians. He then invited Alexander to the city and to the temple area. Josephus recorded the following amazing words:

> ...And when the book of Daniel was shewed him (to Alexander the Great), wherein Daniel declared that one of the Greeks should destroy the empire of the Persians, he supposed that himself was the person intended; and as he was then glad, he dismissed the multitude for the present, but the next day he called them to him, and bade them ask what favors they pleased of him; whereupon the high priest desired that they might enjoy the laws of their forefathers, and might pay no tribute on the seventh year. He granted all they desired; and when they entreated him that he would permit the Jews in Babylon and Media to enjoy their own laws also, he willingly promised to do hereafter what they desired....[1]

… This truly amazing account recorded by Josephus verifies the fulfillment of God's Word. The Jewish leaders knew that the prophecy of Daniel, which had been written when Belshazzar was still reigning in Babylon several hundred years earlier, applied to Alexander the Great in their own day. In exact detail, God fulfills His prophetic word!

So it was with Daniel's vision of the leopard, which had four wings and four heads. The four heads did not represent successive empires, but rather contemporaneous empires which arose after the death of Alexander the Great. The vast Grecian Empire which Alexander had solidified was, upon his death, actually divided into four parts by his four principal generals. Cassander, one of Alexander's generals, assumed control of Macedon and Greece; Seleucus took Syria and upper Asia; Lysimachus became ruler of Asia Minor and Thrace; Ptolemy took possession of Egypt, Palestine, and Arabia. Alexander's wife, mother, son, and brother were all killed.

God, in His sovereignty, used Gentile nations to bring judgment upon Israel for their unbelief, sin, and apostasy. The prophets described the Gentile nations as a lion, a bear, a leopard — and finally as a wild animal. The words of Hosea are significant: "So I will come upon them like a lion, like a leopard I will lurk by the path. Like a bear robbed of her cubs, I will attack them and rip them open. Like a lion I will devour them; a wild animal will tear them apart" (Hosea 13:7, 8).

God literally fulfilled His prophetic word regarding the first three beasts. It seems that He is once again setting the stage of history in a very similar way for His coming judgment. This time the judgment will not be for Israel alone. His judgment will include the great Gentile system of religion, politics, and economics which He used as a rod of chastisement for His chosen people.

ROME AND BEYOND. We read about the fourth beast in Daniel 7:7. The beast described really has no counterpart in the animal kingdom. Hosea described it as a wild animal. Daniel described it in most frightening language: "After that, in my vision at night I looked, and there before me was a fourth beast — terrifying and frightening and very powerful. It had large iron teeth; it crushed and devoured its victims and trampled under foot whatever was left. It was different from all the former beasts, and it had ten horns."

Understanding Daniel's vision of the fourth beast is essential to an understanding of God's prophetic program. It was, in fact, the fourth beast that caught Daniel's attention and is fully described in the interpretation of this vision.

In chapter seven, verses 8 through 10, we read that the prophet saw a little horn coming up among ten horns. (The horn represented a beast, an authority, or a kingdom.) He describes the little horn as having the eyes of a man and a mouth that spoke boastfully against God. He then says he watched as the Ancient of Days took His seat in the heavens. Around the throne he saw a multitude of angels with Him.

The vision continued, and Daniel says he watched as the horn that spoke like a man and blasphemed God was slain and cast into a burning fire. The other beasts (horns, or authorities) were stripped of their power and were ultimately judged by the Ancient of Days as He came in the clouds of heaven. Finally, Daniel saw that the Kingdom of God would be established on the earth and would not be destroyed (Daniel 7:11–14).

After giving Daniel the vision, God gave him the interpretation of the vision. He was told, "'The four great beasts are four kingdoms that will rise from the earth. But the saints of the Most High will receive the kingdom and will possess it forever — yes, for ever and ever'" (verses 17, 18).

The explanation is clear. The beasts represented the kingdoms of the earth, over which The Most High, the LORD God, would ultimately establish His Kingdom and rule forever. We have already identified the first three kingdoms — Babylon, Medo-Persia, and Greece. But what kingdom does this fourth beast represent?

We must recall King Nebuchadnezzar's dream of the great image. In the interpretation of that dream Daniel was told that the fourth empire, represented by the feet and toes, was a complete empire. We identified that empire as the nation of Rome. We also indicated that Rome, as seen in Nebuchadnezzar's image, would be dissipated among the Western nations of the world, but would not completely disappear. It would ultimately form a ten-toed empire just before the LORD, the Messiah, would establish His own empire.

Nebuchadnezzar's dream in Daniel chapter 2, and Daniel's interpretation of the dream, form a "prototype" of Daniel's vision in Daniel, chapter seven. In Daniel's vision, God repeated the same prophetic message He had given to Nebuchadnezzar.

The beast which had no counterpart in the animal kingdom was vicious and terrifying. It represented historical Rome and, ultimately, the nations of the world which will exist before the LORD returns. The political, socio-economic, and religious systems begun in Babylon were further developed during the Medo-Persian Empire, expanded by the Greeks, and carried West by the Roman Empire. Much of this pagan religious system was adopted by the western nations of the world. When the Roman Empire was divided, its political, socio-economic, and religious systems (much of which came from Greece, Persia, and Babylon) was incorporated into Western and Eastern civilizations.

Daniel wrote, "He gave me this explanation: 'The fourth beast is a fourth kingdom that will appear on earth. It will be different from all the other kingdoms and will devour the whole earth, trampling it down and crushing it. The ten horns are ten kings who will come from this kingdom. After them another king will arise, different from the earlier ones; he will subdue three kings'" (Daniel 7:23, 24).

In this explanation the prophet was told that the fourth beast represented a fourth kingdom. This beast (kingdom) would itself trample down the kingdoms of the world in its ascendancy to world power. This was what historic Rome did. In its might and power, it crushed all other nations. Then it forced its own philosophy and religious practices upon these nations.

Daniel was then told that the ten horns represented ten kings who would come out from this fourth kingdom. But the prophet was not given the span of time that would elapse between the rule of the fourth kingdom and the coming into power of the ten kings. It appears from Scripture that these events happen simultaneously. However, this has not happened historically. According to Daniel, chapter nine, a period of time will elapse between the time that the world is conquered and controlled by the fourth beast, and the rise of the final empire composed of the ten horns which will establish world-wide rule just before our LORD returns. (This will be discussed in more detail in the study of Daniel, chapter nine.)

THE TRIBULATION EMPIRE

Comparing the prophecies of Daniel 7:23–25 and Daniel 2, we see that the Roman Empire was described as a mixture of iron and clay, a mixture that would not hold together, yet it would not completely disappear. Instead, the essence of the Roman Empire was to remain intact, ever-present among the nations of the world until the final time of judgment, when it would take the form of a ten-nation (or ten-horned) empire.

According to Daniel's vision, this ten-nation confederacy (ten-horned empire) will arise during the "Great Tribulation." He wrote, "...After them another king will arise, different from the earlier ones; he will subdue three kings. He will speak against the Most High and oppress his saints and try to change the set times and the laws. The saints will be handed over to him for a time, times and half a time" (Daniel 7:24, 25).

The expression "time, times and half a time" literally means "a year, two years, and a half year" that is, a combined period of three and one-half years or 1,260 days. This is clear from Daniel's use of the word, time, in Daniel 4:16. There, he uses the expression, "seven times" to refer to seven years, making the singular "time" to mean one year.

Daniel 9:27 describes a seven year period of time during which Israel and the nations will be judged by God. This span of time is commonly called the "Tribulation." A better name is "Daniel's Seventieth 'Seven'." Daniel wrote, "He will confirm a covenant with many for one 'seven,' but in the middle of that 'seven' he will put an end to sacrifice and offering...."

Revelation 11:2, 3 makes it clear that this seven year span of time is divided into two three-and-one-half-year periods. John wrote, "...the Gentiles...will trample on the holy city for 42 months. And I will give power to my two witnesses, and they will prophesy for 1,260 days,..."

The first three-and-one-half years of this seven-year period are called the "Messianic Woes," the "birth-pangs," or the "beginning of sorrows" (see Matthew 24:8).

The phrases "Messianic Woes" and "Messianic Sufferings" were developed by the writers of Talmud. According to the rabbis, the days preceding the coming of Messiah will be days of great suffering and persecution. Talmud states, "In the footsteps of the Messiah (just before his advent) insolence will increase and honor dwindle...the meeting-place of scholars will be used for immorality...the wisdom of the learned will degenerate, fearers of sin will be despised, and the truth will be lacking; youths will put old men to shame... a son will revile his father, a daughter will rise against her mother...and a man's enemies will be the members of his household...." (Sotah, 49a, 49b).

Talmud further states of Messiah's coming, "Abaye enquired of Rabbah: 'What is your reason (for not wishing to see him)? Shall we say, because of the birth pangs (preceding the advent) of the Messiah?' (these troubles are generally referred to as birth pangs, being the travail which precedes the birth of a new era)" (Sanhedrin 98b).

The second three-and-one-half year period of this seven-year span of time is called the "Great Tribulation." Yeshua said, "For then there will be a great tribulation, such as has not occurred since the beginning of the world until now, nor ever shall be" (Matthew 24:21 NASV). John also spoke of this same period, "...And he said, 'These are they who have come out of the great tribulation; they have washed their robes and made them white in the blood of the Lamb'" (Revelation 7:14).

THE TEN NATION EMPIRE

It is during the second three-and-one-half year period, or the Great Tribulation, that the Beast (the antichrist) and the false prophet reign supreme. The ten-nation confederacy, or ten-horned empire, will also come to life and receive authority to rule the world with the antichrist during the span of time called the Great Tribulation.

Daniel was told that in the last days ten kings would come into power. These ten kings cannot represent the old Roman Empire. At no period in Roman history was the old Roman Empire ever composed precisely of ten kingdoms or governed by ten rulers who fit the description given to Daniel. Daniel was seeing a ten-nation confederacy which would come into existence in the latter days, and rule during the Great Tribulation.

Revelation records that John was given a vision of this same unique ten-horned beast, but his vision had much more detail. History had moved forward from the time of Daniel. Some of the Gentile nations prophesied about by Daniel, had already fallen — Babylon, Medo-Persia, Greece. By the time of John, Rome was ruling the world. John was therefore looking forward from his day to the day of God's final judgment upon the nations. He wrote, "And I saw a beast coming out of the sea. He had ten horns and seven heads, with ten crowns on his horns, and on each head a blasphemous name. The beast I saw resembled a leopard, but had feet like those of a bear and a mouth like that of a lion. The dragon gave the beast his power and his throne and great authority" (Revelation 13:1, 2).

The symbolism in John's vision in Revelation is the same as the symbolism in Daniel's vision. John saw the same ten-horned beast that Daniel saw, only in greater detail. Both saw the beast come up out of the sea (Dan. 7:3,7; Rev. 13:1). However, the beast which John saw was a composite image of the individual beasts seen by Daniel in his vision. John saw the beast in reverse order to Daniel's vision. Rome was in existence when John was writing, and was seen first as the ruthless, diabolical beast. John then mentions the leopard — Greece — which preceded Rome. He mentions the bear — Medo-Persia — and finally he mentions the lion — Babylon, the beast with which Daniel's vision began. John saw the individual empires as a composite whole, bound together by satanic deception and satanic power. When John saw the ten-horned beast there were crowns on each horn, whereas when Daniel saw the same beast it only had horns, with no crowns.

Comparing the visions further, when Daniel saw the ten-horned beast it only had one head (Daniel 7:20). But when John saw it, the beast had seven heads (Revelation 13:1). Why this seeming inconsistency? What is the prophecy trying to reveal?

One must remember that within Scripture, the horn always symbolizes power. The ten horns represent powerful kingdoms. The ten crowns represent the ten kings who will rule over the kingdoms, and the authority and power given to the ten kings. According to Revelation 17, the ten kings will not exercise their authority and power until after the Great Tribulation begins (see Revelation 17:12–18). They will try to destroy the witness and testimony of the Messiah during the Great Tribulation. The crowns which John saw represent the totality of evil and wickedness in existence throughout human history. It is the culmination of the "times of the Gentiles" — that great span of time that began in 586 B.C. when Nebuchadnezzar first captured Jerusalem.

In Daniel's vision the ten-horned beast had only one head because the Gentile system used by God to chastise Israel began with

Nebuchadnezzar. His vision emphasized the beginning of the "times of the Gentiles." At the time of Daniel's vision, God was fulfilling the prophecy of Jeremiah in which the nation of Israel was warned that seventy years of judgment would come upon them if they failed to repent — after which time they would return to their land (see Jeremiah 25:8–14).

When Daniel was given further visions and prophecies, indicating that God's judgment was going to continue, he saw each successive judgment resulting from the one head — Babylon. Since the judgment of Israel began with Babylon, succeeding empires arising to further chastise Israel were seen as an extension of Babylon. Even the writers of Talmud, the rabbis, refer to Israel's successive judgments as coming from Babylon.

John, on the other hand, was looking at world history from a different vantage point. History had moved forward from Daniel's day; evil had progressed; John had a more complete revelation.

John not only saw the "times of the Gentiles," he saw all of the nations God had used, and will use, to chastise Israel. He saw the wickedness of the nations; he saw Satan as the one empowering and deceiving the nations; he saw the final judgment of the nations.

The expanse of John's vision is expressed in Revelation 17:9–11. He wrote, "This calls for a mind with wisdom. The seven heads are seven hills on which the woman sits. They are also seven kings. Five have fallen, one is, the other has not yet come; but when he does come, he must remain for a little while. The beast who once was, and now is not, is an eighth king. He belongs to the seven and is going to his destruction."

THE SEVEN-HEADED BEAST

John was told that the seven heads of the ten-horned beast represented seven kings, or kingdoms. Five of them had already fallen, one was in existence when he was writing, and the other (out of which would come an eighth kingdom) was yet to be established.

Historically, the five kingdoms deceived by Satan and used by God to judge Israel were Egypt, Assyria, Babylon, Medo-Persia, and Greece. The kingdom existing when John wrote the Revelation was the Roman Empire. The kingdom yet to be established — the seventh kingdom — will come into existence during the Tribulation. As previously mentioned, it is also called "Daniel's Seventieth 'Seven.'"

From the seventh empire will come an eighth empire. The eighth empire will be established during the last three-and-one-half years of Daniel's Seventieth 'Seven'— the span of time called the "Great Tribulation." The eighth kingdom will be ruled by the beast (or the antichrist) identified in Daniel 7:8. Daniel wrote, "... another horn, a little one, which came up among them; and three of the first horns were uprooted before it. This horn... spoke boastfully." The beast will speak against the God of gods and the King of kings. Upon this final kingdom, God will bring His judgment during the last part of the Great Tribulation. Scripture reveals that this kingdom will be destroyed when the Messiah returns, in the final battle called Armageddon.

What, then, is this ten-horned empire? Some Bible commentators speculate that it is the European Common Market. However, since the union of these ten nations will occur during the last half of Daniel's seventieth week, the present European Common Market does not fit such a scenario.

Others speculate that the seven hills spoken of in Revelation 17:9 represent the seven hills of Rome. They argue that the final empire is thus the Roman Catholic Church and the papacy. But once again, this interpretation does not seem likely because the seven hills are identified as seven kings who represent the seven kingdoms God used to chastise Israel.

Concerning the ten-nation empire, the seeds for its formation have already been sown on the earth in the form of satanic deception, immorality, and greed for wealth and power.

Revelation 17:12 states that the ten nations (which have not yet received a kingdom, power, or authority) come together during the last part of Daniel's Seventieth 'Seven.' They will come into existence very quickly, and will be given authority very quickly, but they will also fall away very quickly.

In recent times the world witnessed many sudden and major realignments of nations. We witnessed the collapse of the Berlin Wall and the unification of the two Germanies. The western nations watched in amazement as news reports were given concerning the downfall of the government and economy of the Union of Soviet Socialist Republics (USSR). The war with Iraq in the Persian Gulf demonstrated how quickly changes and new alliances can be made. Within a few short weeks the west formed a coalition of nations against Iraq, comprised of such diverse nations as the Soviet Union, the United States, the Arab states, Europe, Japan, and so forth.

During Daniel's Seventieth 'Seven' new alignments of nations will take shape — some very quickly — in order to fulfill the Word of God. Once the beast (antichrist) rules over this religious, political, and economic system of ten-nations, he will utterly destroy three of the ten nations: "I also wanted to know about the ten horns on its head and about the other horn that came up, before which three of them fell — the horn that looked more imposing than the others and that had eyes and a mouth that spoke boastfully.... The ten horns are ten kings who will come from this kingdom. After them another king will arise, different from the earlier ones; he will subdue three kings" (Daniel 7:20, 24).

THE THREE KINGS

Who are the three kings? Commentators are puzzled concerning their identity. Some believe that the king who was "different from the earlier ones" was fulfilled historically by Rome. They contend that the three kings were the nations of Egypt, Africa, and Ethiopia. Others say the three kings were Egypt, Syria, and Selicia.

Like the vision of the ten-horned beast, this passage has not yet been historically fulfilled. Since the ten-nation empire has not yet come into existence, the three kings, likewise, have not yet ascended to power. Their identity will therefore remain a mystery until these great prophetic events unfold.

However, their identity is hinted at in Ezekiel 38 and also in Daniel 11. These passages refer to the alignment of nations which will exist during the Tribulation. Ezekiel 38 describes a battle of Gog and Magog.

Many commentators have identified Gog and Magog exclusively as Russia. But rabbinic literature, as well as Scripture, uses the title Gog and Magog to describe nations which are deceived by Satan (see Revelation 20:7, 8). Thus, Gog and Magog in Revelation 20:7, 8 refers to nations that will exist after the one-thousand-year reign of the LORD Yeshua on the earth, nations that come from the four corners of the earth — nations that are deceived by Satan.

Ezekiel 38 also uses the title Gog and Magog to describe a confederacy of nations which will come into existence during the Tribulation Period (verse 9). These nations will invade Israel. They may well include Russia, but the term Gog and Magog does not exclusively allude to Russia. It refers to the Western nations as well — to a united nations force. Daniel, chapter eleven, states that the antichrist (the Beast) will struggle with the nations to the north and south of Israel. Before the great climactic battle he will also struggle with the nations of the east of Israel.

The ten-horned empire represents a coalition of the Western nations, out of which the Beast (or antichrist) will come. The three kings that are subdued by the antichrist will be the kings of the north, east, and south. It appears that their defeat will occur during the first half of the Tribulation Period, ushering in the antichrist's world-wide control during the last half of the Tribulation, and the ultimate formation of the eighth empire as stated in Revelation 17:11. It also appears that the very nations defeated by the Beast at the beginning of the Tribulation, will rally their armies and, together, will wage war against the Beast (or antichrist), attacking Israel at the conclusion of the Tribulation, ushering in the great and climactic battle called Armageddon (see Revelation 16).

We cannot be dogmatic concerning the details and the alignments of nations during the Tribulation, for Scripture itself is silent on these issues. We can, however, look at the day in which we live and see how God is shaping world history as the nations even today vie for power and authority in the Middle East.

The eleventh horn — the king who will seize control of the ten nations during the last three and one half years of the Tribulation Period — will not remain in power. God declared that his judgment is sure! "But the court will sit, and his power will be taken away and completely destroyed forever. Then the sovereignty, power, and greatness of the kingdoms under the whole heaven will be handed over to the saints, the people of the Most High. His Kingdom will be an everlasting kingdom, and all rulers will worship and obey Him" (Daniel 7:26, 27).

God's great kingdom will be ushered in by the Messiah after the seven-year Tribulation. The great Gentile kingdoms of the world will be utterly destroyed and Satan, the one who empowers them, will be removed. Verses 26 and 27 of Daniel, chapter seven, and this vision, are the basis of premillennial theology.

In Daniel 2:31–35, we are told that a great rock, cut without hands, struck the large statue in Nebuchadnezzar's dream. The statue crumbled, and the stone, not the large statue, became a great mountain that filled the whole earth. We are told that the kingdoms under the whole of heaven will be handed over to the saints, the people of the Most High (see Daniel 7:27). The Scriptures tell us that God's Kingdom is not of this world. Yeshua told this to Pilate (see John 18:36). God's Kingdom is composed of believers who have placed their faith and trust in the Messiah, Yeshua, as Savior and LORD. But God told Daniel that a day was coming when God's Kingdom, now invisible to the human eye, will be made visible. The Kingdom of God will be established on the earth.

Daniel's vision and its interpretation left him deeply troubled, but he wrote that this was the end of the matter (see Daniel 7:28). He kept the matter to himself. He encouraged himself with the realization of God's divine plan for Israel and for the nations. He recognized that in working out that divine plan there would be struggle, strife, warfare, hurt, pain, suffering; the nation of Israel would suffer persecution; there would be attempts to destroy the Jewish people. On a small scale, Daniel's years of exile in Babylon had acquainted him personally with such persecution.

It is human nature to question the injustices seen in life. We ask, "How can God allow this to happen? Why do the righteous suffer and the ungodly seemingly prosper? Why is it that wickedness abounds while righteousness and justice seem difficult to find?"

Daniel recognized that the ultimate answers to life belong to God. He left his questions in the hands of God, just as he had placed his life in the hands of God. By faith, he was confident that the loving, faithful and merciful God who had preserved him time and again would remain faithful.

God's perfect peace can rule in our hearts and minds when we, like Daniel, acknowledge the sovereignty and grace of Almighty God.

NOTES

Chapter 7. Revealing Visions Of World Events
[1] *Works of Josephus,* bk. 11, ch. 8, p 244.

◆

Foretelling Events in Emerging Empires

In the third year of King Belshazzar's reign, I, Daniel, had a vision, after the one that had already appeared to me....

I looked up, and there before me was a ram with two horns, standing beside the canal, and the horns were long. One of the horns was longer than the other but grew up later....

As I was thinking about this, suddenly a goat with a prominent horn between his eyes came from the west, crossing the whole earth without touching the ground.

The goat became very great, but at the height of his power his large horn was broken off, and in its place four prominent horns grew up toward the four winds of heaven.

— Daniel 8:1, 3, 5, 8

Chapters two through seven of Daniel were written in the Aramaic language, while the remainder of the book, chapters eight through twelve, were written in Hebrew. The reason for the change in language seems clear: The prophecies given in Aramaic (chapters 2–7) portray Gentile domination and rule over Israel while the nation was in captivity; the prophecies given in Hebrew (chapters 8–12) relate in their entirety to the Jewish nation — after a remnant had returned to the land, even though still under Gentile dominion.

God's hand of protection and blessing extends to the Jewish people whether they are in the land, or out of the land (in the Diaspora). It had been revealed to Daniel that ultimately Israel would once again be in the place of blessing God had promised!

A SECOND VISION

Daniel's second vision is of Antiochus Epiphanes' ascendancy to power, and his desecration of the rebuilt (the Second) temple in Jerusalem. The date of this vision is given in Daniel 8:1: "In the third year of King Belshazzar's reign I, Daniel, had a vision, after the one that had already appeared to me."

The vision came approximately two years after his first vision (see chapter 7). The second vision came toward the end of the Babylonian Empire — just prior to Belshazzar's great sin and abomination in using the sacred vessels in worship to his pagan gods.

In Daniel's first vision, he stated that as he was dreaming, a vision of four beasts passed through his mind (7:1). In his second vision, he was not dreaming. Instead, he was carried off in the spirit to the great fortress of Shushan (Susa): "In my vision I saw myself in the citadel of Susa, in the province of Elam; in the vision I was beside the Ulai Canal" (Daniel 8:2).

Josephus claimed that Daniel was not present in Susa in spirit, but that he was actually there in body.[1] Such tradition has led to the speculation that the tomb of Daniel was located near Susa; several sites in and around Susa are said to be the location of his tomb. This tradition led the great Jewish doctor, Benjamin of Tudela, to visit Susa in 1172 in search of Daniel's tomb.

Susa was one of the three royal cities of the great Achaemenids, the ruling house of ancient Persia. Three biblical books mention the city of Susa: Nehemiah 1:1; Daniel 8:2; and the book of Esther. In fact, Susa was the setting for the book of Esther. It was city where King Xerxes ruled.

Susa was located in the province of Elam, a mountainous region in western Asia. The area was originally occupied by the Cushite race. One of its earliest kings was Kedorlaomer, mentioned in Genesis 14:1–24.

Elam achieved independence from Babylon in 2280 B.C. It grew to such an extent that soon afterward its warriors were able to attack and loot Babylon; they carried off the famous Code of Hammurabi.

It is uncertain whether Elam was a part of the Babylonian Empire at the time of Belshazzar. We do know that Susa became a part of the Persian Empire under Cyrus and was, from the time of Darius (521–486 B.C.), a capital of the first world empire — together with Persepolis, Ecbatana, and Babylon. Susa became the winter residence for the Persian kings.

To the south and to the east of Susa flowed the two rivers, Choaspes and Coprates. These were connected by a large artificial canal called the Ulaius. This artificial canal, the Ulai, was approximately nine hundred feet wide. It is claimed that when Ashurbanipal (king of Syria) invaded Elam in 640 B.C., the waters turned red with the corpses of the men and horses that his army had slain.

It was by this canal, the Ulai, that Daniel saw the vision recorded in Daniel eight. Some commentators have suggested that the word "Ulai" is a play on words — a pun based on the Hebrew word "oolai," which means "perhaps." If this is so, this vision signaled a change in God's program for the Israelites, indicating their future deliverance and miraculous return to the land.

Background information is important if one is to glean more insight into the character and the spiritual life of Daniel — this man of God — God's man in Babylon!

According to his vision, Daniel actually experienced, by divine revelation, the Persian Empire and, later, the Grecian empire — both of which impacted the people of Israel after their return to the land. Daniel knew that the days of Belshazzar were numbered; he knew the days of the ruling Gentile empires were numbered. Because of his vision, Daniel knew that ultimately God, and all who had faith in God (Jew or Gentile) would be victorious.

THE TWO-HORNED RAM

Daniel saw a most unusual two-horned ram standing beside the Ulai Canal: "...the horns were long. One of the horns was longer than the other but grew up later" (8:3). Continuing, he said, "I watched the ram as he charged toward the west and the north and the south. No animal could stand against him, and none could rescue from his power. He did as he pleased and became great" (8:4).

One of the elements making this vision unique was the symbolism used for the Persian kingdom — the ram. C.F. Keil and F. Delitzsch, in their commentary on the book of Daniel, wrote, "...in *Bundehesch* the guardian spirit of the Persian kingdom appears under the form of a ram with clean feet and sharp-pointed horns, and,...the Persian king, when he stood at the head of his army, bore, instead of the diadem, the head of a ram (cf. Hav.)."[2] Persian coins were embossed with the figure of the ram and Persian kings wore a golden, jeweled ram's head on their heads instead of the usual crown. The ram came to symbolize Persia.

It is not without significance that the two horns in Daniel's vision are different from each other. One horn comes up later and grows stronger and longer than the other. Within the Scriptures, horns can symbolize power and kingdoms. Daniel was told, "The two-horned ram that you saw represents the kings of Media and Persia" (8:20; see also 8:3).

Persia, under King Cyrus, became the dominant influence in the dual kingdom; it was represented by the growth of the larger horn. Susa, after being ruled for a time by Babylon, was attacked by the Median Empire and finally by the Persian Empire, being ruled by the latter until the Medo-Persian Empire fell.

The direction of the attack of the two-horned ram is also significant. It attacked from the west, the north, and the south (8:4). The Persian Empire came from the land east of Babylon. Today it is the modern country of Iran, located to the east of the Tigris-Euphrates River. The first direction of attack was toward the west. Persia conquered Babylon, Syria, and Asia Minor. After conquering these empires, Persia conquered the northern empires of Colchis, Armenia, and Iberia. Finally, Persia moved south and conquered Egypt, Ethiopia, Libya, and Israel.

In this vision God revealed to Daniel, in full detail, the extent of the Persian Empire and its conquest of Babylon and of the then-known world. Being the recipient of such an awesome revelation, Daniel was both encouraged and alarmed. He was encouraged by the knowledge that God will one day judge the wicked nations for their sin and unrighteousness. He found comfort in God's promise that even though Babylon was going to be destroyed, Daniel himself — as well as the Jewish people exiled in the Babylonian Empire — would be preserved. He was also alarmed. He recognized that the time was short; God's judgment was about to fall on the Babylonian Empire.

As believers study God's prophetic word, and see events in the Middle East rapidly shaping the stage of world history for the return of the Messiah, they, too, should be both encouraged and alarmed. Like Daniel, they should rejoice in the knowledge that God is a covenant-keeping God. The Messiah, Yeshua, will return in fulfillment of God's prophetic program! But their hearts should be alarmed because of the shortness of the hour. Many have not heard the Good News of salvation. An understanding of God's prophetic truth should spark within believers a desire to exhibit their faith through actions — an urgency to proclaim the Gospel to all peoples.

Understanding God's prophetic word is not an intellectual exercise; it is not a "spiritual exercise." Prophecy is not truth to be contemplated. Rather, understanding God's prophetic truth should provoke believers into action. God is acting in history! Judgment is coming! Daniel lived his life in the light of the privilege that was his in understanding God's prophetic program. Likewise, understanding God's prophetic Word is a privilege for the believer today — a privilege accompanied by the great responsibility to share the gospel with all peoples.

A Uni-horned Goat

Daniel's vision recorded in Daniel 8 dealt with more than just the Medo-Persian Empire. He wrote: "As I was thinking about this, suddenly a goat with a prominent horn between his eyes came from the west, crossing the whole earth without touching the ground. He came toward the two-horned ram I had seen standing beside the canal and charged at him in great rage. I saw him attack the ram furiously, striking the ram and shattering his two horns. The ram was powerless to stand against him; the goat knocked him to the ground and trampled on him, and none could rescue the ram from his power. The goat became very great, but at the height of his power his large horn was broken off, and in its place four prominent horns grew up toward the four winds of heaven" (Daniel 8:5–8).

This vision of Daniel's is most unique because it foretold the shifting of Gentile power from the east to the west!Daniel saw the ram (representing the Medo-Persian Empire) charge from the east and conquer the west, the north, and the south (Dan. 8:4). In the next verse, he saw the ram being attacked *from the west* by a goat with a great horn (8:5). Verse 21 reveals that the shaggy goat was none other than the king of Macedon (Philip of Macedon) and that the large horn between his eyes was Philip's son, Alexander the Great.

Once again, history verifies the accuracy of the Bible. The goat's horn represented Greece under the leadership of Alexander the Great, its first king, who conquered the kingdom of Persia (the ram). Greece's conquest of Persia marked the first time in history that a nation from the west had conquered a nation to the east. Also, up to that time the Gentile domination of Israel was always controlled from the east. But since the victory of Alexander the Great to the present day, Israel has been controlled by the nations of the west.

In the final conflict, which will occur during the Seventieth 'Seven' of Daniel, the western nations of the world will be involved in the invasion of Israel and the nations to the north, east, and south.

Daniel's vision of the he-goat "coming from the west, crossing the whole earth without touching the ground" (verse 5) was remarkably fulfilled in every detail. But before proceeding with our discussion of Daniel's vision we need to digress to take a closer look at Alexander the Great.

Alexander the Great

Although Alexander the Great is not mentioned by name in Scripture, he is mentioned by name in 1 Maccabees 1:1: "And it happened, after that Alexander *son* of Philip, the Macedonian, who came out of the land of Chettiim, had smitten Darius king of the Persians and Medes, that he reigned in his stead, the first over Greece, And made many wars, and won many strong holds, and slew the kings of the earth, And went though to the ends of the earth, and took spoils of many nations, insomuch that the earth was quiet before him; whereupon he was exalted, and his heart was lifted up. And he gathered a mighty strong host, and ruled over countries, and nations, and kings, who became tributaries unto him."[3]

Philip, king of Macedon, had trained his son, Alexander, for a military career. At the early age of sixteen, Alexander took part in the campaign against the Illyrians. In 336 B.C., when Philip was assassinated, Alexander was confirmed as the leader of the Hellas army to fight against Darius, the leader of the Persian army.

History has recorded the swiftness with which the Persian Empire was destroyed by Alexander the Great — six short years. He wanted revenge for the atrocities his people had suffered at the hands of the Persian king, Xerxes. Thus, after his father's death, Alexander began his illustrious military career by securing all of Greece. He then gathered his army at Pella and crossed the Hellespont to fight against the Persians. He successfully routed the Persian army, slaughtering many of the troops and chasing the rest into Asia Minor. But, he was unable to capture Darius. When he heard that Darius had re-grouped his forces and was coming to meet him in battle with over a half-million men Alexander is said to have hastened with all speed to meet him.

"Rapidity of motion (symbolized in Dnl. 8:5 by the 'he-goat' that 'came from the west...across the face of the whole earth, without touching the ground') was Alexander's great strength. In 333 B.C. the two armies met in the relatively narrow plain of Issus. Here the Persians lost, to a great extent, the advantage of their numbers; they were defeated with tremendous slaughter, Darius himself being put to flight. Alexander pursued the defeated army only far enough to break it up utterly. He then began his march southward along the seacoast of Syria toward Egypt..."[4]

While he was in Egypt, Alexander went to the oracle of Jupiter Amon (Amen-Ra). Afterward, the Egyptians declared him to be the son of their god; they ascribed to him divine origin, thus making him more than a mere man. Coins were struck with Alexander's image, depicting him with "two ram's horns". This image of Alexander was carried over into the Koran, which calls him "Iskander du al-qarnain" (Alexander of the Two Horns).

Some Bible commentators therefore assign a late date to the book of Daniel, or they state that the ram seen in Daniel 8:3 does not refer to the Medo-Persian Empire, but to Alexander instead. History refutes this interpretation, however, as does the Word of God, in that Persia was historically symbolized by the ram (see Daniel 8:20, 21). The ram's horns given to the image of Alexander only symbolized the Egyptians' attempt to make him a god — perhaps explaining Daniel's vision of the large horn (Alexander) on the head of the goat as he defeats the ram (Persia).

Having subdued Egypt, and having received god-like status, Alexander set out on his last campaign to utterly defeat Darius and the Medo-Persian Empire. He was determined that Darius, who had slipped through his fingers twice before, would not slip away again. Scripture declares that Alexander "charged at him in great rage" (Daniel 8:6). He wanted to utterly destroy the Persian army. Once again, Darius was forced to gather a large army. The Persian army, which this time assembled on the plains of the Tigris River, was no match for Alexander's small army. Alexander's troops overwhelmed the Persians and slaughtered almost the entire army, resulting in the total submission of the Medo-Persian Empire to Alexander.

The vision of Daniel was completely and totally fulfilled: "I saw him attack the ram furiously, striking the ram and shattering his two horns. The ram was powerless to stand against him; the goat knocked him to the ground and trampled on him, and none could rescue the ram from his power" (Daniel 8:7). The Persian Empire, which had taken years to consolidate, was completely conquered by Alexander in only six short years.

After conquering the Persian Empire, Alexander continued to pursue Darius into India. Alexander would have followed Darius into the Far East, but his Macedonian army would not go with him, so he returned to Babylon.

Daniel then noted that the goat, which we are told represented the king of Greece, became very great, and that the great horn, which represented Greece's first king, Alexander the Great, was broken off at the apex of its strength and power. "The goat became very great, but at the height of his power his large horn was broken off, and in its place four prominent horns grew up toward the four winds of heaven" (Daniel 8:8).

Once again history has recorded the exact fulfillment of Daniel's vision and prophecy. Like other kings of Babylon, Alexander began to live a drunken, licentious life. He was struck with malaria, and because of his poor health, brought on by his sinful and dissolute life, he died after being ill for only eleven days. Thus ended the career of Alexander the Great, the brilliant 32-year-old king who had ascended the throne of Greece only twelve years earlier.

Alexander failed to recognize God's hand upon his life. Through all of his conquests and victories he had many opportunities to see and to acknowledge God's involvement in the affairs of men. One such opportunity occurred when Alexander and his army approached Jerusalem and were met by the high priest and the elders of Israel. Alexander was shown the scroll of Daniel in which he, Alexander the Great, was symbolized as a leopard that would conquer the world. It is likely that Alexander was flattered by the words of the high priest. However, he failed to recognize that every God-given privilege brings with it responsibility. He ignored the fact that, as a human being, he was clay in the Master's hands. It is God's desire to shape and mold us as His instruments of righteousness in the world (see Isaiah 64:8; Jeremiah 18:1–11).

The God of Israel gave Alexander an opportunity to recognize Him, to worship Him, to acknowledge Him as sovereign. Instead, in his pride and sin, Alexander lifted himself up and gloried in the worship of men, refusing to acknowledge the One who had made him and who had given him his position and station in life.

There was a time when Israel had a similar problem. The prophet Isaiah addressed the nation saying, "You turn things upside down, as if the potter were thought to be like the clay! Shall what is formed say to him who formed it, 'He did not make me'? Can the pot say of the potter, 'He knows nothing?'" (Isaiah 29:16).

Perhaps Yeshua, knowing the incident of Alexander the Great's visit with the high priest, and knowing that the Jews in Jerusalem were also very familiar with the story, had Alexander in mind when He told the crowds and His disciples, "What good is it for a man to gain the whole world, yet forfeit his soul?" (Mark 8:36). Alexander the Great had conquered the then-known world, but from all indications he died in his own sins — he lost his own soul.

What a stern warning Alexander's fate should be! The Word of God is freely taught in our society. Through television, radio, the printed page, and the pulpits of our land, the Gospel message goes forth. On the final day of judgment mankind will be without excuse.

After Alexander's death in 323 B.C., a great struggle began for the control of his vast empire. God had told Daniel that the empire would be divided in four directions. "The goat became very great, but at the height of his power his large horn was broken off, and in its place four prominent horns grew up toward the four winds of heaven" (Daniel 8:8).

History records that Alexander had two legal heirs: One was a half-witted son named Philip. The other was born after Alexander's death; he was named Alexander, after his father. Neither son had a chance of becoming king. In his book "Israel and the Nations," F.F. Bruce describes in vivid detail what happened to Alexander's heirs: "Within a few years Philip Arrhidaeus and his wife Eurydice had been put to death by Olympias; Olympias in turn was put to death by Cassander, son of Antipater, who controlled Macedonia and Greece, and later on Cassander also murdered Roxane and her young son, Alexander. As all Alexander's legitimate heirs had thus been removed, there was no longer any need to maintain the pretense of guardianship and regency, and a scramble began for the succession."[5]

ALEXANDER'S EMPIRE DIVIDED

The scramble for the empire ended when an agreement was made to divide it among Alexander's four generals —Cassander, Lysimachus, Seleucus, and Ptolemy. Cassander took Macedonia, Thessaly, and Greece. Lysimachus took Thrace, Cappadocia and northern Asia Minor. Seleucus took Syria, Babylonia and Media. Ptolemy took Egypt and Cyprus. Thus four empires were formed, an exact fulfillment of Daniel's vision.

In Daniel 7, Alexander the Great's empire was symbolized as a leopard with four heads and four wings; whereas in Daniel 8, it was symbolized as a goat. The symbolism for Medo-Persia is likewise different in Daniel chapters seven and eight. In chapter seven, Medo-Persia was seen as a bear with three ribs in it's mouth; whereas in chapter eight, it was depicted as a ram with two horns. Why the change in symbolism for the same empires?

The symbolism used by God was divinely appointed, based upon God's intents and purposes in revealing prophetic truth to Daniel. In chapter seven, Daniel was given a vision concerning the succession of world empires — empires that would exist during a great period of time called the "Times of the Gentiles" (see Luke 21:24). These Gentile nations were to come into existence and exercise authority, power, and privilege as the result of Israel's sin and disobedience. God chose rapacious beasts to symbolize these nations because He wanted to depict their character and attitudes toward one another, as well as toward Israel and the

Jewish people. The bear, the lion, the leopard, and the horrible beast with iron teeth, were animals that could kill and completely devour their prey.

The nations of the world, deceived by Satan and blinded by their own sin, have always sought to destroy the Jewish people. History has been written and punctuated with Jewish blood, shed by the nations of the world as they have sought to destroy the Jews. These animals symbolized the ferocity as well as the speed and power of the nations, deceived by Satan, as they had sought, and would continue to seek, to destroy Israel.

God warned Israel that its sin and disobedience would bring it under the bondage and control of the nations. He told Moses, "Then the LORD will scatter you among all nations, from one end of the earth to the other. There you will worship other gods — gods of wood and stone, which neither you nor your fathers have known. Among those nations you will find no repose, no resting place for the sole of your foot. There the LORD will give you an anxious mind, eyes weary with longing, and a despairing heart. You will live in constant suspense, filled with dread both night and day, never sure of your life. In the morning you will say, 'If only it were evening!' and in the evening, 'If only it were morning!' — because of the terror that will fill your hearts and the sights that your eyes will see" (Deuteronomy 28:64–67).

These rapacious beasts symbolizing anti-Semitic nations are created beings. As such, they are under the power and authority of God Himself. God is sovereign over all His creatures and over all the nations, which can only rise and fall as God permits.

Each of these beasts, with the exception of the last beast (the one with the iron teeth representing the final empire of Gentile domination over Israel), could be tamed. In Daniel's day, it was common to have such beasts as part of the royal court. Even today we find trained bears, lions, and leopards. The fact that these animals could be tamed indicates that not all Gentile nations would seek to destroy the Jews. Nations can only be tamed through the power of the Holy Spirit and the Word of God.

We have seen, and will see, that within nations where the leaders have accepted the Word of God, the Jewish people have not suffered persecution. However, within the untamed nations — nations that refuse to accept the authority of God's Word — there are those who seek to destroy the Jewish people. This is why the last beast, the final beast which represents the Tribulation Empire, was depicted as being something that was not an ordinary animal. This beast symbolized Satan's presence and power, which cannot be tamed, since Satan will never accept God's Word. For that, he will be cast into the Lake of Fire.

In Daniel, chapter eight, the symbolism changed because the emphasis was different. Here, God began to reveal to the prophet the direct effect these untamed nations would have on Israel and the Jewish people. A ram and a he-goat can be dangerous, but they are not beasts of prey. In other words, although the nations symbolized as rapacious beasts in chapter seven were deceived by Satan, and would try to destroy the Jewish people, they would not succeed. God promised Israel that He would not put a complete end to the nations, even though He would chastise them for their sins (see Jeremiah 5:18). Thus, the ram and he-goat with horns symbolized the power and authority of nations that God would use to chastise Israel for its sin and disobedience. However, they would not be permitted to utterly destroy Israel.

Having thus seen a vision of Alexander's empire being given over to his four generals, Daniel then saw the rise of yet another conqueror. "Out of one of them came another horn, which started small but grew in power to the south and to the east and toward the Beautiful Land" (Daniel 8:9).

We see God's great precision and detail in the image of the horns. Daniel states that he saw one of the horns grow another horn. This new horn began small but continued to grow until it conquered the south, the east, and finally the "Beautiful Land" (a reference to the land of Israel).

Once again, history records the precise fulfillment of Daniel's visions and prophecies. Almost all Christian and Jewish scholars believe that the little horn that grew up out of one of the four horns refers to Antiochus Epiphanes, who came from the Syrian kingdom of Seleucus. Antiochus Epiphanes was a younger son of Antiochus III (Antiochus the Great) (242 B.C.).

HELLENISM VERSUS JUDAISM

In order to understand the visions and prophecies in Daniel, chapters eight and eleven, we must understand something of the history of that period. After the break-up of Alexander the Great's empire, his four generals, not content with the territories given to them, engaged in warfare with one another. The Seleucid empire which ruled Syria, sought to capture Coelesyria, which was controlled by Ptolemy II of Egypt. The small country of Judea had the misfortune of being caught in the middle of these conflicting empires. Judea was caught as well between two conflicting religious and social ideologies — Judaism and Hellenism. Hellenism was the influence of Greek culture. The Seleucid empire sometimes required mandatory submission to Hellenistic culture, literature, language, and the arts, as well as political, economic, and religious beliefs. Hellenistic beliefs directly contradicted rabbinic Judaism and synagogue and temple worship.

The struggles between the Seleucid empire and the Ptolemies of Egypt continued, and it was this ongoing conflict that became the background for Daniel's prophecies concerning the kings of the north and the south (see Daniel 11:2–35).

Whenever the Seleucids were victorious, they sought to Hellenize the conquered territories. Whenever Egypt was victorious, it also sought to impose its own religious, political, and economic reforms upon the subjugated territories. Such were the struggles facing the inhabitants of Judea (Israel), who were constantly being pulled one way or the other by the opposing forces. As a result, Judaism as a religious, political, and economic system was being subtly changed. Hellenism began to penetrate synagogue and temple worship, as well as to affect the priesthood and the political rulers. The debilitating effects of this ideological struggle eventually weakened both the Seleucid and the Ptolemaic empires, thus allowing Rome to conquer both.

Antiochus III became king of the Seleucid empire after the murder of his brother, Seleucus III Soter in 223 B.C. Antiochus was a warrior king, and although his first campaigns against Egypt were successful, he lost a most decisive battle near Rafi'ah (Rafa) located south of Gaza. As a result of this loss, he was forced to give up much of the territory he had conquered. Josephus wrote:

Now it happened that in the reign of Antiochus the Great, who ruled over all Asia, that the Jews, as well as the inhabitants of CoeleSyria, suffered greatly, and their land was sorely harassed; for while he was at

war with Ptolemy Philopater, and with his son, who was called
Epiphanes, it fell out that these nations were equally sufferers, both
when he was beaten and when he beat the others: so that they were very
like to a ship in a storm, which is tossed by the waves on both sides: and
just thus were they in their situation in the middle between Antiochus'
prosperity and its change to adversity.[6]

By the year 198 B.C., the Jewish leaders within Judea decided that
the inhabitants of the region could no longer tolerate living under the
struggle between the Ptolemaic rule (Egyptian) and the Seleucid (Hellenistic) empires. They decided living under the Seleucid rule would be pref-
erable to living under the Ptolemaic rule. Therefore, when Antiochus III
sought to liberate the cities of Coelesyria, including Samaria and Judea,
the Jewish leaders of Jerusalem opened the gates of Jerusalem to the
armies of Antiochus and helped them defeat the Egyptian garrison which
the Ptolemies had placed there.

Josephus recorded, "...Yet was it not long afterward when Antiochus
overcame Scopas [general of the Ptolemaic armies], in a battle fought at
the fountains of Jordan, and destroyed a great part of his army. But afterward, when Antiochus subdued those cities of Coelesyria which Scopas
had gotten into his possession, and Samaria with them, the Jews, of their
own accord, went over to him, and received him into the city [Jerusa-
lem] and gave plentiful provision to all his army, and to his elephants,
and readily assisted him when he besieged the garrison which was in the
citadel of Jerusalem."[7]

As a reward for the help and assistance Antiochus had received from
the Jewish leadership and for the "splendid reception" he received from
the Jewish people, Antiochus allowed the Jews to form their own government, after their own laws. They were exempt from the "Hellenization" policy he had established for all other conquered territories and
countries. He also exempted the Jews from paying taxes to the Seleucid
empire. Instead, they were allowed to pay their taxes to the "temple
Fund," so that temple worship and Judaism as a political and religious
system could be maintained.

Josephus recorded the following letter sent by Antiochus III to
Ptolemy of Egypt:

Since the Jews, upon our first entrance on their country, demonstrated their friendship towards us; and when we came to their city, [Jerusalem,] received us in a splendid manner, and came to meet us with their senate, and gave abundance of provisions to our soldiers, and to the elephants, and joined with us in ejecting the garrison of the Egyptians that were in the citadel, we have thought fit to reward them, and to retrieve the condition of their city, which hath been greatly depopulated by such accidents as have befallen its inhabitants, and to bring those that have been scattered abroad back to the city; and, in the first place, we have determined, on account of their piety towards God, to bestow on them, as a pension, for their sacrifices of animals that are fit for sacrifice, for wine and oil, and frankincense, the value of twenty thousand pieces of silver,...and these payments I would have fully paid them, as I have sent orders to you. I would also have the work about the temple finished, and the cloisters, and if there be anything else that ought to be rebuilt; and for the materials of wood, let it be brought them out of Judea itself, and out of the other countries, and out of Libanus, tax-free; and the same I would have observed as to those other materials which will be necessary, in order to render the temple more glorious; and let all of that nation live according to the laws of their own country; and let the senate and priests, and the scribes of the temple, and sacred singers, be discharged from poll-money and the crown-tax, and other taxes also; and that the city may sooner recover its inhabitants, I grant a discharge from taxes for three years to its present inhabitants, and to such as shall come to it,...We also discharge them for the future from a third part of their taxes, that the losses they have sustained may be repaired; and all those citizens that have been carried away, and are become slaves, we grant them and their children their freedom; and give order that their substance be restored to them.[8]

Antiochus III then issued another decree forbidding foreigners (Hellenized pagans) from killing and sacrificing unclean animals in Jerusalem. Josephus recorded the decree of Antiochus III as follows:

...It shall be lawful for no foreigner to come within the limits of the temple round about; which thing is forbidden also to the Jews, unless to

those who, according to their own custom, have purified themselves. Nor let any flesh of horses, or of mules, or of asses, be brought into the city, whether they be wild or tame; nor that of leopards, or foxes, or hares; and, in general, that of any animal which is forbidden for the Jews to eat. Nor let their skins be brought into it; nor let any such animal be bred up in the city. Let them only be permitted to use the sacrifices derived from their forefathers, with which they have been obliged to make acceptable atonements to God. And he that transgresseth any of these orders, let him pay to the priests three thousand drachmae of silver.[9]

Thus, for a short time under Antiochus III the Jews of Israel and of Jerusalem had respite from outside influences. However, the struggle within the country between Hellenist Jews and the traditional Jews continued. Jews who wanted to bring their sacrifices to the temple were permitted to. They were allowed to maintain their own religious practices and form of government. But the respite was temporary.

The great victories over the Ptolemies of Egypt by Antiochus III had brought him to the attention of Rome. As Daniel had prophesied, Rome also had designs on Judea; in fact, on the entire Middle-East. When word spread that Antiochus III wanted to add Greece to his expanding empire, Rome took action to stop Antiochus III.

In 190 B.C. Antiochus III suffered a major defeat at the hands of the Romans near Magnesia (a city in Asia, near Ephesus), and he was forced to sign a treaty with the victorious Romans. His son Antiochus IV (later called Antiochus Epiphanes) was taken hostage by Rome. Perhaps the Romans thought that holding the son of Antiochus III would give them more control in the situation. However, this was not the case. The threat of Rome evoked such fear among the inhabitants in the eastern provinces of the Seleucid empire that they revolted against Antiochus III. In trying to put down the revolt, Antiochus was killed (or murdered) while he was trying to sack the temple treasuries of Elymias.

After Antiochus III's death, Seleucus IV, his eldest son (also called Philopater), ascended the throne in 187 B.C. Almost immediately Seleucus increased taxes to pay for his father's wars. He also expressed his intentions to lift the tax exemptions his father had granted to the Jews, thus ensuring that the Jews would pay their share of the tax burden. When the Hellenist Jews in Jerusalem heard of Seleucus' new policies, they told him about the fabulous treasure stored at the temple in Jerusalem, saying it would be more than sufficient to pay their share of the taxes. Seleucus immediately sent his official treasurer, Heliodorus, to Jerusalem to confiscate the temple treasury.

According to Jewish tradition, the high-priest met Heliodorus when he arrived in Jerusalem and tried to discourage him from confiscating the temple treasury, but Heliodorus would not be dissuaded. Jewish tradition goes on to say that when Heliodorus attempted to enter the temple, a miracle happened. He saw a vision of a horse with an armed rider. The horse and rider struck him, and two young men beat him nearly to death. This vision so unnerved Heliodorus that he lost consciousness, collapsed, and had to be carried out of the temple. When he regained strength he returned empty-handed to Seleucus and told him about the "divine power" that protected the temple treasure.

The Hellenist Jews in Jerusalem continued to pressure Seleucus to take the treasure rather than to tax the people. However, before Seleucus was able to seize the treasure, Heliodorus, his trusted treasurer, poisoned him (175 B.C.) and attempted to take the throne for himself. Perhaps Seleucus sensed that his life was in danger and that he was in need of help, for he had dispatched his own son, Demetrius, to Rome in exchange for Antiochus Epiphanes IV (Seleucus' brother) who had been taken as a hostage to Rome some fourteen years earlier. In fact, Antiochus Epiphanes was returning to Syria when he heard that his brother, Seleucus, had been murdered by Heliodorus, who had subsequently usurped the throne.

The news of his brother's death infuriated Antiochus. While in Rome, Antiochus had learned how Rome used force, political intrigue, and religion, as well as savage brutality to impose its will on conquered territories. Immediately, Antiochus made political alliances with two men who had been his father's enemies — Eumenes, King of Pergamum, and his brother, Attalas. These two men had supplied Antiochus with armies and financial aid in his fight against Heliodorus. Before long, the armies of Antiochus prevailed, and Heliodorus was captured and cruelly slain. Demetrius, Seleucus' son and rightful heir to the throne, was left in Rome, and Antiochus proclaimed himself to be the rightful king of Syria and Asia (including Judea).

ANTIOCHUS EPIPHANES

Daniel prophesied of Antiochus Epiphanes, "He [Seleucus] will be succeeded by a contemptible person [Antiochus Epiphanes] who has not been given the honor of royalty. He will invade the kingdom when its people feel secure, and he will seize it through intrigue" (Daniel 11:21).

Thus, through intrigue, Antiochus Epiphanes, a man who was not entitled to be king, became one of the most influential and powerful kings of the Middle East. He was known for his love of cruelty and for his love of Hellenism. He was also an immense egoist, equating himself with the gods by giving himself the title, "Epiphanes" ("the illustrious" or "majestic one"). The Jews of Judea, however, made a subtle change in his title, calling him among themselves "Antiochus Epimanes" (the madman).

The reign of Antiochus Epiphanes from 175 to 164 B.C. marks a turning point in Jewish history. He was a man dedicated to the task of restoring the strength of the Seleucid empire, determined to accomplish his goal through an intense program of Hellenization. He was determined to enforce his particular brand of paganism upon all of the territories under his rule. This policy eventually resulted in a head-on collision with the Jews, for although some of them subscribed to some forms of Hellenism, none were really ready to subscribe to Antiochus' form of Hellenism. However, by the time the Hellenistic Jews discovered the extreme nature of the Hellenism which Antiochus was promoting, it was too late and they were already in its trap.

Soon after Antiochus Epiphanes came into power the Hellenistic Jews of Jerusalem offered him a large sum of money if he would remove Onias III, the high-priest, from office and transfer the high priesthood to Onias' brother, Jason. Onias was a strict Orthodox Jew, but Jason leaned toward Hellenism. Antiochus was delighted with their proposal. He needed the money they offered, to settle the debts he had incurred in his coup against Heliodorus. Acting on their suggestion, Antiochus had Onias, the legal high-priest, deposed and imprisoned. In 173 B.C., Antiochus appointed Jason as the new high-priest.

The Hellenistic Jews asked their new high-priest, Jason, to petition Antiochus to allow them to build a gymnasium in Jerusalem so that all Judeans who had been trained in the Greek games could participate. Antiochus, the Hellenist, was delighted. Further, the Hellenistic Jews wanted all Jewish participants in the Greek games to register themselves as residents of Antioch, or as Macedonians, thus insuring their full participation in Greek society. In 172 B.C. Jason selected the Acropolis on the northwest side of the temple as the site for the Olympian games and the gymnasium.

The selection of this site for the gymnasium added further stress to an already explosive situation. Orthodox Jews were not only opposed to Jason being the high-priest, they were also opposed to every form of Hellenism. Participation in the games required that every athlete compete in the nude, thus necessitating that Judean participants in the games appear nude in sight of the temple. It also meant Judean participants would have to go through the painful operation of disguising their circumcision, the mark of God's covenant. To remove this mark was, in effect, to become non-Jewish. To most Jews this was unthinkable. But many in Israel wanted to be like the nations and now, in Antiochus, they had a king who would force them to be like the nations. God had told Daniel that "a little horn would arise" and He said this little horn (in the form of Antiochus Epiphanes) would trample down the temple and it's worship (see Daniel 8:10–12).

Even Jason could not bear the deliberate violation of the Law and of Jewish tradition that would result from the Jewish athletes' participation in the Olympian games. When the Judeans were sent to participate in the games being held at Tyre, money was to be sent as a contribution toward the sacrifices being made to the pagan god Hercules, but Jason balked. He could not go so far as to sacrifice to a pagan deity. The Hellenists in Jerusalem were furious at Jason, and they began to devise ways to depose him from the high priesthood.

Once again the high priesthood was sold. This time it was purchased by Onias Menelaus, a Benjaminite and therefore not a legitimate heir to the high priesthood. Onias was an outright Hellenist who was in total agreement with the policies of Antiochus. The Orthodox Jewish community of Jerusalem was infuriated. The gates of the temple would be opened to idolatry because of another false high priest, a usurper. They despised the sight of Jewish priests garbed in Greek robes, officiating at the idolatrous rites of the Greeks. Jerusalem was fast becoming a Hellenistic city, and Antiochus and the Hellenistic Jews were delighted.

Without conscience, they did what was right in their own eyes, giving no thought to the judgment of God that would soon fall.

God's Word warns us that He always judges sin. How strange that the Jewish religious leaders, who had full knowledge of Daniel's prophecies, and had even used those prophecies to influence Alexander the Great, evidently no longer believed them or, at least, did not apply them to their present situation. Such is the blindness that sin brings to the heart and mind.

The small Orthodox Jewish community in Jerusalem that opposed the Hellenistic influences infecting the larger Jewish community in Jerusalem, expressed their opposition in ways similar to the Hellenists, the very group they opposed. They entered into alliances, seeking out their old enemies, the Ptolemies of Egypt. Instead of trusting God, both groups, Hellenists and Orthodox Jews, put their faith in man.

Man, by his very nature, seems to turn to God only as a last resort. Israel would not have experienced much of its painful history had its leaders turned to God first.

God told the prophet Daniel exactly what Antiochus Epiphanes would do: "It [the little horn] grew until it reached the host of the heavens, and it threw some of the starry host down to the earth and trampled on them. It set itself up to be as great as the Prince of the host; it took away the daily sacrifice from him, and the place of his sanctuary was brought low. Because of rebellion, the host of the saints and the daily sacrifice were given over to it. It prospered in everything it did, and truth was thrown to the ground" (Daniel 8:10–12).

Striving to restore the prestige and position of the Seleucid empire, Antiochus built more Greek cities than any of his predecessors. His goal was to conquer the world, to become more powerful than Rome. He had given himself the title of "Epiphanes," meaning "Illustrious One" or "God Manifest" because he believed himself to be divine; he believed himself to be a descendant of the gods. He issued coins bearing his own portrait in the image of the Olympian god, Zeus. He demanded that statues of him be erected in all the temples and that all of the people worship his image. He held lavish spectator sports, going so far as to import the Roman gladiatorial events to the capital in Syria. At his parties and orgies he danced naked with his royal entertainers. All of this was done to impose his rule over his subjects and to force his particular brand of Hellenism on the countries he had conquered. His successes had gone to his head.

With the Hellenistic high priest, Onias Menelaus, established in Jerusalem, Antiochus turned his attention to Egypt. He wanted to subdue Egypt, to bring it under his form of Hellenism, and unify his empire. In the summer of 169 B.C. Antiochus invaded Egypt with a huge army. His campaign was successful. He quickly deposed the young Egyptian king and declared himself king over a unified empire, but his grandiose plans did not last long. On his way to Memphis Antiochus was met by a Roman ambassador who served him with papers notifying him that Rome had issued him an ultimatum: Withdraw from Egypt or face an immediate attack from Rome. Antiochus knew his battle-weary troops would be no match for the well-armed and well-trained Roman army, so he and his troops withdrew from Egypt. It was a humiliating experience for Antiochus, who considered himself to be "a god."

In Jerusalem rumors began to spread that Antiochus had been killed. Jason, the first high priest whom Antiochus had appointed for a fee, saw this as his opportunity to overthrow Menelaus (the high priest Antiochus had appointed in Jason's place). Jason was supported in his efforts by the Orthodox Jews of Jerusalem and by those who were opposed to Hellenism, a group of one thousand men. He attacked the city and was able to penetrate the walls of Jerusalem, forcing Menelaus' supporters to retreat and take refuge in the Acra (a strong fortification near the temple site). Jason entered Jerusalem and killed many of his fellow countrymen in his attempt to regain the office of high priest.

The rumors of Antiochus' death soon dissipated. Word spread that he was very much alive and that he was livid over the revolt taking place in Jerusalem. He took it personally, believing that Jason and the Jews were revolting against him and against his Hellenization policy. First being humiliated by Rome, and then by Jason in Jerusalem, Antiochus left Egypt in great haste and in a vengeful rage. He ordered his troops to massacre the Jews of Jerusalem, without regard to age or sex, slaughtering friend and foe alike. An account of this slaughter is given in 2 Maccabees:

Now when this that was done came to the king's ear, he thought that

Judea had revolted: whereupon removing out of Egypt in a furious mind, he took the city by force of arms,

And commanded his men of war not to spare such as they met, and to slay such as went up upon the houses.

Thus there was killing of young and old, making away of men, women, and children, slaying of virgins and infants.

And there were destroyed within the space of three whole days four-score thousand, whereof forty thousand were slain in the conflict; and no fewer sold than slain.

Yet was he not content with this, but presumed to go into the most holy temple of all the world; Menelaus, that traitor to the laws, and to his own country, being his guide:

And taking the holy vessels with polluted hands, and with profane hands pulling down the things that were dedicated by other kings to the augmentation and glory and honor of the place, he gave them away.[10]

According to Jewish tradition, Antiochus blasphemed the God of Israel because God did nothing to stop his desecration of the temple. He reasoned that if God was omnipotent, as the Jews proclaimed, He would have prevented the sacrilege of His temple. Jewish tradition also states that Antiochus spread lies about the Jews. These lies caused much hatred and anti-Semitic feelings toward the Jewish people.

...Antiochus declared that he had seen in the holy of holies the statue of a man with a long beard, mounted on an ass, holding a book in its hand. He believed it to be the statue of the law-giver Moses, who had given the Judaeans inhuman, horrible laws to separate them from all other peoples. Amongst the Greeks and Romans the rumour was spread that Antiochus had found the head of an ass made of gold in the temple, which the Judaeans venerated, and that consequently they worshipped asses. Antiochus was probably the author of another horrible lie invented to blacken the Judaeans: it was said that he had discovered, lying in bed in the temple, a Greek, who entreated to be released, as the

Judaeans were in the habit of killing a Greek every year, and feeding on his intestines, meanwhile swearing hatred against all Greeks, whom they were determined to destroy.[11]

Through the centuries of time the lies of Antiochus have continued to haunt the Jewish people — lies that continued to be spread by the Romans, by the Crusaders, and by Hitler. The same lies are still used by anti-Semites today. The Scriptures tell us that in the Tribulation, God will send a strong delusion upon the people and "they shall believe the lie" (see 2 Thessalonians 2:11). It is believing "the lie" that ultimately will bring God's judgment down upon the nations.

The origin and source of all lies is Satan. Scriptures calls him the "father of lies" (see John 8:44). It is his lie that says to the human heart, "The Jews are not the chosen people of God" and "God is finished with the Jews," even though God clearly chose Israel as a means of revealing His promises, first in the Old Testament and then in the New.

Since the continued existence of the Jews validates the authenticity of the Bible, and since the reason for Messiah's return is to establish a Kingdom for the Jews, Satan's plan is to destroy the Jew and thereby invalidate the promises of God, the Word of God. Ever since that first lie to Eve, Satan has continued to seek to replace God's holy Kingdom with his own ungodly kingdom. He wants his "chosen people" to replace God's chosen people. But the Scriptures tell us that Satan will not succeed. He has already been defeated through the death, burial, and resurrection of our Messiah Yeshua. Still, he spreads his lies, deluding men and women into believing that all evil, hardship, trouble, and tribulation in the world is caused by the Jews. His lie to the hearts of mankind is that the world would be a better place if mankind would rid themselves of the Jews. Pharaoh believed the lie. Haman believed the lie. Antiochus Epiphanes believed the lie. Hitler believed the lie. Many people today believe the lie. Scripture tells us that the nations will believe the lie in the Tribulation.

A HISTORIC ANTICHRIST

Antiochus Epiphanes believed the lie, and spreading it became his personal crusade. It is no wonder, then, that Scripture, in selecting a type of the Beast (or the antichrist) chose Antiochus Epiphanes. It was

Antiochus Epiphanes who set up the first "abomination of desolation" in the temple. Yeshua referred to the "abomination that causes desolation" in Matthew 24:15. The Bible characterizes what the Beast, the political ruler in the Tribulation, will be like and what he will do. Notice what Daniel says of Antiochus Epiphanes:

(1) He casts down the host of heaven and tramples on them. (See Daniel 8:10 and compare with Revelation 12:13–17.)

(2) He sets himself up to be greater than the Prince of the Host. (See Daniel 8:11 and compare with 2 Thessalonians 2:3–12.)

(3) He takes away the daily sacrifice. (See Daniel 8:11 and compare with Daniel 9:27 and Matthew 24:15.)

(4) He causes an abomination to be placed in the temple. (See Daniel 8:11, 12 and compare with Daniel 9:27; 11:31; Matthew 24:15; and 2 Thessalonians 2:3.)

(5) He has a false prophet (priest) who will do his bidding. (Daniel 8:12 and compare with Revelation 13:11–17 [i.e., the Beast out of the earth].)

(6) He throws truth to the ground, making people believe the "lie". (See Daniel 8:12 and compare with 2 Thessalonians 2:3–12 and Revelation 13:4, 14.)

These verses described in advance the actions taken by Antiochus Epiphanes to bring the Jewish people under his control.

Antiochus never forgot how Rome had humiliated him by forcing him to leave Egypt after he had conquered that country. In 168 B.C., while Rome was bogged down in a war in Macedonia, Antiochus saw his chance to avenge his humiliation. He quickly entered Egypt, progressing as far as Alexandria. Once again, the King of Egypt was able to dispatch envoys to Rome, and once again, Rome told Antiochus to leave Egypt. But this time he refused. When Rome had successfully put an end to the Macedonian war on June 22, 168 B.C., three deputies were immediately dispatched to inform Antiochus that the full Roman Senate had commanded him to leave Egypt at once. Antiochus asked for more time. History records that the Roman deputy, Popillius Laenas, drew a circle in the sand around Antiochus. He then purportedly told Antiochus that before he stepped out of the circle, he had to state whether he wanted war or peace with Rome. Antiochus chose peace and returned to his capital in Syria, once again humiliated by the Romans.

As the knowledge spread of Antiochus' humiliation and defeat at the hands of the Romans (though not even one battle had been fought), Antiochus began to look for a scapegoat. He found one in the Jews in Judea. They had proclaimed, or so he believed, that it was their God who had humiliated him. Antiochus vowed he would show the Jews of Jerusalem that he was more powerful then their God so he sent Apollonius, the former governor of Mysia and one of his loyal subjects, to Jerusalem. The writer of the Maccabees described what happened when Apollonius entered Jerusalem:

> *He sent also that detestable ringleader Apollonius with an army of two and twenty thousand, commanding him to slay all those that were in their best age, and to sell the women and younger sort:*
> *Who coming to Jerusalem, and pretending peace, did forbear till the holy day of the sabbath, when taking the Jews keeping holy day, he commanded his men to arm themselves.*
>
> *And so he slew all them that were gone to the celebrating of the sabbath, and running through the city with weapons slew great multitudes.*
>
> *But Judas Maccabaeus with nine others, or thereabout, withdrew himself in the wilderness, and lived in the mountains after the manner of beasts, with his company, who fed on herbs continually, lest they should be partakers of the pollution.*[12]

Antiochus had told Apollonius to kill and destroy the Jews' property but not to touch the temple. Antiochus wanted to desecrate the temple himself to prove he was greater than the God of the Jews. He looted the temple, taking away all of its treasure, sacred vessels, curtains, and furnishings. He then turned it into a fortified citadel. But his hatred of the Jews, and of their God, was so intense he still was not satisfied. He yearned to wreak yet more havoc on the Jews. Menelaus, the Hellenistic high priest, presented him with a plan. It seemed that Menelaus was growing tired of being the high priest over a temple where no one could worship, so he suggested that Antiochus pass laws forbidding Jews from keeping the law of Moses, and commanding them to adopt the Greek faith. In other words, the Jews were to be completely Hellenized, or destroyed.

Antiochus liked Menelaus' plan because Antiochus would not only be the king over the Judean people, he would also prove once and for all that he was more powerful than the Jewish God. Antiochus issued his infamous decrees that were to put an end to the Jewish nation. In order to make the Jews like other people, he declared as illegal the three religious rites that ostensibly kept the Jews separated from the nations — circumcision, keeping the Sabbath and the festivals, and abstinence from unclean food.

The writer of the Maccabees described the results of Antiochus' decrees:

Moreover king Antiochus wrote to his whole kingdom that all should be one people,

And every one should leave his laws: so all the heathen agreed according to the commandment of the king.

Yea, many also of the Israelites consented to his religion, and sacrificed unto idols, and profaned the sabbath.

For the king had sent letters by messengers unto Jerusalem and the cities of Juda, that they should follow the strange laws of the land,

And forbid burnt offerings, and sacrifice, and drink offerings, in the temple; and that they should profane the sabbaths and festival days:

And pollute the sanctuary and holy people:

Set up altars, and groves, and chapels of idols, and sacrifice swine's flesh, and unclean beasts:

That they should also leave their children uncircumcised, and make their souls abominable with all manner of uncleanness and profanation:

To the end they might forget the law, and change all the ordinances.

And whosever would not do according to the commandment of the king, he said, he should die.

In the selfsame manner wrote he to his whole kingdom, and appointed overseers over all the people, commanding the cities of Juda to sacrifice, city by city.

Then many of the people were gathered unto them, to wit, every one that forsook the law; and so they committed evils in the land;

And drove the Israelites into secret places, even wheresoever they could flee for succour.

Now the fifteenth day of the month Casleu, in the hundred forty and fifth year, they set up the abomination of desolation upon the altar, and builded idol altars throughout the cities of Juda on every side;

And burnt incense at the doors of their houses, and in the streets.

And when they had rent in pieces the books of the law which they found, they burnt them with fire.

And wheresoever was found with any the book of the testament, or if any consented to the law, the king's commandment was, that they should put him to death.

Thus did they be their authority unto the Israelites every month, to as many as were found in the cities.

Now the five and twentieth day of the month they did sacrifice upon the idol altar, which was upon the altar of God.

At which time according to the commandment they put to death certain women, that had caused their children to be circumcised.

And they hanged the infants about their necks, and rifled their houses, and slew them that had circumcised them.

Howbeit many in Israel were fully resolved and confirmed in themselves not to eat any unclean thing.

Wherefore they chose rather to die, that they might not be defiled with meats, and that they might not profane the holy covenant: so then they died.

And there was very great wrath upon Israel.[13]

The Abomination of Desolation which Antiochus erected in the Holy of Holies was a statue of Jupiter. He is identified with the Greek god, Zeus, and represents the god who rules over all other gods. It was the image of the Olympian god Zeus that Antiochus had struck on all the coins he issued throughout his empire — but he had replaced the face of Zeus with his own image. Antiochus even sought to change the name of Jerusalem and of the temple itself. The writer of Maccabees wrote, "And to pollute also the temple in Jerusalem, and to call it the temple of Jupiter Olympus; and that in Garizim, of Jupiter the Defender of strangers, as they did desire that dwelt in the place."[14]

The vision of the little horn given to Daniel (Daniel 8:9–12) was fulfilled in every detail by Antiochus Epiphanes. He prospered in everything he did, and truth was thrown to the ground (8:12). God, in His permissive will, allowed sin to run rampant. From all outward appearances, it seemed that God had forsaken Israel and that Antiochus was in control. A similar situation will arise during the Tribulation. Just as Antiochus trampled down Jerusalem, so will the Beast, or antichrist, trample the city in the Tribulation. As Antiochus' false priest, Menelaus, was directing the people to worship Antiochus' image, so also will the Beast's false priest proclaim and enforce the Beast's lies. Just as Antiochus set up an Abomination of Desolation in the temple, so, too, will the Beast defile the temple. The Beast, like Antiochus, will demand that all worship him, and anyone refusing to do so will suffer death.

Some may ask why God allowed Antiochus to usurp such power, and why He will allow the Beast to do the same thing. God gave the prophet Daniel His reason, which is found in Daniel 8:12: "Because of rebellion, the host of the saints and the daily sacrifice were given over to it…"

Although this verse is difficult to translate, the inference in the Hebrew language is that God allowed Antiochus to defile the temple and to remove the daily sacrifice because of the rebellion of God's people. In other words, it was because of the sin of rebellion (disobedience) within the Jewish nation that God brought such a great judgment, and it will be for the same reason that God will bring the Great Tribulation upon Israel and the nations.

Like the sin of lying, the sin of rebellion is satanic. Satan was the first to rebel against God. In essence, rebellion is the declaration of the inner man saying, "I am going to do it my way; I will not submit my will to your will." Rebellion is diametrically opposed to obedience. It cannot exist alongside faith. Both sins — lying and rebellion — were present in the Garden of Eden, and both Adam and Eve succumbed to these sins.

First Eve was deceived by Satan's lie; then after eating the fruit she convinced Adam to eat it too. But the Scriptures state that when Adam ate of the fruit he deliberately disobeyed God (see 1 Timothy 2:14; compare Romans 5:12–14). God wanted the children of Israel to be obedient to Him, to trust Him. Some within Israel had forgotten this, and others deliberately declared they wanted to do things their own way. Instead of trusting God, they put their trust in man and in man-made alliances.

The visions described in this portion of the book of Daniel refer to God's dealings with Israel in history. After Israel had returned from Babylon the Israelites continued to sin. The prophets Haggai and Zechariah spoke directly to the people and in caustic language upbraided them because of their sin, but even then the people did not want to worship God in His way. Instead, they wanted to hold on to the superstitions and rituals they had developed in Babylon. Instead of being willing and anxious to work on the temple, the House of the LORD, they wanted to complete their own houses. They wanted to work on things that would satisfy themselves, placing God in second place in their lives.

God had made a promise to Israel. He told the people if they would return unto Him, that is, repent, He would return unto them, and His glory, which had left Solomon's temple, would return and dwell in the temple that Zerubbabel was building (see Zechariah 1:1–2:13). The temple was rebuilt but God's presence, His glory, never returned to the temple Zerubbabel built. Instead, Antiochus Epiphanes erected his Abomination of Desolation in it.

Disobedience and rebellion cannot exist alongside obedience and faith. God's presence cannot occupy a sanctuary that is defiled by sin. This is why it is so very important for believers to live lives that are righteous and holy. Their bodies are the temple of the Holy Spirit. God resides within the believers. He demands their obedience, their faith, their trust.

Time and time again God extended His grace to the people of Israel, but they responded with rebellious and stiff-necked pride. Only a faithful few, a remnant of faithful ones, responded to God's grace. Such obedience often meant cruel death. I believe the writer of Hebrews referred to this remnant of faithful believers in Israel when he wrote:

113

"who through faith conquered kingdoms, administered justice, and gained what was promised; who shut the mouths of lions, quenched the fury of the flames, and escaped the edge of the sword; whose weakness was turned to strength; and who became powerful in battle and routed foreign armies. Women received back their dead, raised to life again. Others were tortured and refused to be released, so that they might gain a better resurrection. Some faced jeers and flogging, while still others were chained and put in prison. They were stoned; they were sawed in two; they were put to death by the sword. They went about in sheepskins and goatskins, destitute, persecuted and mistreated—the world was not worthy of them" (Hebrews 11:33–38).

Although a remnant remained faithful, for the most part the religious leaders and political rulers became arrogant and rebelled against God. The result of that rebellion was the judgment of God upon Israel through Antiochus Epiphanes, or, as the Jews called him, Antiochus Epimanes, the madman.

God revealed to Daniel exactly when the little horn, Antiochus Epiphanes, would come into power. He also told Daniel precisely how long Antiochus would reign! He did this to assure those who were trusting in Him that truth would not always be "thrown to the ground" (Daniel 8:12). God is victorious. He is sovereign. Satan is a defeated foe. He cannot be the ultimate winner.

GOD'S JUDGMENT FINAL

This is a pattern throughout the Scriptures: When God foretells a coming judgment, He places a constraint of time upon His judgment. For example, long before God led Israel into Egypt, He told Abram that his descendants would be strangers in a country not their own. He said that this captivity would be for a specific time (400 years), and that He would deliver them at the end of the 400 years (see Genesis 16:13–16). Much later, when Israel continued to sin as a nation, God told the Israelites that they would be taken into captivity for seventy years. But He also promised that at the end of the seventy years He would deliver them (see Jeremiah 25:8–14; 27:22). God has even foretold the exact length of the coming Tribulation, after which the Messiah would return to establish

His kingdom (see Daniel 9:27; Revelation 11:1, 2).

It should therefore not surprise us that God told Daniel exactly how long Antiochus would pollute the temple. We read, "Then I heard a holy one speaking, and another holy one said to him, 'How long will it take for the vision to be fulfilled — the vision concerning the daily sacrifice, the rebellion that causes desolation, and the surrender of the sanctuary and of the host that will be trampled underfoot?' He said to me, 'It will take 2,300 evenings and mornings; then the sanctuary will be reconsecrated'" (Daniel 8:13, 14).

Note very carefully what Daniel was told, because confusion about the meaning of the phrase "2,300 evenings and mornings" has caused a great deal of misunderstanding of God's Word. Some individuals have used the 2,300 evenings and mornings to attempt to set a date for Messiah's return. Mr. William Miller and Ellen G. White, founders of the "Adventist" movement, interpreted these verses to mean 2,300 years. They began their calculations with the year 457 B.C. and calculated that 2,300 years later, in the year 1844 C.E., Yeshua would return and cleanse a rebuilt temple in Jerusalem. Their teaching caused quite a stir among Christians, and when the year 1844 approached, many looked for Yeshua's return. When He failed to come back the Adventist movement changed its interpretation, teaching instead that He had come to cleanse the Heavenly Sanctuary rather than the earthly sanctuary. However, nothing in Scripture supports such teaching.

Others apply the 2,300 evenings and mornings to modern Israel. Once again, the 2,300 evenings and mornings are calculated as years. Individuals who hold to this interpretation contend that God would use this time to chastise Israel. They conclude that the 2,300 evenings and mornings (symbolizing years) begin or end at various points in history — for instance, the signing of the Balfour declaration in 1917, or the establishment of the nation of Israel in 1948, or the capture of Jerusalem in 1967, or the Yom Kippur war in 1973. Thus, according to where they begin their calculations, they can make these verses refer to almost any future or past event.

All such calculations are incorrect because they ignore the simple statements of Scripture. In context, Daniel was told that the 2,300 evening and mornings related directly to the "daily sacrifice" — precisely, to its removal (cf. Daniel 8:13). Notice that God did not say "2,300 days." Nor did He say "2,300 years." Rather, He said, "2,300 evenings and mornings." He was referring to the required daily sacrifice of which there were two:

> *This is what you are to offer on the altar regularly each day: two lambs a year old. Offer one in the morning and the other at twilight. With the first lamb offer a tenth of an ephah of fine flour mixed with a fourth of a hin of oil from pressed olives, and fourth of a hin of wine as a drink offering. Sacrifice the other lamb at twilight with the same grain offering and its drink offering as in the morning — a pleasing aroma, an offering made to the LORD by fire. For the generations to come this burnt offering is to be made regularly at the entrance to the Tent of Meeting before the LORD. There I will meet you and speak to you; There also I will meet with the Israelites, and the place will be consecrated by my glory (Exodus 29:38–43).*

The 2,300 evenings and mornings is a direct reference to the two daily sacrifices in the temple, representing 1,150 days (2,300 divided by 2). Since a biblical year equals 360 days, 1,150 days represent three years and a few days — the exact length of time that Antiochus Epiphanes defiled the temple in Jerusalem. According to the writer of the Maccabees, Antiochus defiled the temple on 15 Kislev 145 (168 B.C.) and the Maccabees rededicated the altar on 25 Kislev 148 (165 B.C.) — exactly three years and a few days later, precisely fulfilling Daniel's prophecy about the "little horn," Antiochus Epiphanes.

The writer of the Maccabees recorded the cleansing of the temple and the rededication of the altar in this way:

> *Then said Judas and his brethren, Behold, our enemies are discomfited: let us go up to cleanse and dedicate the sanctuary.*
>
> *Upon this all the host assembled themselves together, and went up unto mount Sion.*
>
> *And when they saw the sanctuary desolate, and the altar profaned, and gates burned up, and shrubs growing in the courts as in a forest, or in one of the mountains, yea, and the priests' chambers pulled down;*

They rent their clothes, and made great lamentation, and cast ashes upon their heads,

And fell down flat to the ground upon their faces, and blew an alarm with the trumpets, and cried toward heaven.

Then Judas appointed certain men to fight against those that were in the fortress, until he had cleansed the sanctuary.

So he chose priests of blameless conversation, such as had pleasure in the law:

Who cleansed the sanctuary, and bare out the defiled stones into an unclean place.

And when as they consulted what to do with the altar of burnt offerings, which was profaned;

They thought it best to pull it down, lest it should be a reproach to them, because the heathen had defiled it: wherefore they pulled it down,

And laid up the stones in the mountain of the temple in a convenient place, until there should come a prophet to shew what should be done with them.

Then they took whole stones according to the law, and built a new altar according to the former;

And made up the sanctuary, and the things that were within the temple, and hallowed the courts.

They made also new holy vessels, and into the temple they brought the candlestick, and the altar of burnt offerings, and of incense, and the table.

And upon the altar they burned incense, and the lamps that were upon the candlestick they lighted, that they might give light in the temple.

Furthermore they set the loaves upon the table, and spread out the veils, and finished all the works which they had begun to make.

Now on the five and twentieth day of the ninth month, which is called the month Casleu [Kislev], in the hundred forty and eighth year, they rose up betimes in the morning,

And offered sacrifice according to the law upon the new altar of burnt offerings, which they had made. . . .

And so they kept the dedication of the altar eight days, and offered burnt offerings with gladness, and sacrificed the sacrifice of deliverance and praise. . . .

Moreover Judas and his brethren with the whole congregation of Israel ordained, that the days of the dedication of the altar should be kept in their season from year to year by the space of eight days, from the five and twentieth day of the month Casleu [Kislev], with mirth and gladness.[15]

The dedication of the altar by the Maccabees is still celebrated on 25 Kislev by Jewish people. It is called Hanukkah, the Feast of Dedication, or the Festival of Lights. It is celebrated for eight days, just as the Maccabees established.

Hanukkah, the Feast of Dedication, is only mentioned once in the Scriptures. It is a most interesting reference: "Then came the Feast of Dedication (Hanukkah) at Jerusalem. It was winter, and Yeshua was in the temple area walking in Solomon's Colonnade" (John 10:22, 23).

Yeshua had been ministering in the temple. (This temple, called Herod's temple, was an enlarged version of the temple cleansed and re-dedicated to God by the Maccabees.) The Jewish leaders came to Yeshua asking Him if He was indeed the Messiah. Yeshua responded that they should know He was the Messiah by the miracles He had performed in His Father's name. He then went on to tell them that He and the Father were one (see John 10:22–30). Upon hearing Yeshua's declaration that He and His Father were one, the Jewish leaders picked up stones to stone Him (see John 10:31–33). The significance of this incident not only involves Yeshua's declaration that He was equal to and one with the Father, but the Jewish leaders' reaction: They were going to stone Him for blasphemy. Three questions come to mind. (1) Why did Yeshua wait until this particular Festival, Hanukkah, to declare His deity? (2) Why did He make this declaration in the temple? (3) What stones did the Jewish leaders use in their attempt to stone Him?

God had promised that His glory would return to His temple in Jerusalem. Yeshua was the visible manifestation of God's glory. John wrote, "We have seen his glory, the glory of the one and only Son, who came from the Father, full of grace and truth" (John 1:14). Yeshua chose to declare His deity in the temple on Hanukkah so the Jewish leaders would know that He was the Son of God and so they would see that God's glory had returned. Sadly, however, religious tradition and the sin of unbelief had so blinded the hearts of the Jewish leaders that they refused to listen to His message. They refused to accept Him as the Messiah, the prophet like unto Moses, whom they were to listen to and obey (see Deuteronomy 18:14–20). So, when Yeshua declared Himself to be equal with God, they picked up stones to stone Him.

When the Maccabees were cleansing the temple, which had been desecrated by the Hellenistic priests of Antiochus, the workers pulled down the altar and put all the stones to one side. The account in 1 Maccabees stated: "…wherefore they pulled it (the altar) down, And laid up the stones in the mountain of the temple in a convenient place, until there should come a prophet to shew what should be done with them."[16] Perhaps the stones the Jewish leaders picked up were the very altar stones that had been set aside by the Maccabees, awaiting the prophet who would tell them what should be done with them. The Prophet came, but they would not listen to Him. God's glory was once again rejected. The priests and the people who were celebrating Hanukkah, the festival honoring the cleansing of the temple, celebrated in a defiled sanctuary. Such is the blindness which sin brings to the heart. Judgment for that sin came a few short years later (in 70 C.E.) when the army of Titus marched into the city of Jerusalem, destroying the temple and scattering the priests and the people to the far flung regions on the then-known world.

God's word is accurate. It is authoritative. It is infallible. What God speaks, He brings to pass. His Word is a reliable guide for everyone. Believing His Word brings life. Rejecting His Word brings death and judgment.

Both Daniel and Yeshua prophesied that the temple standing during the Tribulation would also be defiled by an "abomination of desolation" (see Daniel 9:27; Matthew 24:15). Both Daniel and John in the Revelation addressed the issue of the duration of this "desolation," which they said would last, ironically, three and one-half years, approximately the same length of time that Antiochus defiled the sanctuary (see Daniel 12:11; Revelation 11:1, 2).

When God gave Daniel the vision of the little horn (Daniel 8:9–12), He made no reference to the old Roman Empire. The reason was that this vision was fulfilled by Antiochus Epiphanes when he polluted the temple and trampled the sanctuary underfoot. The actions taken by Antiochus historically prefigure the activities of the Beast (antichrist) during the Tribulation. The vision in Daniel 8:9–12 had a dual prophetic significance and fulfillment: It spoke of *a* tribulation as well as of *the* Tribulation.

CONFIRMED BY A HEAVENLY MESSENGER

Such a long-term future fulfillment of the Daniel 8:9–12 prophecy became clear as Daniel's vision continued. He said: "And I heard a man's voice from the Ulai calling, 'Gabriel, tell this man the meaning of the vision.' As he came near the place where I was standing, I was terrified and fell prostrate. 'Son of man,' he said to me, 'understand that the vision concerns the time of the end'" (Daniel 8:16, 17).

Earlier in chapter eight (Dan. 8:2), Daniel said he was standing by the Ulai canal when he first received this vision. Evidently he had not moved. The fulfillment of this vision spans a corridor of time which held great significance for Israel's future. Because of the significance of this vision, God sent Gabriel to interpret it for Daniel.

The name Gabriel means "strong man of God." It is the name of an angel or messenger from God. Gabriel is mentioned only four times in the Scripture: twice in Daniel (Dan. 8:16; 9:21) and twice in Luke (Luke 1:19; 1:26).

Gabriel's name also appears in the noncanonical writings of Enoch. He is referred to as one of the four archangels in Enoch 9:1. He is called the holy angel who presides over Ikisat, over paradise, and over the cherubim (Enoch 20:7). [Ikisat appears to be a proper name. In another edition, this word is translated 'the serpents'.] He is also referred to as one of the four "presences," the one presiding over all that is powerful (Enoch 40:3–9).

It was Gabriel who gave Daniel the interpretation of the visions recorded in Daniel 8 and 9 (the latter vision concerned the Seventy Weeks). Gabriel also announced the birth of Messiah, Yeshua, to Mary and Joseph. In Luke 1:19 we are told that Gabriel is the angel who stands in the very presence of God. The intervention of the angel Gabriel at that point in time indicates that this vision has great future significance: Gabriel was sent to reveal God's program of judgment as well as His program of redemption. Note the phrases: "the time of the end" (verse 17); "I am going to tell you what will happen later in the time of wrath, because the vision concerns the appointed time of the end" (verse 19); and "The vision of the evenings and mornings that has been give you is true, but seal up the vision for it concerns the distant future" (verse 26).

Within Scripture, a specific revelation, by a specific messenger of God, carries with it special significance and often has a near fulfillment as well as a future fulfillment. In this vision Daniel was not only being shown what would take place historically when the little horn (Antiochus Epiphanes) would come upon the scene of history, but also that the actions of this historical person would foreshadow events which would take place at a later period of time — during the Tribulation. Just as the coming of the Messiah Yeshua at His first advent did not complete the prophecies of His coming (He is to return to establish His kingdom and to judge the world), God's program of judgment for Israel did not end when Antiochus defiled the temple in 168 B.C. The significance of the vision given to Daniel is that it had both an immediate fulfillment, as well as a future fulfillment.

Daniel was told: "In the latter part of their reign [the four generals unto whom Alexander gave his kingdom], when rebels have become completely wicked, a stern-faced king, a master of intrigue, will arise. He will become very strong, but not by his own power. He will cause astounding devastation and will succeed in whatever he does. He will destroy the mighty men and the holy people. He will cause deceit to prosper, and he will consider himself superior. When they feel secure, he will destroy many and take his stand against the Prince of princes. Yet he will be destroyed, but not by human power" (Daniel 8:23–25).

John's vision of the Beast who would rule and reign during the "time of the end" (or during the Great Tribulation — the last three and one half years of Daniel's Seventieth Week) reveals the same truths about the Beast: he will receive his power and authority from Satan himself; he will be greater than Antiochus — more wicked, more cruel, more ruthless; he will seek to utterly destroy the nation of Israel and all who trust in the Messiah, Yeshua (see Revelation 13:1–10).

Daniel was told that this stern-faced, ruthless king would be destroyed

— not by human power, but by the Prince of Princes, the Messiah. John's vision confirms that this is exactly the way the Beast (antichrist) will be destroyed when the Messiah returns (see Revelation 19:11–20:3).

Gabriel then told Daniel that the vision concerning the 2,300 evenings and mornings belonged to the near future and would surely happen as God had revealed them to Daniel, but the vision relating to the fierce king (the Beast [Satan incarnate]) concerned the distant future so Daniel was told to seal up the vision (see Daniel 8:26). Although God did reveal more concerning those "future days" in the visions given to John, the vision is still sealed in our day and the identity of the Beast remains a mystery.

At this point the visions and prophecies of Daniel pause and we are given a glimpse into the character and the feelings of Daniel, the man. How easy it is to forget the humanity of the prophets of God. Reading the Scriptures, we see them as such heros of the faith, so in touch with God. But I believe the Holy Spirit directed the writers of Scripture to include glimpses into their humanity because God knew that without such insights we would have great difficulty identifying with them.

Daniel was given a vision of the future as it concerned his people, Israel. The few broad strokes that God revealed to him were enough to make him literally sick. He wrote: "I, Daniel, was exhausted and lay ill for several days....I was appalled by the vision; it was beyond understanding" (Daniel 8:27).

Put yourself in Daniel's place. Imagine that you have just been told the worst news you have ever heard concerning your family and loved ones. You have been told that many of them are going to be killed and that the descendants of those who survive will face suffering and persecution so that their fate will be worse than their ancestors before them. Imagine that the individual telling you this terrible news is a representative of the highest governmental authority in the universe. He tells you that laws have been established to accomplish the events he has described, and that because of those laws the outcome cannot be changed. What would your reaction be? Most of us, like Daniel, would be "appalled." We would be emotionally and mentally drained. We would literally be ill.

It is the grace of God that keeps the future sealed. God, in His mercy, does not want us to know it. He wants us, instead, to place our confidence in Him. He wants us to trust Him for each day, and for the future. God entrusted this vision of the future to Daniel because He knew Daniel had learned to trust Him in every circumstance of life. Daniel purposed in his heart to turn over everything in his life — the good and the bad — to God. Then he went on with life. We read that despite physical exhaustion and vexation of heart, he "got up and went about the king's business" (see Daniel 8:26, 27). Daniel's resolve to trust in God brought him strength from God. God's promises are sure. His Word declares:

So do not fear, for I am with you; do not be dismayed, for I am your God. I will strengthen you and help you; I will uphold you with My . righteous right hand (Isaiah 41:10).

NOTES

Chapter 8. Foretelling Events In Emerging Empires

1   Flavius Josephus, *Antiquities X*, 11.7.

2   Keil & Delitzsch, *Commentaries on the O.T.—Daniel,* p 290.

3   *The Apocrypha*, I Maccabees 1:1–4, (New York: American Bible Society, Printed in Great Britain: Eyre & Spottiswoode, n.d.).

4   *The International Standard Encyclopedia*, Vol. 1, (Grand Rapids, MI: Wm. B. Eerdmans, 1979), p 88.

5   F. F. Bruce, *Israel and the Nations*, (Grand Rapids, MI, Wm. B. Eerdmans Publishing Co., 1963), p 123.

6   *Works of Josephus*, bk. 12, Ch. 3, p 251.

7   *Works of Josephus*, bk. 12, Ch. 3, p 251.

8   *Works of Josephus*, bk. 12, Ch. 3, p 252.

9   *Works of Josephus*, bk. 12, ch. 3, p 252.

10 *Apocrypha*, II Maccabees 5:11–16.

11 Heinrich Graetz, *History of the Jews*, Vol. 1, (Philadelphia, PA: The Jewish Publication Society of America, 1967), p 452.

12 *Apocrypha*, II Maccabees 5:24–27.

13 *Apocrypha*, I Maccabees 1:41–64.

14 *Apocrypha*, 2 Maccabees 6:2.

15 *Apocrypha*, I Maccabees 4:36–59.

16 *Apocrypha*, I Maccabees 4:45–46.

♦

Revealing God's Divine Timetable

In the first year of Darius son of Xerxes (a Mede by descent), who was made ruler over the Babylonian kingdom — in the first year of his reign, I, Daniel, understood from the Scriptures, according to the word of the LORD given to Jeremiah the prophet, that the desolation of Jerusalem would last seventy years.

— Daniel 9:1, 2

Daniel was a man who had learned to pray and to fully trust in God. Rather than worry over the visions of the future that had been revealed to him by God, Daniel prayed and searched the Scriptures. He knew God heard and answered prayer, and he knew the answers to his questions about God's program and plan for his life, as well as for the lives of his people, Israel, could be found within the revealed Word of God.

The visions of Daniel have not been arranged in a chronological sequence. Rather, they have been arranged to specifically show how God will deal with Israel once Israel has returned to the land. Daniel's visions denote God's redemptive and judgmental programs which He will bring upon Israel, and upon the nations through Israel.

Daniel had been reading the prophecies of Jeremiah at the time when Darius, son of Xerxes (a Mede), ascended the throne (Daniel 9:1, 2). It was during the first year of Darius' reign —after the Persians had taken control of the Babylonian empire. Darius began his reign sometime during the spring of 538 B.C., and continued his reign until the spring of 537 B.C. These dates and names are important because the seventy years of captivity, which God had promised through the prophet Jeremiah, were drawing to a close. Nearly forty-nine years of the captivity had elapsed. To those not looking through the "eyes of faith," there seemed to be no end in sight. The Gentile empires were growing in strength, not weakening, and persecution and hatred of the Jews was increasing, not decreasing. Daniel was driven to the Word of God to seek answers for the problems that were perplexing him. In contrast with others, who look for answers to life's problems in every source — except the Word of God — Daniel knew exactly where to look. He knew God's Word held the answers, and he went directly to the prophet Jeremiah.

Daniel was a young teenager when Jeremiah uttered his message of doom in Jerusalem, in the year 605 B.C., during the reign of King Jehoiakim. After the invading Babylonian army swept Daniel and his people away to Babylon, Jeremiah's prophecy took on new meaning for Daniel! He had predicted:

Therefore the LORD Almighty says this: 'Because you have not listened to my words, I will summon all the peoples of the north and my servant Nebuchadnezzar king of Babylon,' declares the LORD, 'and I will bring them against this land and its inhabitants and against all the surrounding nations. I will completely destroy them and make them an object of horror and scorn, and an everlasting ruin. I will banish from them the sounds of joy and gladness, the voices of bride and bridegroom, the sound of millstones and the light of the lamp. This whole country will become a desolate wasteland, and these nations will serve the king of Babylon seventy years.

But when the seventy years are fulfilled, I will punish the king of Babylon and his nation, the land of the Babylonians, for their guilt,' declares the

LORD, *'and will make it desolate forever. I will bring upon that land all the things I have spoken against it, all that are written in this book and prophesied by Jeremiah against all the nations. They themselves will be enslaved by many nations and great kings; I will repay them according to their deeds and the work of their hands' (Jeremiah 25:8–14).*

The prophecy of Jeremiah indicated that when the seventy years had expired, God would punish the Babylonians and restore the Jewish people to their land. He stated:

This is what the LORD says: 'When seventy years are completed for Babylon, I will come to you and fulfill my gracious promise to bring you back to this place. For I know the plans I have for you,' declares the LORD, 'plans to prosper you and not to harm you, plans to give you hope and a future. Then you will call upon me and come and pray to me, and I will listen to you. You will seek me and find me when you seek me with all your heart. I will be found by you,' declares the LORD, 'and will bring you back from captivity. I will gather you from all the nations and places where I have banished you,' declares the LORD, 'and will bring you back to the place from which I carried you into exile' (Jeremiah 29:10–14).

How specific this prophecy is! It states, "When seventy years are completed for Babylon,..." Daniel was perplexed. If the seventy years began before the destruction of Jerusalem, and if those years were literally fulfilled when Babylon fell in 539–538 B.C., why weren't the Jews returning to Israel as God had promised? On the other hand, if the seventy year prophecy began with the destruction of Jerusalem in 586 B.C., how could a literal fulfillment of this prophecy have taken place, seeing that with the fall of Babylon in 539–538 B.C., only forty-seven to forty-eight years had elapsed? Had God made a mistake? Was the word of the prophet Jeremiah accurate and true? Would the Jews remain in captivity throughout all of the empires that had been revealed?

Daniel knew God's Word was reliable. He knew God's promises could not be broken. He knew it was far more important for him to exercise trust in God than to seek after an understanding of God's timetable. At the same time, however, he realized that if the seventy years had elapsed,

God would keep His promise to restore His people to their land. Daniel knew God would listen to them, if they would heed the words of Jeremiah to "come and pray to me."

Convinced that God's promises could be trusted, Daniel donned sackcloth and ashes and turned to God in prayer, petition, and fasting (Daniel 9:3). He earnestly sought God, believing God would reveal to him the mystery of the seventy years, and of the future of his people, Israel.

A MEDIATOR

As a representative for his nation, Daniel began making intercession for the sins of the people of Israel. His heart was filled with anguish as he confessed the sins of the nation against the Righteous One and he cried out to God for help. Pleading for an extension of life for the nation, Daniel's intercessory prayer was similar to the prayer of Moses when he descended from Mount Sinai and saw the people of Israel worshipping the golden calf. Moses was so concerned for the nation, he was willing to have his own name blotted out of God's Book of Life rather than to see the people perish. The book of Exodus records these awesome words: "So Moses went back to the LORD and said, 'Oh, what a great sin these people have committed! They have made themselves gods of gold. But now, please forgive their sin—but if not, then blot me out of the book you have written!'" (Exodus 32:31, 32).

God's response to Moses was one of grace, but it was also a response that called for judgment of sin. He reminded Moses that every man and woman is responsible for his or her own sin; He told Moses that although Moses could not be a substitute for the sins of the people (a sinbearer), he would be the leader God had promised. God said: "Now go, lead the people to the place I spoke of, and my angel will go before you. However, when the time comes for me to punish, I will punish them for their sin" (Exodus 32:34).

Like Moses, Daniel knew God had called him to a place of leadership among his people. He felt responsible for them and he carried a weight of responsibility for their sins within himself. As he interceded on their behalf, like Moses, he offered himself in the place of his people. This was a righteous and loving gesture, but only God's Messiah could be the true mediator. Only He could be the true sin bearer. Moses and

Daniel could not, for they were sinners. However, it was the knowledge of their own sinfulness, and the wonder of the grace of God in forgiving their sins, that drove both Moses and Daniel to intercessory prayer on behalf of the people.

The wonder of God's grace, providing forgiveness of sin in our own lives should provoke in every believer a desire to see others forgiven. Prayer does change things. It changes attitudes toward God, toward self, and it changes attitudes toward the treatment of others. Prayer accomplishes God's will in the lives of believers and in the lives of others.

In his study of the Word of God, Daniel had most likely given close attention to God's words of warning to Israel. His words warning Israel of impending judgment if they were disobedient and if they refused to repent must have deeply stirred Daniel's heart. As he read and meditated upon the warnings in Leviticus, he likely endeavored to calculate the length of Israel's time of the judgment. God had said:

> *I will turn your cities into ruins and lay waste your sanctuaries, and I will take no delight in the pleasing aroma of your offerings.*
>
> *I will lay waste the land, so that your enemies who live there will be appalled.*
>
> *I will scatter you among the nations and will draw out my sword and pursue you. Your land will be laid waste, and your cities will lie in ruin.*
>
> *Then the land will enjoy its sabbath years all the time that it lies desolate and you are in the country of your enemies; then the land will rest and enjoy its sabbaths.*
>
> *All the time that it lies desolate, the land will have the rest it did not have during the sabbaths you lived in it (Lev. 26:31–35).*

God's judgment upon Israel would accomplish a two-fold purpose (1) It would judge Israel for their sins. (2) It would allow the land to rest; the land would enjoy the Sabbath rest which Israel had forsaken.

The judgment of seventy years, incurred because of the people's failure to live righteously in the land, was in direct proportion to the length of the Sabbath rest which God had promised to bestow upon the land of

Israel. Whenever Israel has been exiled from the land, the land has remained fallow and returned to desert conditions. But when the people of Israel return to the land, it blossoms. Every nation conquering the land of Israel has found the land infertile and unproductive. Prior to the establishment of the State of Israel in 1948, pictures portray, and the accounts describe, a dry, barren land. In every case, the nations that occupied the land were unable to make the desert blossom or produce. Yet, when Israel returned, the land yielded; the desert bloomed. God keeps His promises.

God told Israel: "If you remain hostile toward me and refuse to listen to me, I will multiply your afflictions seven times over, as your sins deserve" (Leviticus 26:21).

The Word of God is precise and accurate. It is true in every detail and thus, wholly trustworthy. "All Scripture is God-breathed and is useful for teaching, rebuking, correcting and training in righteousness" (2 Timothy 3:16). The "all" includes dates which record events. They, too, are a part of the inspired text. Although an exact date may not be recorded within Scripture, dates can be determined according to the reigns of certain kings, or by special events spoken of. It is through this method of deduction scholars know Solomon dedicated his temple to the LORD in the year 950 B.C.; they know that the temple stood for approximately three hundred sixty-four years before it was destroyed by Nebuchadnezzar in 586 BC.

God had declared that He would use the judgment of His people as a "Sabbath rest" for the land, and that he would "multiply their affliction seven times over, [or seventy times] as their sins deserve." These words are an extraordinary coincidence. Seventy (the length of God's judgment upon Israel) multiplied by three hundred sixty-four (the length of time the temple stood before its destruction) equals 25,480 days. Using the Biblical year of 360 days, and allowing for the intercalation of days (based on a lunar/solar calendar) and the leap years (as the Jewish calendar indicates) the length of time is 25,480 days, or seventy years — the exact number of days prophesied in the seventy year captivity.

God's Holy Word was literally fulfilled. He brought judgment upon Israel and, as He had warned, they were sent into exile in Babylon for exactly seventy years, allowing the land to have its Sabbath rest.

2 Chronicles 36:21 states: "The land enjoyed its Sabbath rests; all the time of its desolation it rested, until the seventy years were completed in fulfillment of the word of the LORD spoken by Jeremiah."

It was God's desire not only to have the land enjoy its Sabbath rest; He desired that the people would be drawn to a spiritual rest in Him. Sadly, the writer of the Book of Hebrews reminds us that Israel failed to enter into their Sabbath rest (see Hebrews 3:7–18). Instead, they continued to rebel against God. The writer of Hebrews subsequently issues both a warning and an invitation to readers of every age. The invitation to all who will heed is to enter into God's rest through the finished work of our Messiah at Calvary (see Hebrews 4:1–13). The warning is to learn from Israel who, because of unbelief and rebellion, came under God's judgment (see Hebrews 3:12–18).

AN INTERCESSORY PRAYER

Convinced, through his study of God's Word, that the seventy years had expired and that God's judgment upon Israel was complete, Daniel began his great intercessory prayer. It is a prayer which should be studied in depth, for it contains the elements of true prayer which can serve as a model prayer for all believers. Daniel's prayer includes praise (worship), confession of sin, thanksgiving, and petition. A study of this prayer reveals similarities to the prayer Solomon made when he dedicated the temple (see 1 Kings 8:22–53). It is conceivable that Daniel, thinking of the temple and of God's promises to Israel, recalled portions of the remarkable prayer of Solomon. Likewise, Daniel's prayer may have served as a model for the prayers of Nehemiah (see Nehemiah 1:5–11) and Ezra (see Ezra 9:5–15). It is very likely that it was Daniel's prayer which served as model for the prayers and supplications found in the writings of Baruch, one of the Apocryphal books that was written around 70 C.E. (but claimed to be written much earlier).[1] In some instances it seems that the writer of Baruch borrowed almost word-for-word from Daniel's prayer.

Before Daniel uttered one word, he prepared himself to approach God by clothing himself in sackcloth and ashes (see Daniel 9:3). He comes before Almighty God in an attitude of humility. After clothing himself in humility, Daniel began his prayer with the recognition of God's unfailing grace to those who are undeserving. He says: "...O LORD, the great and awesome God, who keeps his covenant of love with all who love him and obey his commands, we have sinned and done wrong. We have been wicked and have rebelled; we have turned away from your commands and laws. We have not listened to your servants the prophets, who spoke in your name to our kings, our princes and our fathers, and to all the people of the land" (Daniel 9:4–6).

Daniel marvels at God's grace; he addresses Him as great and awesome. He comes before God with the attitude of a petitioner, rather than with the attitude of one who is exercising his "rights" — demanding that his rights be recognized. How different this is from the prayers of some today who seem to believe that "equal rights" means "rights on demand." Individuals today are often encouraged to "demand their rights" in the work place and in their homes. This attitude is carried into houses of worship. In some circles, Christians are encouraged to "claim" their promise — exercising their faith — reminding God of His responsibility to fulfill His promises.

This was not the attitude of Daniel! Instead, this great man of God, dressed in the royal robes of the court of the Persian king, laid aside those symbols of power and authority (the symbols that gave him certain rights within the kingdom). In the place of those royal robes Daniel put on sackcloth and ashes, the sign of one in mourning, of one who has absolutely no rights. Recognizing God's greatness, and his own unworthiness, Daniel humbly petitioned God.

Daniel went before the Throne of God in the same way our Messiah came to us. He, too, laid aside His robes (of glory) when He came in the likeness of man. He willingly set aside His glory, and the prerogatives of His deity to become the suffering servant, the obedient servant of His Father. He set aside His divine rights to become the mediator between God and man (see Philippians 2:1–11).

Successful prayer begins with the attitude of the heart. Prayer is not answered on the basis of "rights." It is answered on the basis of God's grace, His mercy, and on the basis of His unfailing love. Prayer is answered because of the finished work of the LORD, Yeshua, at Calvary.

Daniel continued his prayer with confession of sin and a rehearsal of all that God had done on behalf of Israel. The emphasis Daniel places upon the confession of sin cannot be missed. It is a primary element. His prayer is approximately sixteen verses in length, and in those sixteen verses confession of sin is made over twenty times. In each instance, he uses the personal pronouns "we," "us," "our." Never once does Daniel exclude himself from the sins of the nation. Never once does he blame the people, while claiming to be exempt from their sin problem. Daniel knew he was just a sinner who had been saved by the grace of Almighty God. He recognized that he was no better than the least or the worst in Israel. He realized that as long as he was alive, he, too, was subject to the consequences and judgment of sin. In his book, "The Climax of the Ages," Dr. Frederick A. Tatford writes:

The prophet [Daniel] then burst into a frank confession of the sins of the people, identifying himself with them. There was no tautology in the prolific accumulation of expressions he used: it was rather that he sought to express by every possible word the enormity of the guilt and contumacy of himself and his people. They had sinned in wandering from the right, they had dealt perversely in their wilful impiety, they had done wickedly in their sheer infidelity, they had rebelled in deliberate refractoriness, they had turned aside from the Divine commandments and ordinances. Their cup of iniquity was full. Their guilt was accentuated by the fact that prophets had been sent to them with the Divine message and they had refused to listen. All were implicated — rulers, leaders (the term 'fathers' being used, of course, in a metaphorical rather than in a literal sense), and people. God was perfectly just, but a shameful countenance betrayed their own guilt. Nor was the confusion of face limited to Judah and Jerusalem: it was true of all Israelites throughout the world. Indeed, their scattering was in punishment for their own unfaithfulness to God. Daniel associated himself completely with his people in acknowledging their wrong-doing and freely confessed that their shamefacedness was due to perfectly justified corrections: they had sinned against God.[2]

Daniel's complete and total identification with the people of Israel is seen by his continuous use of the plural personal pronouns, indicating that he never separated himself from the nation. Israel's shame was his shame. Israel's plight was his plight. Israel's judgment was his judgment.

He prayed:

> LORD, *you are righteous, but this day we are covered with shame — the men of Judah and people of Jerusalem and all Israel, both near and far, in all the countries where you have scattered us because of our unfaithfulness to you. O LORD, we and our kings, our princes and our fathers are covered with shame because we have sinned against you. The LORD our God is merciful and forgiving, even though we have rebelled against him; we have not obeyed the LORD our God or kept the laws he gave us through his servants the prophets. All Israel has transgressed your law and turned away, refusing to obey you (Daniel 9:7–11a).*

While Daniel identified with the sin of the nation, he, unlike the nation as a whole, had experienced the grace, mercy, and forgiveness of God. He said: "The LORD our God is merciful and forgiving, even though we have rebelled against him" (verse 9). What wonderful words! God has always promised to extend His grace and His mercy to every individual, to every sinner, who is willing to recognize his sin and his need of God's forgiveness. Daniel knew this. He had experienced it in his own life.

Daniel's words reveal that he had grasped something else about God's mercy and forgiveness; he understood that God's mercy and forgiveness is extended to sinners. God does not wait for us to become perfect before He extends His forgiveness. If He did, no one would ever experience His forgiveness. Scripture says while we were yet sinners, our Messiah died for us (Romans 5:8). Daniel knew his people were still sinners. He was very much aware that they were still rebelling against God, and he knew the nation would perish if God's mercy and His forgiveness was not extended to them even though they were still sinners. He rehearsed to God how His judgment had come upon Israel because of their sin, yet His grace had always been there to deliver them, to establish them, and to keep them. He prayed:

> *Therefore the curses and sworn judgments written in the Law of Moses, the servant of God, have been poured out on us, because we have sinned against you. You have fulfilled the words spoken against us and against our rulers by bringing upon us great disaster. Under the whole heaven*

nothing has ever been done like what has been done to Jerusalem. Just as it is written in the Law of Moses, all this disaster has come upon us, yet we have not sought the favor of the LORD our God by turning from our sins and giving attention to your truth. The LORD did not hesitate to bring the disaster upon us, for the LORD our God is righteous in everything he does; yet we have not obeyed him.

Now, O LORD our God, who brought your people out of Egypt with a mighty hand and who made for yourself a name that endures to this day, we have sinned, we have done wrong. O LORD, in keeping with all your righteous acts, turn away your anger and your wrath from Jerusalem, your city, your holy hill. Our sins and the iniquities of our fathers have made Jerusalem and your people an object of scorn to all those around us (Daniel 9:11b–16).

Did Daniel give this rehearsal of the deeds of God to remind God of something He'd forgotten, or as evidence that He needed to act? Certainly not. He rehearsed God's deeds as a reminder to himself of God's nature, of His character, and of His promises. Reviewing what God has done for us, rehearsing His faithfulness to us, is a building block upon which faith is built. Faith, as defined in the Scriptures, is being sure of what "we hope for and certain of what we do not see" (see Hebrews 11:1). Faith is strengthened through experience.

God is omniscient. He is all-knowing. He does not forget the past, and He is well aware of the present and the future. Yeshua told us that He knows when a sparrow falls from heaven, and He knows the exact number of hairs on our heads. Daniel was not rehearsing God's deeds as a reminder to God of something He had forgotten. The reminder was to himself. Daniel encouraged himself by recalling to his memory those things which he knew about his God — that He is a covenant-keeping God; He is faithful; He is true to His word.

All of life's experiences should be "schoolmasters." Someone has said repetition is the mother of learning, and so it is. Believers need to reflect upon and rehearse God's blessings and His chastisement in their lives. They need to review circumstances and events of their lives, to remind themselves of His divine intervention, His Faithfulness, His divine lessons. God's children need to build upon the events of life which prove

His love and grace toward them.

Daniel knew that everything in life is ordered by God. He knew God is Sovereign. God is Lord. God is in control. He knew God was not only aware of everything that had happened to Israel, He had allowed it. He also knew, from experience, that God would not forsake Israel because of their disobedience, but would save them in spite of themselves. So Daniel rehearsed the supernatural events, the blessings, and the judgment of God which demonstrated His daily involvement with His people. He rehearsed the miracles which demonstrated that God was, indeed, real and concerned for the people of Israel, and as he did so, Daniel's faith, trust, and confidence in God was renewed. God had been faithful in the past and He had shown Himself faithful in the present. Daniel was therefore confident that God would be faithful in the future.

Having clothed himself in humility, and having confessed his sin and the sins of the nation, requesting God's forgiveness; and having further rehearsed God's deeds toward Israel, offering up praise to God for His unfailing grace and faithfulness, Daniel concludes his petition, praying:

Now, our God, hear the prayers and petitions of your servant. For your sake, O Lord, look with favor on your desolate sanctuary. Give ear, O God, and hear; open your eyes and see the desolation of the city that bears your name. We do not make requests of you because we are righteous, but because of your great mercy. O Lord, listen! O Lord, forgive! O Lord, hear and act! For your sake, O my God, do not delay, because your city and your people bear your Name (Daniel 9:17–19).

Notice the basis upon which Daniel makes his petition and request. He says "We do not make requests of you because we are righteous, but because of your great mercy" (verse 18). It is clear that Daniel did not come before the Lord demanding that God keep His promises. He did not come before God "claiming his rights," demanding God's intervention because of his standing as a believer. Daniel petitioned God to act based on His great mercy. Daniel petitioned God to bestow His unqualified favor on an undeserving and sinful nation.

But Daniel's petition went beyond just a request for mercy for the nation of Israel; it was also a request that God be glorified in all that He does. Daniel knew from his study of the Word of God that God's program of redemption for Israel, and for the Gentile nations, involved two things. First, it involved the return of God's glory to the city of Jerusalem and to the Holy of Holies within the temple. Secondly, it involved the indwelling presence of God's glory in the lives of His people. Daniel did not tell God how to accomplish this, nor did He tell God why He should accomplish this. He simply states, "…O LORD, look with favor on your desolate sanctuary…. open your eyes and see the desolation of the city that bears your name" (Daniel 9:17, 18).

Daniel knew that God, in His grace, His mercy, His love, would work out all of the details of His program of redemption. He knew God's program of redemption involved Jerusalem and involved the Jewish people. He trusted the God of the universe to "do right."

God's program of redemption, which He began with Israel, is still in effect. It has not changed through the centuries of time. During this Church Age, all who become children of God through belief in His Son, are indwelt with the "glory of God." He no longer dwells in a building made of stones and mortar, but now dwells in individuals (Jew and Gentile alike) who have confessed Yeshua as LORD and Savior. When the LORD Yeshua returns to establish His kingdom on the earth, God will once again establish His glory in Jerusalem, and in the temple, and ultimately He will establish His glory within the Jewish people.

The Psalmist declared: "Pray for the peace of Jerusalem" (see Psalm 122:6). In his petition Daniel, too, was praying for the peace of Jerusalem as he prayed for the return of God's glory, and prayed that God would once again dwell in Jerusalem.

All believers, like Daniel and the Psalmist, should be praying for the peace of Jerusalem. They should be praying for the salvation of the Jewish people; they should be actively involved in sharing the Gospel with them. God's glory needs to reside in Jewish hearts as well as in Gentiles' hearts. The Body of Messiah, the Church, is composed of "Jew and Greek, bond and free, and male and female" (Galatians 3:28). This is God's desire for this age, and just as Daniel prayed earnestly for God's glory to return to Jerusalem, believers today should be earnestly praying for God's glory to reside in the hearts of Jew and Gentile. The only way this can happen is through the preaching of the Gospel. There is no other way.

This is why it is so urgent that we bring the Gospel message to the ends of the earth. This is why it is so vital we be faithful in intercessory prayer.

If believers today would begin to pray like Daniel, and devote themselves to intercessory prayer for the peace of Jerusalem (for the indwelling presence of God in the lives of Jews and Gentiles), revival would sweep across our nation, and across the nations of the world!

Daniel's prayer expressed the deepest concerns of his heart. His words were not the formal petition of a rote prayer, or words of selfish concern. Daniel wanted God to be honored. He wanted God's glory, honor, and reputation restored in this world.

GOD ANSWERS

God's answer to Daniel's prayer came immediately. Daniel wrote:

While I was speaking and praying, confessing my sin and the sin of my people Israel and making my request to the LORD God for his holy hill — while I was still in prayer, Gabriel, the man I had seen in the earlier vision, came to me in swift flight about the time of the evening sacrifice (Daniel 9:20, 21).

Prayer moves God to action. It is not that He is inactive, just waiting for us to petition Him so that He will have something to do, or have some decision to make. Nor is He perplexed and unsure of what to do with us, or how to use us, and therefore waiting for some suggestions from us. How absurd a notion that is! God knows the end from the beginning. His plan for our lives is not simply some cosmic kaleidoscope which changes every time we pray, or forget to pray. God's plan for our lives is complete. He is Sovereign, Omnipotent, Omniscient, and Omnipresent. He knows our every need and is eager to show His loving kindness to His children. The prophet Isaiah recognized this truth when we wrote: "Before they call I will answer; while they are still speaking I will hear" (Isaiah 65:24).

Why then does God respond to our prayers? Because prayer is the acknowledgement of His very Being, His Sovereignty, His Omnipresence, His Omnipotence, His Omniscience. Prayer allows our spirits to draw near to God, who is Spirit. Through prayer we exercise the faith

God has given us, so that as we grow in Him we begin to see that His will for us is what is best in this life and through eternity. Prayer does change things. It changes us! It moves us to recognize and to accept God's sovereign rule in our lives. Prayer instills confidence that what God does, He does for our good and for His glory. Prayer always accomplishes the Divine plan of God.

The Scriptures teach us that answers to our prayers may come in a variety of ways. In the case of Daniel's prayer, the answer was immediate. In the case of Abraham's servant who stood praying by the well of Nahor, the answer was given before he had finished praying, and when he finished speaking "Rebekah came out" (see Genesis 24:15). There are other instances when God's answers are delayed because of spiritual conflict in heavenly places (see Daniel 10:7–11:1; Ephesians 6:10–18; Revelation 12:7–12). There are times when the answer is given, but the answer is not recognized or is simply accepted without notice or thanks — as was the case when Peter was released from jail (see Acts 12:11–16). Answers to prayer can also be delayed because of some unconfessed sin in our lives (see Isaiah 59:2). James gives yet another reason for unanswered petitions: "you do not have, because you do not ask God" (James 4:2).

Prayer is the life-line of faith between God and the believer. God delights in our prayers because in true prayer we are agreeing with Him about His sovereignty and rule over our lives. In the book of Revelation the prayers of the saints are portrayed as ascending before the very throne of God. There are no idle prayers, but there are effective and ineffective prayers.

Daniel prayed in faith, believing the Word of God. He was willing to accept God's will, because he had confidence that God knew what was best for himself and for the people of Israel. God responded to Daniel's prayer by sending the angel Gabriel to him. The answer to Daniel's prayer was visual proof that God is a covenant-keeping God; He keeps His promises; His compassion and mercy upon Jerusalem and His Jewish people will never cease.

The fact that Gabriel came to Daniel in "swift flight" has led some Bible scholars to believe that Gabriel was sent quickly in answer to Daniel's prayer. However, it would appear that Gabriel was sent "swiftly" because of Daniel's physical, emotional, and spiritual state. Daniel was an old man by this time, and he was emotionally, physically, and spiritually drained from his intense time of study and intercessory prayer. He was weary in well-doing. His previous vision had left him ill for several days (see Daniel 8:27).

How full of grace our God is! He could have given Daniel another vision, but instead he sent His messenger (Gabriel) who not only explained God's program to Daniel, he also gave him the emotional and spiritual support he needed at that time.

God knows our needs, and oftentimes He meets them by sending His special messengers our way. Gabriel told Daniel, "...Daniel, I have now come to give you insight and understanding. As soon as you began to pray, an answer was given, which I have come to tell you, for you are highly esteemed. Therefore, consider the message and understand the vision..." (see Daniel 9:23).

"As soon as you began to pray, an answer was given." What encouraging words! He also told Daniel he was a man "highly esteemed." Daniel saw himself as a worthless sinner. He identified himself completely with the sinful nation, and in humility he had put on sackcloth and ashes before approaching a holy and righteous God. But God saw Daniel as a precious jewel in the crown of His glory. In God's sight every believer is "highly esteemed" because they have been purchased with the shed blood of His Son, our Messiah, the LORD Yeshua. God sees believers as "highly esteemed" because they are clothed in His Son's righteousness.

Gabriel came to Daniel at the time of the evening oblation, or about three in the afternoon. This was the time of day when the Passover lamb was killed, and the time of day when our Messiah was put to death. Perhaps this was why Gabriel was sent at this particular hour. When the temple was destroyed, prayer took the place of the daily sacrifice and for Daniel, who prayed three times a day, this hour was one of his regular times for prayer. In so doing, Daniel faithfully sacrificed in his prayer life and God faithfully responded. Daniel would receive an answer concerning Israel's captivity.

Seventy 'Sevens'

The angel told Daniel, "Seventy 'sevens' are decreed for your people and your holy city to finish transgression, to put an end to sin, to atone for wickedness, to bring in everlasting righteousness, to seal up the vision and prophecy and to anoint the most holy" (Daniel 9:24). Daniel was told that God has an exact timetable for the nation of Israel and the Jewish people.

Some time ago scientists investigating the "aging process' came across an amazing discovery. They had begun growing cultures from the tissue of human fetal lung cells in glass bottles and they noticed that as the cells divided they would continue up to fifty total population doublings, which occurred between the seventh and the ninth month. After that, the cells decayed and died. They discovered that an automatic time clock has been built into the human cell which stops further division after a total of fifty population doublings. The scientists had no rational explanation for their findings and observations but individuals who know the Word of God know that God has allotted a time for everything in His creation. The aging process is the result of sin. The Bible tells us it is appointed unto man once to die and after that the judgment (see Hebrews 9:27). The Book of Ecclesiastes tells us:

> *There is a time for everything, and a season for every activity under heaven: a time to be born and a time to die, a time to plant and a time to uproot, a time to kill and a time to heal, a time to tear down and a time to build, a time to weep and a time to laugh, a time to mourn and a time to dance, a time to scatter stones and a time to gather them, a time to embrace and a time to refrain, a time to search and a time to give up, a time to keep and a time to throw away, a time to tear and a time to mend, a time to be silent and a time to speak, a time to love and a time to hate, a time for war and a time for peace (Ecclesiastes 3:1–8).*

God in His infinite wisdom and grace has set a time clock upon all of life, including a time clock upon the nation of Israel and the Jewish people. The angel Gabriel told Daniel that an exact period of time, seventy 'sevens,' had been decreed by God to complete His program of redemption for Israel.

It must be remembered that in his intercessory prayer, Daniel had asked that God be glorified, not only in Jerusalem, but also in the lives of the Jewish people themselves. God's time clock for Israel was not established with the fall of man in the Garden of Eden, nor with the judgment of the world at the flood of Noah's day, nor even with the formation of the nation of Israel in Egypt, or with their deliverance which is celebrated by the commemoration of Passover. God establishes the date for the beginning of His prophetic time clock with the return of the Jewish people after the seventy year Babylonian captivity. The judgment of the seventy years is to be symbolic of a greater judgment which God declared He would bring upon Israel if they continued in disobedience and sin.

The "seventy 'sevens'" were to represent the immediate future of Israel if, as a nation, they repented and became obedient to God's commands, or they would represent the distant future of Israel if they continued in their unbelief and disobedience of the commandments of God.

Some readers may respond that their King James translation of the Bible says "seventy weeks" and not "seventy 'sevens.'" Although the King James version does read "seventy weeks," the most competent of Hebraists all agree that the Hebrew word for seven, which was translated "weeks" in the King James version, should be understood in its generic sense, simply meaning "seven." Technically it is called a "heptad" or "hebdomad."

Dr. S.P. Tregelles, a noted Hebrew scholar, makes the following observation:

Daniel had made inquiry about seventy years of the captivity in Babylon; the answer speaks also of seventy periods, which in our English translation are called 'weeks'; the word, however, does not necessarily mean seven days, — but a period of seven parts: of course it is much more often used in speaking of a week than of anything else, because nothing is so often mentioned as a week which is similarly divided. The Hebrews, however, used a septenary scale as to time, just as habitually as we should reckon by tens; the sabbatical years, the jubilees, all tended to give this thought a permanent place in their minds. The denomination here is to be taken from the subject of Daniel's prayer; he prayed about years, he is answered about periods of seven years, i.e., the recurrence of sabbatical years.[3]

The same Hebrew word "seven" translated "weeks" in the King James version, is the same Hebrew word used in Genesis 29:27 where Jacob is told to "Finish out his daughter's bridal week;..." To do this he had to work for Laban for seven years (cf. Genesis 29:28). Thus, to the Hebrew mind, as Dr. Tregelles indicates, Daniel's statement is a reference to seventy periods of seven. The reason for this is clear from the prophecy itself. Just as each week is divided into exact periods of time called "days," this revelation of the seventy sevens is also divided into separate periods of time.

It is helpful to recall, as was stated earlier, that God had numbered the exact time of the seventy year captivity to the sins and transgressions of the Jewish people. The land itself was to remain at rest, or to have its "sabbath" during the period of time when the people were in captivity. With that seventy year period coming to a close, God tells Daniel, in answer to his prayer, that the seventy year captivity symbolized the extended period of time — an extended period of judgment which was yet to come upon Israel before He would ultimately restore His glory in Jerusalem. Sadly, the people had not repented. But in spite of their unbelief, God's promise could not be broken and He was bringing the immediate captivity to a close. The distant future, and the extended period of God's intense judgment, would be conditional — based upon the disobedience or obedience of the people. This becomes very important to the understanding of seventy 'sevens.' There are gaps, or periods of time, between some of the periods of seven. It is as if God pauses, and reaches out to His people in grace and mercy, asking them to repent so further judgment might be spared.

Why Seventy 'Sevens'?

Daniel is told several things about these seventy periods of seven. First, he is told that they are necessary to finish transgression. The idea expressed in the Hebrew is to literally restrain or arrest the national transgression of Israel. The nation had sinned. This was the reason they were in captivity and under the domination of the Gentiles. It was their national sin of rejecting God and His Messiah, Yeshua, that caused Israel's further captivity and judgment many years after the Babylonian captivity.

God's promise to Daniel was that despite their national sin and disobedience, a day would come when He would put an end to their national sin. In the Hebrew text the definite article appears before the word "transgression" so that it reads, "the transgression." This is a direct reference to "the national transgression" when the nation rejected God, culminating in their rejection of God's Messiah, Yeshua.

Secondly, Daniel is told the seventy 'sevens' were necessary to make an end of sin. The idea expressed literally in the Hebrew is to "restrain" or "seal up" the deliberate wickedness of the people of Israel. The prophet Ezekiel expressed it this way, "They will no longer defile themselves with their idols and vile images or with any of their offenses, for I will save them from all their sinful backsliding, and I will cleanse them. They will be my people and I will be their God" (Ezekiel 37:23). In other words, the matter of sin will be concluded.

Sometimes the phrases "to make an end of" or "to seal" were used by official secretaries to indicate the closing of a letter. When the letter was complete, the king would place his royal seal upon it, thus indicating that the matter was closed and there would be no further discussion. The affixing of his seal made it official.

Third, the seventy 'sevens' were necessary to atone for Israel's wickedness, to make provision for the nation's guilt. For God's glory to dwell permanently in Jerusalem, or in the lives of His people, it was necessary that someone pay the price for the penalty of Israel's sin, and thus the sin of the whole world. The judgment for sin is death. Thus, provision for sin required a substitute who would bear the sins of the world before the Kingdom of God could be established upon the earth. This "sin bearer" would be rejected by Israel.

As strange as it may seem, Israel's captivity provided the means for God to extend His grace and His provision of salvation to all nations. While Israel was in their land God dwelled among them and worked with them, but once they were scattered among the nations God began to work among the nations as well. The nations were sanctified by having the Jewish people in their midst (see Ezekiel 36:16–23).

This is Paul's argument in Romans 9–11. He states that the fall of Israel brought salvation to the Gentiles (see Romans 11:11–24). Within God's Divine program of redemption the scope of His grace went beyond the nation of Israel to include the Gentile nations as well, and He used the dispersion of Israel to reach the Gentiles with His Truth. In so doing, God has placed upon the Gentiles the responsibility of seeing that the Jewish people themselves are also included as the message of His Divine program of redemption is shared. Failure to do so will result in God's judgment upon the Gentiles.

Fourth, the seventy 'sevens' were necessary in order to usher in everlasting righteousness, when the very righteousness of the eternal God would be visible here on earth. This righteousness is called eternal because it originates from the eternal God, and because it is eternal in its duration. This eternal dimension to God's righteousness dwelling upon the earth is in contrast to the transitory gifts of righteousness, grace, and mercy that were seen throughout God's dealings with Israel. Daniel was given a glimpse of the wonderful future Messianic kingdom that could only be established by a Messiah who was both God and man.

The prophet Jeremiah spoke of a New Covenant which God would establish with the House of Israel. He said this New Covenant would be entirely different from the one God had established with His people at Mount Sinai. Unlike the Mosaic Covenant, this New Covenant would provide forgiveness for sin; it would provide for the removal of sin. Jeremiah spoke of the wonderful conditions of this covenant when he said:

> 'The time is coming,' declares the LORD, 'when I will make a new covenant with the house of Israel and with the house of Judah. It will not be like the covenant I made with their forefathers when I took them by the hand to lead them out of Egypt, because they broke my covenant, though I was a husband to them,' declares the LORD. 'This is the covenant I will make with the house of Israel after that time,' declares the LORD. 'I will put my law in their minds and write it on their hearts. I will be their God, and they will be my people. No longer will a man teach his neighbor, or a man his brother, saying, "Know the LORD," because they will all know me, from the least of them to the greatest,' declares the LORD. 'For I will forgive their wickedness and will remember their sins no more.' This is what the LORD says, he who appoints the sun to shine by day, who decrees the moon and stars to shine by night, who stirs up the sea so that its waves roar — the LORD Almighty is his name: 'Only if these decrees vanish from my sight,' declares the LORD, 'will the descendants of Israel ever cease to be a nation before me.' This is what the LORD says: 'Only if the heavens above can be measured and the foundations of the earth below be searched out will I reject all the descendants of Israel because of all they have done,' declares the LORD (Jeremiah 31:31–37).

The promise made by the angel Gabriel must have taken on great significance for Daniel, who had already been reading and studying the prophet Jeremiah. Not only did God promise everlasting righteousness, He stated that the seventy 'sevens' were necessary to seal up the vision and the prophecy. These words not only express the idea that God was vindicating the truth of the vision which he had given to the prophet, thus establishing beyond any question the authenticity of the prophet's words, but it also refers again to that Messianic Kingdom. At the time when the Messiah will rule and reign in righteousness upon the earth there will no longer be a need for visions and for prophecy because they will have been fulfilled.

There is a further aspect in view, as suggested by the use of the word "seal." The Septuagint (the Greek translation of the Hebrew Old Testament) translates the Hebrew word for seal with the Greek word for seal, "sphiragazo." This is the word the New Testament uses in Ephesians 1:13, 14 and in Ephesians 4:30 with reference to the Holy Spirit's ministry in the life of the believer. In the references in Ephesians, the seal is the "mark" of the Holy Spirit in the life of the believer, "...guaranteeing our inheritance until the redemption of those who are God's possession — to the praise of his glory" (Ephesians 1:14). It is the indwelling presence of the Holy Spirit who gives and energizes the gifts of the Spirit within the life of the believer. In a very real way this indwelling presence of the Holy Spirit, and the gifts that He gives, allow believers in this age to experience a "little bit of heaven right here on earth."

Visions and prophecy were gifts of the Spirit. When the Holy Spirit came at Pentecost, and took up permanent residence in the lives of those who accepted Yeshua as the Messiah and Savior, the gifts of visions and prophecy were a sign of His indwelling presence. These sign gifts verified and vindicated the authenticity of the New Testament and the death, burial, and resurrection of Yeshua, God's Messiah. The fact that God told the prophet Daniel these gifts would be sealed is a further promise of the indwelling presence of the Holy Spirit within the lives of believers. While these sign gifts may not be necessary today, because of the completed revelation of God's redemptive program in the New Testament, Scripture indicates that sign gifts will once again be evidenced in the last days (see Joel 2:28–32).

Finally, Daniel is told that the seventy 'sevens' were necessary to anoint the most holy. The word translated "anoint" is the Hebrew word "Meschiach," from which we get our English word "Messiah." The Greek word is "Christos," from which we get our English word, "Christ." The word Messiah, or Christ, simply means anointed.

This verse is a dual fulfillment — the anointing of the most holy, or the anointing of the Holy of Holies, referring to the return of the visible glory of God to the temple in Jerusalem. God's visible glory had departed prior to the destruction of the temple by the armies of Nebuchadnezzar in 586 B.C. (see Ezekiel 8:6; 9:3; 10:3–5; 10:18, 19; 11:22, 23). God had promised that He would be a sanctuary to Israel in all the countries where they were scattered (see Ezekiel 11:16). He said He would bring them into their own land and give them an undivided heart and a new spirit (Ezekiel 11:18–20). He further promised that His glory would return to the rebuilt temple in Jerusalem (see Ezekiel 43:1, 2; 44:1, 2). It is this final return of God's glory, His anointed, which is referred to in the statement "to anoint the most holy."

For God to be a Sanctuary to the Jewish people in all the nations where they were scattered, it was necessary that He dwell among them. He did this at Pentecost (Shevuoth), when the Holy Spirit came and indwelt the 120 Jews to whom Peter preached (see Acts 2). He did so when the Holy Spirit came and indwelt Cornelius, a Gentile (see Acts 10). God is now dwelling among His people as He indwells believers, both Jew and Gentile. Since Pentecost, God has been building a Sanctuary for His name among the Jews wherever they have been scattered (Ephesians 2:19–22). Through the centuries since Pentecost, it has been the true believers who have lovingly helped, protected, and provided sanctuary for the Jewish people whenever they have faced persecution from the nations. Sadly, Christianity has also had many professing Christians who have brought shame to the One they claim to follow, and who have behaved like wolves in sheep's clothing. Such Christians, who follow Christ in name only, have never showed any love for the Jewish people, and in many cases they have been the instigators of hatred and persecution against the Jewish people.

Within the program of God, His glory returned to Israel in His Messiah, Yeshua, but He was rejected and was put to death. As He ascended into heaven the promise was given that He would return (Acts 1:8–11). When He returns, Jerusalem will be rebuilt, the temple will be rebuilt, and God's glory will once again dwell in the temple in Jerusalem. It is most remarkable that God would sum up His program of redemption and judgment, and reveal it to Daniel in six phrases. This is significant because within the Bible the number six is the number for man. Man was created on the sixth day. In the book of the Revelation the number "666" is ascribed to the Beast and we are told "that it is the number of a man" (Revelation 13:18).

In these six aspects of His redemptive program, God reveals that mankind will be completely redeemed, Israel will be restored, and Jerusalem will be established as the place of God's glory. God will have completed and sealed up all prophecy.

God revealed to Daniel that these six elements of His redemptive and judgmental program are inexorably linked to the Jews and to Jerusalem. He said these things are decreed upon "your people" and "your holy city." Every system of interpreting Biblical prophecy must include the Jew, Israel, and Jerusalem.

It is no wonder, then, that Bible scholars like Sir Edward Denny have called the "Seventy 'Sevens'" of Daniel "the back-bone of prophecy."[4] Every system of eschatology that includes a future for Israel must take into consideration some kind of interpretation of Daniel's prophecy of the seventy 'sevens.' A literal interpretation of these seventy 'sevens' will lead one inexorably to the conclusion that Yeshua is the Messiah.

The angel Gabriel revealed an overview of God's program of redemption and judgment to Daniel and he revealed the time framework in which it would be fulfilled. Daniel was then told: "Know and understand this: From the issuing of the decree to restore and rebuild Jerusalem until the Anointed One, the ruler, comes, there will be seven 'sevens,' and sixty-two 'sevens.' It will be rebuilt with streets and a trench, but in times of trouble" (Daniel 9:25).

THE FIRST PERIOD OF SEVEN

The period of seventy 'sevens' is to begin with a decree to restore and rebuild Jerusalem. There were four separate and distinct decrees that were issued in connection with the restoration of Jerusalem at the conclusion of the Babylonian captivity.

The first decree was issued by Cyrus in 536 B.C. This is recorded for us in 2 Chronicles 36:22–23, and repeated in the book of Ezra (see Ezra 1:1–4). These decrees stated: "In the first year of Cyrus king of Persia, in order to fulfill the word of the LORD spoken by Jeremiah, the LORD moved the heart of Cyrus king of Persia to make a proclamation throughout his realm and to put it in writing: 'This is what Cyrus king of Persia says: The LORD, the God of heaven, has given me all the kingdoms of the earth and he has appointed me to build a temple for him at Jerusalem in Judah. Anyone of his people among you — may the LORD his God be with him, and let him go up'" (2 Chronicles 36:22, 23).

This same decree was repeated by Ezra. It stated: "In the first year of Cyrus king of Persia, in order to fulfill the word of the LORD spoken by Jeremiah, the LORD moved the heart of Cyrus king of Persia to make a proclamation throughout his realm and to put it in writing: 'This is what Cyrus king of Persia says: The LORD, the God of heaven, has given me all the kingdoms of the earth and he has appointed me to build a temple for him at Jerusalem in Judah. Anyone of his people among you — may his God be with him, and let him go up to Jerusalem in Judah and build the temple of the LORD, the God of Israel, the God who is in Jerusalem. And the people of any place where survivors may now be living are to provide him with silver and gold, with goods and livestock, and with freewill offerings for the temple of God in Jerusalem'" (Ezra 1:1–4).

Careful examination of this decree will reveal that it is limited specifically to the restoration of the temple. Daniel was then told that the decree which would begin the Seventy 'sevens' would include a decree to "restore and rebuild Jerusalem."

The second decree, made by Darius, is recorded in Ezra 6:1–5 and Ezra 6:8–12. It stated:

King Darius then issued an order, and they searched in the archives stored in the treasury at Babylon. A scroll was found in the citadel of Ecbatana in the province of Media, and this was written on it: Memorandum: In the first year of King Cyrus, the king issued a decree concerning the temple of God in Jerusalem: Let the temple be rebuilt as a place to present sacrifices, and let its foundations be laid. It is to be ninety feet high and ninety feet wide, with three courses of large stones and one of timbers. The costs are to be paid by the royal treasury. Also, the gold and silver articles of the house of God, which Nebuchadnezzar took from the temple in Jerusalem and brought to Babylon, are to be returned to their places in the temple in Jerusalem; they are to be deposited in the house of God (Ezra 6:1–5).

Moreover, I hereby decree what you are to do for these elders of the Jews in the construction of this house of God: The expenses of these men are to be fully paid out of the royal treasury, from the revenues of Trans-Euphrates, so that the work will not stop. Whatever is needed — young bulls, rams, male lambs for burnt offerings to the God of heaven, and wheat, salt, wine and oil, as requested by the priests in Jerusalem — must be given them daily without fail, so that they may offer sacrifices pleasing to the God of heaven and pray for the well-being of the king and his sons.

Furthermore, I decree that if anyone changes this edict, a beam is to be pulled from his house and he is to be lifted up and impaled on it. And for this crime his house is to be made a pile of rubble. May God, who has caused his Name to dwell there, overthrow any king or people who lifts a hand to change this decree or to destroy this temple in Jerusalem.

I Darius have decreed it. Let it be carried out with diligence. (Ezra 6:8–12)

A close examination of this decree reveals that it is just a re-confirmation of Cyrus' original decree to rebuild the temple, and has nothing at all to do with the rebuilding of the city and its walls.

A third decree was issued by Artaxerxes. This decree was issued in the seventh year of his reign. Artaxerxes ruled the Persian empire from 465 B.C. to 424 B.C. The seventh year of Artaxerxes reign would therefore have been 458 B.C. Once again, this decree contained nothing about the rebuilding of the city. It emphasized only the rebuilding of the temple and the re-establishment of the temple services and judicial arrangements which would administrate the land. This decree stated:

This is a copy of the letter King Artaxerxes had given to Ezra the priest and teacher,…Now I decree that any of the Israelites in my kingdom, including priests and Levites, who wish to go to Jerusalem with you, may go. You are sent by the king and his seven advisers to inquire about Judah and Jerusalem with regard to the Law of your God, which is in your hand. Moreover, you are to take with you the silver and gold that the king and his advisers have freely given to the God of Israel, whose dwelling is in Jerusalem, together with all the silver and gold you may obtain from the province of Babylon, as well as the freewill offerings of the people and priests for the temple of their God in Jerusalem. With this money be sure to buy bulls, rams and male lambs, together with their grain offerings and drink offerings, and sacrifice them on the altar of the temple of your God in Jerusalem.

You and your brother Jews may then do whatever seems best with the rest of the silver and gold, in accordance with the will of your God. Deliver to the God of Jerusalem all the articles entrusted to you for worship in the temple of your God. And anything else needed for the temple of your God that you may have occasion to supply, you may provide from the royal treasury.

Now I, King Artaxerxes, order all the treasurers of Trans-Euphrates to provide with diligence whatever Ezra the priest, a teacher of the Law of the God of heaven, may ask of you — up to a hundred talents of silver, a hundred cors of wheat, a hundred baths of wine, a hundred baths of olive oil, and salt without limit. Whatever the God of heaven has prescribed, let it be done with diligence for the temple of the God of heaven. Why should there be wrath against the realm of the king and of his sons? You are also to know that you have no authority to impose taxes, tribute or duty on any of the priests, Levites, singers, gatekeepers, temple servants or other workers at this house of God.

And you, Ezra, in accordance with the wisdom of your God, which you possess, appoint magistrates and judges to administer justice to all the people of Trans-Euphrates — all who know the laws of your God. And you are to teach any who do not know them. Whoever does not obey the law of your God and the law of the king must surely be punished by death, banishment, confiscation of property, or imprisonment (Ezra 7:11–26).

Although none of these decrees fulfilled the requirements necessary to begin the period of seventy 'sevens,' they did allow for a man by the name of Nehemiah to visit Jerusalem. When he arrived in the holy city he found the walls of the city broken down and its gates destroyed by fire. Before embarking on his visit to Jerusalem, Nehemiah went before King Artaxerxes in fear and trembling, requesting permission to go to Jerusalem for the specific purpose of rebuilding the city. Scripture states:

"In the month of Nisan in the twentieth year of King Artaxerxes, when wine was brought for him, I took the wine and gave it to the king. I had not been sad in his presence before; so the king asked me, 'Why does your face look so sad when you are not ill? This can be nothing but sadness of heart.' I was very much afraid, but I said to the king, 'May the king live forever! Why should my face not look sad when the city where my fathers are buried lies in ruins, and its gates have been destroyed by fire?'

"The king said to me, 'What is it you want?' Then I prayed to the God of heaven, and I answered the king, 'If it pleases the king and if your servant has found favor in his sight, let him send me to the city in Judah where my fathers are buried so that I can rebuild it.'

"Then the king, with the queen sitting beside him, asked me, 'How long will your journey take, and when will you get back?' It pleased the king to send me; so I set a time" (Nehemiah 2:1–6).

Based upon Nehemiah's request to rebuild the city, and the King's willingness to grant his request, there was a modification of the original decree that was issued by King Artaxerxes. This modification allowed Nehemiah not only to rebuild the temple, but to rebuild the walls of the city —to rebuild Jerusalem. This was the fulfillment of the requirement that God had told Daniel was necessary to begin the period of seventy 'sevens.' Nehemiah 2:2 reveals the exact time when Nehemiah appeared before the King, and the exact time when the King's decree was modified to include the rebuilding of Jerusalem; it was in the month of Nisan, in the twentieth year of the reign of King Artaxerxes.

The original decree to rebuild the temple was issued in July, 446 B.C., and the modification of the decree allowing Nehemiah to rebuild Jerusalem was in the year 445 B.C. Since the modification of the original decree was in the month of Nisan, there is an exact starting point (Nisan 445 B.C.) to begin calculating the period of time that the seventy 'sevens' would cover.

Daniel 9:25 states: "Know and understand this: From the issuing of the decree to restore and rebuild Jerusalem until the Anointed One, the ruler, comes, there will be seven 'sevens,' and sixty-two 'sevens.' It will be rebuilt with streets and a trench, but in times of trouble."

From the issuing of the decree there would be a period of seven 'sevens,' then there would be an additional sixty-two 'sevens,' and finally there would be a final period of one seven (9:27). Daniel is told that the total of seventy 'sevens' is divided into three distinct periods of time.

The first period of seven 'sevens' represented a period of forty-nine years (7x7=49). The second period of sixty two 'sevens' represented a period of 434 years (62x7=434). The final period of one seven, represented seven years (7x1=1). It is important to the understanding of the prophecy to recognize these as three distinct time periods, as this is the way the seventy 'sevens' were presented to Daniel.

When the Scriptures speak of "years" within a prophetic context, the writers of Scripture have in mind a year composed of 360 days, rather than 365. This is based upon the use of the lunar Jewish calendar comprised of twelve months of thirty days each. Hence, the book of Revelation speaks of forty-two months as being comprised of 1260 days, or three and one-half years (see Revelation 11:2; 12:6).

The first period of seven 'sevens,' or forty-nine years, covered the period of time from the modification of the decree issued by King Artaxerxes in Nisan 445 B.C. to Nisan 396 B.C. During this time Daniel was told that the walls around Jerusalem would be rebuilt, the streets would be rebuilt, and a trench, or moat, would be built. He was told these would all be built in troublous times. This is the way the book of Nehemiah describes the rebuilding of Jerusalem. Historical evidence of that time reveals that it took approximately forty-nine years to accomplish this. Throughout this time the Jewish people faced spiritual struggles and national troubles, and they were engaged in continual battles with the Samaritans and with the rulers in Persia and surrounding countries. Nevertheless, in fulfillment of the prophecy given to Daniel, the city and walls were rebuilt.

The Second Period of Seven

The second period of sixty-two 'sevens,' or 434 years, began after the completion of the rebuilding of the city of Jerusalem. This period spanned the years from 396 B.C. to Nisan 33 C.E. The 434 years are represented by years comprised of 360 days per year — a biblical year. (360 days times 434 years is equal to 156,240 days.) The solar/lunar year of 365 days, which allows for leap years, divide into the 156,240 days represented by the biblical year, calculates to a total of 428 calendar years.

God had told the prophet Daniel that after the 434 biblical years, or 428 calendar years, which would be Nisan in 33 C.E., His Anointed One would be cut off. Only one person in all of Jewish history, or for that matter in all of world history, could have fulfilled this prophecy in every detail. That person was Yeshua of Nazareth. The word "Anointed" is the Hebrew word for Messiah. Daniel is told exactly when the Messiah, whom God promised to send to Israel, would be "cut off."

Luke said that Yeshua began His ministry, revealing Himself to be God's Messiah for Israel, in the 15th year of Tiberias Caesar (see Luke 3:1). Tiberias became Emperor on August 19, 14 C.E. It can therefore be deduced that 30 C.E. was the fifteenth year of his reign. The first Passover in Yeshua's ministry was at Nisan (March/April) 30 C.E. The Scriptures confirm that Yeshua kept four Passovers during the course of His ministry. The fourth Passover was the Last Supper which He kept with His disciples. The following day, April 6, 33 C.E., He was crucified, "cut off." When Yeshua rode into Jerusalem on the foal of a donkey during that last Passover week, in fulfillment of the prophecy of Zechariah 9:9, the people cried out "Hosanna, Hosanna, (Save us, Save us) blessed be He who comes in the name of the LORD," in fulfillment of the prophecy of Psalm 118:25, 26. Is it any wonder that Yeshua said, "If the people don't cry out, the very stones will" (see Luke 19:40). God had a precise timetable for Israel's redemption and for our salvation which could only be fulfilled through the death of His Messiah.

The words, "cut off," in Daniel 9:26 are translated from a word that normally refers to the death penalty. Inherent in the original Hebrew word is the idea of suffering a violent death. The word is used this way in Leviticus 7:20, where it speaks of one who has been defiled, or who has eaten unclean animals and is therefore to be "cut off" from the people of Israel. This word is also used in Psalm 37:9, where the Psalmist speaks of evil men who would be "cut off."

Daniel is not only told that the Messiah would be cut off, he is also told that the Messiah would "have nothing." In this context, to "have nothing" means to have no children, no progeny, no one to carry on one's name. To the religious Jew in Daniel's day, or even in our own day, the thought of not having children, or of being put to death before physical descendants were born, was the greatest of all tragedies. Without earthly descendants a family's name and heritage was in danger of being eradicated, and ultimately such privation could destroy the Jewish nation as a whole.

This unique prophecy of a Messiah who would be "cut off," and without progeny, is even more amazing when placed alongside Isaiah's prophecy of a "Suffering Servant" in Isaiah 53. In verse 8, Isaiah prophesied: "By oppression and judgment, he was taken away. And who can speak of his descendants? For he was cut off from the land of the living; for the transgression of my people he was stricken."

Daniel is told that with the death of the Messiah, transgression would be finished; His death would make an end to sin and atone for wickedness. Through the death of the Messiah, everlasting righteousness would be ushered in and God would seal up the vision and prophecy and anoint the Most Holy.

That Yeshua saw Himself as the fulfillment of the Messianic role, as seen in Daniel 9, is apparent in both His deeds and His words. Not only did Yeshua refer to the prophet Daniel (see Matthew 24:15), He also applied one of the prophecies of Daniel to Himself. He said: "Therefore I tell you that the kingdom of God will be taken away from you and given to a people who will produce its fruit. He who falls on this stone will be broken to pieces, but he on whom it falls will be crushed" (Matthew 21:43, 44).

Yeshua made a direct reference to Psalm 118:22, 23 and had applied it to Himself. He claimed to be the "Stone the builders rejected." He continued His analogy, saying that the "rejected Stone" will crush everyone upon whom it falls. This is a direct reference to the great image of a man which King Nebuchadnezzar saw, and to the "great stone cut without hands" which Nebuchadnezzar saw crush the feet of the great idol, causing it to come crashing down (see Daniel 2). The implication of the text is clear: God is sovereign. Whether Jewish or Gentile, all mankind must come to God in His way. All mankind must accept God's program of redemption. There is no other. Those who accept the "rejected Stone,"

God's Messiah, find His blessings as their lives are built upon the solid Rock of God's grace. Those who reject the Messiah will be crushed in judgment by the "rejected Stone."

THE LAST PERIOD OF SEVEN

The period of the sixty-two 'sevens', or 434 years, has caused many problems for the Jewish community because it so clearly sets forth Yeshua as the Messiah. Within the Christian community, however, it has been the last period of "one seven" that has been troublesome to scholars. If the "sixty-two periods of seven" is understood and accepted as having been fulfilled in Yeshua, the questions arise, "When was this last period of one seven fulfilled?" and, "If it was not fulfilled, when will it be fulfilled?" To answer these questions, one must look closely at Daniel 9:25–27. Daniel was told:

Know and understand this: From the issuing of the decree to restore and rebuild Jerusalem until the Anointed One, the ruler, comes, there will be seven 'sevens,' and sixty-two 'sevens.'... After the sixty-two 'sevens,' the Anointed One will be cut off and will have nothing. The people of the ruler who will come will destroy the city and the sanctuary. The end will come like a flood: War will continue until the end, and desolations have been decreed. He will confirm a covenant with many for one 'seven,' but in the middle of the 'seven' he will put an end to sacrifice and offering. And one who causes desolation will place abominations on a wing [of the temple] until the end that is decreed is poured out on him.

When Daniel wrote his prophecy, under the inspiration of the Holy Spirit, there were no verse or chapter divisions. These were later additions. Punctuation marks indicating the end of a verse, such as the period which appears at the end of verse 25 in our modern translations, do not allow for completion of the thought. This leads to misunderstanding. The meaning of the text would be clearer if the thought of verse 25 were allowed to come to its conclusion after the first phrase of verse 26. Verse 25 would then read: "Know and understand this: From the issuing of the decree to restore and rebuild Jerusalem until the Anointed One, the ruler, comes, there will be seven 'sevens,' and sixty-two 'sevens.' It will be rebuilt with streets and a trench, but in times of trouble. After the sixty-two 'sevens,' the Anointed One will be cut off and will have nothing." Verse 26 would continue saying, "The people of the ruler who will come will destroy the city and the sanctuary. The end will come like a flood..."

The "Anointed One" spoken of in Daniel 9:25 is the same "Anointed One" mentioned in the first part of verse 26. However, the "ruler" of verse 25 is not the same "ruler who will come" spoken of in verse 26. The "ruler" of verse 25 is a reference to the Messiah, who was Jewish. However, the reference to the "the ruler who will come" is a reference to the Roman armies under Titus. This is clear from the history of that period. Approximately forty years had elapsed between the fulfillment of: "...the Anointed One will be cut off and will have nothing" and "...the ruler who will come." This forty year period represents the time from the death of Yeshua to the destruction of Jerusalem by Titus in 70 C.E.

Individuals who believe that this last period of seven has been fulfilled completely, claim that it was fulfilled either by Yeshua, or by Antiochus Epiphanes. Those who hold to the position that it was fulfilled by Yeshua, argue that the "prince" mentioned in verses 25 and 26, refer to the same individual. They say, "If the Messiah, the 'prince' of verse 25, is Yeshua, then the 'prince' mentioned in verse 26 must also refer to Yeshua." They further state that the references to a "covenant," in verses 26 and 27, refer to the New Covenant which Yeshua made at His last Passover. One major difficulty with this interpretation stems from the fact that the covenant, mentioned in verses 26 and 27, will last for a period of seven years, or one period of seven. It will then be broken in the middle of this last period of seven, or after three and one half years.

The New Covenant inaugurated by Yeshua at the Last Passover, however, is an everlasting, unconditional covenant. It cannot be broken. The New Covenant of Yeshua is the covenant spoken of in Jeremiah 31:31–37. Therefore, this temporary covenant cannot be a reference to the New Covenant which Yeshua inaugurated.

If the covenant mentioned in Daniel 9:26 and 27 is not the New Covenant, there is no basis within the context to maintain that the ruler (prince) spoken of in verse 25 must necessarily be the same ruler spoken of in verses 26 and 27. In fact, the language of the prophecy given to Daniel seems to preclude this. It is clear that the ruler mentioned in verse 25 is the Anointed One (Messiah), who will be cut off. However, in verses 26 and 27, Daniel speaks of the "ruler that will come." If the ruler is killed after the sixty two periods of seven, as declared in verse 25, he cannot be the one spoken of as "coming" in verse 26. Thus, it could be concluded that the ruler spoken of in verses 26 and 27 is not a reference to the Messiah. And that covenant is not the New Covenant.

On the other hand, the time frame of the seventy 'sevens' will not allow for an interpretation asserting that the ruler spoken of in verses 26 and 27 are references to Antiochus Epiphanes. It has already been established that the ruler of verses 26 and 27 is to come after the sixty-two periods of 'seven'. Antiochus Epiphanes died as an insane man in 164 B.C., long before the fulfillment of the sixty-two sevens, or 434 years, that were prophesied.

THE RULER WHO WILL COME

Three questions are left. Who is this ruler who will come? When will he come? What covenant will be made and broken with the people of Israel?

In seeking answers to these questions, let us first note that the word translated "ruler" or "prince" in verses 25, 26, and 27 is the Hebrew word "nahgeed." It is the less common word for "prince" or "ruler." The most widely used word for "prince" or "ruler" is the Hebrew word "Sar," and it is the word "Sar" that is used of the Chief ruler, the Mighty Prince, etc. This is the word that is used of the Messiah in Isaiah 9:6, where He is called the "Sar Shalom" (Prince of Peace).

If the word Sar is the more popular usage of prince, why didn't the Holy Spirit use the word 'Sar' in Daniel 9:25, rather than the weaker word 'nahgeed,' when speaking of the prince? Two possible explanations come to mind. One is that the Holy Spirit chose the word "nahgeed" because, in His first coming, our Messiah came not as the Mighty Prince, but as the "suffering Servant" who would be "cut off" for the sins of people. He came as the Lamb of God who would take away the sin of the world. But when He returns, He will return as Prince of Peace, Lord of lords, King of kings! He will come as the Lion of the Tribe of Judah. He will establish His kingdom and, indeed, the government will be upon His shoulders.

The other explanation for the Holy Spirit's choice of the Hebrew word "nahgeed" was that this word is used in Ezekiel 28:2, speaking of the

Prince of Tyre. In Ezekiel 28, the Prince of Tyre is seen as an incarnation of Satan (see Ezekiel 28:11–19). He is referred to as the "anointed cherub," the "one who was in the 'Garden of God' and was blameless until sin was found in him." This explanation best fits the context. This means the ruler (or prince) referred to as the "ruler who will come" in verse 26 is a reference to Satan.

Scriptures tell us that Satan is the "prince of the power of the air" (Ephesians 2:2). Believers wrestle against wickedness in the heavenlies. They are in a war against spiritual powers of wickedness (Ephesians 6:10–18). Angelic beings themselves are involved in spiritual warfare. Gabriel would have come sooner in answer to Daniel's prayer, but he was prevented by the "prince of persia." The Archangel Michael intervened so that Daniel's prayer could be answered (see Daniel 10).

Daniel had already been given the vision of Antiochus Epiphanes — the prototype of the antichrist (the Beast) who would make war on Israel in the last days. Now he is told another ruler (prince) will come. This ruler will make a seven-year covenant with Israel, and after three and one half years he will break it. Because of him, desolations have been determined upon the holy city of Jerusalem until the end. This ruler (prince) will be used by Satan in his attempt to destroy the nation of Israel. Satan failed in his attempt to destroy the Messiah. The Messiah was "wounded" for the sins of His people. He was "cut off" because of the sins of His people. But death could not hold Him. He was victorious over death — He was not destroyed!

Since Satan was not able to destroy the Messiah, he now attempts to destroy the people unto whom the Messiah will return. John sees a vision of a woman clothed with the sun, with the moon under her feet, and with twelve stars in her crown. This is a picture of Israel. It is similar in detail to the dream that Joseph had (see Genesis 37:9, 10). The woman represents Israel, the twelve stars represent the twelve tribes, the moon, and the nations. The woman gives birth to a man-child, the Messiah. A great red dragon, representing Satan, seeks to destroy her child but he cannot. Instead, he is caught up into heaven. The scene then changes, and John is told there is a great war in heaven, and Satan is cast down to the earth where he tries to destroy the woman and her seed (Israel) (see Revelation 12:1–17).

The latter part of Daniel 9:26 and verse 27 tell about things that would happen to Israel after the Messiah was cut off. These verses are a vision of Satan's continuing attempt to destroy the nation of Israel and to thereby invalidate the Word of God and the promises of God.

THE PEOPLE OF THE RULER

The following phrase in verse 26 is significant: "...The people of the ruler (prince) who will come will destroy the city and the sanctuary...." If the ruler (prince) is an individual who will be deceived and empowered by Satan, who are the "people of the ruler"? One suggestion is that the people are those who are Satanically blinded to the truth of God's Word. Satan is the god of this age who blinds men's hearts to the Gospel (see 2 Corinthians 4:4). He is the one who blinded the hearts of the Jewish people so they would reject their Messiah. He continues to blind the hearts of Jewish and Gentile people so that they continue to reject God.

The nation of Israel rejected the Messiah and cried out for His crucifixion, but it was the Gentiles, the Romans, who carried out the act of crucifixion. Under Roman law the Jews were not permitted to practice crucifixion as a means of punishment. Further, crucifixion was forbidden by Jewish law, and had never been a means of Jewish punishment. The Talmud allowed for two prescribed methods of dealing with capital offenders—stoning or hanging. In their acquiescence to the cries of the Jewish leaders to "crucify Him" the Romans were just as responsible for the death of the Messiah as the Jews (see Acts 4:27). They could have refused, but they did not.

Because the Jews rejected God, they also rejected His Messiah, and because the Gentiles rejected the God of Israel they, too, rejected His Messiah. In their sinfulness, the Jewish leaders and the Jewish people rejected God before 586 B.C. and, as God had promised through the warnings of the prophets, the Jewish people were led into captivity and their temple was destroyed. The rejection of God's Messiah, Yeshua, was a continuation of that same rejection of God. The return of the Jewish people to their land after seventy years of Babylonian captivity was not intended to be the final regathering of the Jewish people to usher in the Messianic kingdom. The return of the Jewish people after the Babylonian captivity fulfilled the promise of God and served as an hiatus during which God would reveal His total program of redemption. The Messiah had to come. He had to be the sinbearer of the world. He had to be rejected by both Jew and Gentile. His rejection was pictured in the desolation that was to come upon Jerusalem, until He would return to restore the city and the temple.

Within a generation after the death of the Messiah, Yeshua, the city of Jerusalem was destroyed by the Roman armies of Titus in the year 70 C.E. Its destruction came in fulfillment of the words of the prophet. The end came like a flood. The Jewish historian, Josephus, describes how hordes of Roman soldiers wantonly sacked and burned the Holy City, killing its inhabitants and taking its leaders captive.

Daniel 9:26 predicted: "...The end will come like a flood: war will continue until the end, and desolations have been decreed." This is a most unique prophecy. It states that the city of Jerusalem, the city of peace, will know no peace until the end, or until Messiah returns to establish His kingdom. Until then, the city of Jerusalem will either be in desolation or in conflict. Yeshua told his disciples the same thing when they questioned Him about the destruction of Jerusalem and about the temple (see Matthew 24:1–32; Luke 21:5–36). He said there would be continual warfare, famine, diseases, false prophets, and deceit. He told His disciples when they saw Jerusalem surrounded by the Gentiles they should flee into the wilderness. Ironically, when the armies of Titus surrounded Jerusalem many of the believers in Yeshua, believing that this was the fulfillment of Daniel's prophecy which Yeshua had referred to, fled to Pela (a few miles from Jerusalem in the wilderness). Members of the Jewish community who did not believe Yeshua was the Messiah saw the flight of the Jewish believers as disloyalty, prompting them to take steps to isolate the Jewish believers from the synagogues and from Jewish life within the community.

Satan's seeds of deception took root in the hearts of Jews, Gentiles, and even within the hearts of some who professed to be Christians. The result has been a long period to time with continuing destruction of Jerusalem, continued ravaging of the land of Israel, and increased hatred of the Jewish People. God told the prophet Daniel that "desolations had been decreed," and his prophecy was being fulfilled.

When Hadrian became emperor of the Roman Empire, he granted

the Jews permission to rebuild the temple. Then he changed his mind, and in 123 C.E. he issued decrees against the Jews in which he forbade them to hold Sabbath services, or to practice the mikvah (ritual bath) or the bris (circumcision). He then made plans to rebuild Jerusalem as a secular city, complete with a temple for worshiping Jupiter on the very site where the Jewish temple had stood. His plans were interrupted, however, by a revolt of the Jews under Bar Kochba. In this revolt Bar Kochba successfully conquered Jerusalem, once again making it a free Jewish city.

Bar Kochba ruled Jerusalem from 133 C.E. to 135 C.E. He even minted coins with his picture on them. Rabbi Akiva was so impressed with Bar Kochba's victories over the Romans that he declared him to be the Messiah. Rabbi Akiva soon realized his mistake, but by then it was to late. The damage had already been done. Rome once again attacked. This time Bar Kochba lost Jerusalem and he fled to Betar. He fought the Roman legions for three more years and was finally killed in battle, along with 580,000 Jews who were slain by the Roman soldiers.

With the death of Bar Kochba, Rome moved swiftly to attack and destroy other Jewish cities throughout Israel. Much of the Jewish population was killed indiscriminately by the Roman soldiers. Some of the Jews were captured and sold as slaves. During this time Rome forbade the Jews from burying their dead. Rome expelled all Jews, as well as all Jewish believers in the Messiah, from the city of Jerusalem and Judaism was banned as an official religion. Any Jew caught entering Jerusalem, or practicing his religion, was put to death or imprisoned.

The massacres of the Jews continued under the Roman Emperor Rufus II, until he felt the total destruction of the Jewish people and their religion was complete. Jerusalem was then rebuilt by the Romans and was renamed "Aelia Capitolina." As a pagan Roman city, no Jews or Christians were allowed to enter the city. It had become a city of desolation, just as God had told the prophet Daniel it would.

Satan continued to sow his seeds of deception and hatred. Under the Roman empire Christianity and Judaism were despised "unofficial" religions, and adherents of either group were targets of persecution at the whim of the emperor or ruler. In an attempt to escape persecution, and succumbing to the deception of Satan, the Christian leaders began to petition Rome to become an official religion, separate from Judaism. In order to make themselves distinct from the Jews, and from their practices, the Christians began to claim that they were the true Israel, and they began to interpret Scriptures applying the blessings to themselves and the curses to the Jews.

Deceived by Satan, and in contrast to the true believers, a counterfeit Christianity gradually incorporated Judaism's monotheism, its morality, its eschatology, its liturgy, and most of its ceremonies—including its feasts and fasts. However, each Holy day, and each feast and fast, such as Passover, the Sabbath, and Shevuoth (Pentecost) was soon divested of its Judaic origin. When Pope Victor I (189–99 C.E.) convened the first Roman Senate, he threatened to excommunicate the bishops of Asia if they continued to observe Easter on the date of Passover (the 14th of Nisan). Worship on the Sabbath was forbidden, and was officially moved to Sunday in commemoration of the resurrection of Yeshua. The early Church Fathers advocated that all Christians should take biblical names such as Israel and Jacob, as a means of proving that they were really the genuine Israel of God.

A reading of early Church history reveals that the early Church Fathers' perception of Jews was that they were all like Herod, slayers of the innocent. They were all like Judas, the betrayer of Yeshua. They saw all Jews as being anti-Christ. On the other hand, they saw themselves as being the legitimate heirs of all the promises of God. Blinded by sin and Satanic deception, Rome stripped the Jewish people of their land and laid the country-side waste. Ironically, Satanic deception also led the early Church Fathers within Christianity (not true Christianity) to strip the Jews of their spiritual homeland — the promises of God, and thus rob them of the knowledge of the true Messiah, Yeshua.

The prophet Daniel declared there would be desolations declared upon the Holy City until the time of the end, and so it happened, and continues to happen, because the end has not yet come. Even though the Jewish people living in the State of Israel have, in our day, conquered the city of Jerusalem, and are rebuilding the land, they are still under what the Scriptures call the "Times of the Gentiles" (times of the nations), and they will continue under the "Times of the Gentiles" until the Messiah, Yeshua, returns (see Romans 11:25–27; Luke 21:24).

The "people of the ruler (prince) who will come" refers, then, to those individuals who are satanically blinded to the truth of God's Word in this age. The formation of this group of people began with the Romans, after the Messiah was "cut off," and this group will continue to exist until its culmination with the coming of the Beast, or the antichrist and in his armies. This is why this unique phrase occurs. In the other visions of Daniel, specific nations have been identified (i.e., Babylon, Persia, Greece, etc.) but here, the destruction is seen as coming from the "people of the prince (ruler)." The destruction and desolations will continue until the end.

THE LONG GAP

The vision of the "one seven," the final seven, is about to be revealed. Daniel is told: "He will confirm a covenant with many for one 'seven,' but in the middle of that `seven' he will put an end to sacrifice and offering. And one who causes desolation will place abominations on a wing [of the temple], until the end that is decreed is poured out on him" (Daniel 9:27).

God had already told the prophet Daniel that after the second period of sixty-two 'sevens' the Messiah would be cut off — after which Jerusalem would be destroyed by the people of the ruler (prince) who would come. The prophet was further told that wars would continue to exist until the final abomination was fulfilled.

Jerusalem was destroyed in 70 C.E. by the Romans. Since that time, wars have continued to engulf Israel, the Middle East, and the city of Jerusalem. The Jewish people themselves have been the subjects of hatred and persecution.

The prophet is now told that a covenant will be made with "many" within the nation of Israel. For such a covenant to be made, Israel must exist as a nation. Was such a seven year covenant ever made with "many" within the nation of Israel before the destruction of Jerusalem by Titus, or before the final dispersion of the nation of Israel by the Romans? No. Israel was dispersed from the land and was scattered among the nations until 1948. No covenant was made with Israel during those years. However, now that Israel has been re-established as a nation, and now that Israel has control of the city of Jerusalem, it is possible that such a covenant could now be made. This means that between the second period of 'sevens' (the sixty-two 'sevens') and the last period of one 'seven,' almost 2000 years of history have gone by. Why this great gap of time between the fulfillment of the sixty-two 'sevens' and this last period of one seven? This is a question that has long puzzled Bible scholars.

It should not surprise us to find gaps of time between single verses in the Bible. This occurs in several instances. The original Hebrew texts did not include punctuation; this was added much later by scribes and translators. The placement of commas, periods, or the breaking of a paragraph, as inserted by scribes or translators, can cause confusion over the original intent of the text. An example of this can be found in Isaiah, where the prophet says: "The Spirit of the Sovereign LORD is on me, because the LORD has anointed me to preach good news to the poor. He has sent me to bind up the brokenhearted, to proclaim freedom for the captives and release from darkness for the prisoners, to proclaim the year of the LORD's favor and the day of vengeance of our God, to comfort all who mourn," (Isaiah 61:1, 2).

The prophet Isaiah was speaking of a day when the Messiah, God's Redeemer, would come and literally make an end of sin. He would bind the broken hearted, proclaim freedom to the captives, proclaim the vengeance of God, and comfort all who mourn. In reading the prophet's words, it would appear that all of this was to be accomplished when the Messiah came. However, when the Messiah, Yeshua, attended the synagogue in Nazareth, He did an extraordinary thing. Luke records the incident in this way:

> *He went to Nazareth, where he had been brought up, and on the Sabbath day he went into the synagogue, as was his custom. And he stood up to read. The scroll of the prophet Isaiah was handed to him. Unrolling it, he found the place where it is written: 'The Spirit of the LORD is on me, because he has anointed me to preach good news to the poor. He has sent me to proclaim freedom for the prisoners and recovery of sight for the blind, to release the oppressed, to proclaim the year of the LORD's favor.' Then he rolled up the scroll, gave it back to the attendant and sat down. The eyes of everyone in the synagogue were fastened on him, and he said to them, 'Today this scripture is fulfilled in your hearing (Luke 4:16–21).*

Yeshua, reading from Isaiah 61, read verse one in its entirety, but He stopped right in the middle of the verse two. He did not complete the reading. He then startled the crowd by proclaiming, "Today this scripture is fulfilled in your hearing." By stopping in the middle of the verse, proclaiming that the first part of this passage was being fulfilled in Him at the very time He was speaking, He was also implying the last part of verse two was not to be understood as being fulfilled in Him at that time. The last part of Isaiah 61:2 reads, "and to proclaim the day of the vengeance of our God."

The phrase, "the day of the vengeance of our God," was a phrase that had to do with the judgment of God. It is a reference to the Tribulation. Because of the fuller revelation of truth in the New Testament, it appears that the "day of vengeance of our God" will not take place until Yeshua returns at the end of the Tribulation, to bring judgment and to establish His Kingdom.

In Isaiah 61:2, where the scribes and translators inserted a comma (indicating a pause to readers), God inserted two thousand years of time. A similar gap of time exists between Genesis 1:1 and Genesis 1:2. Verse one states that God created the heavens and the earth. Verse two tells us the earth was in chaos. Most evangelical Bible scholars agree that a great gap of time exists between verse one and verse two.

It should not surprise us, then, to find an extended gap of time between the fulfillment of the sixty-two 'sevens' in Daniel, and the seventieth seven in Daniel. This span of time has been called the "Church Age." It began at Pentecost, when the Holy Spirit came and indwelt the disciples (see Acts 2), and it will end with the rapture of the Church, the Body of Christ (see 1 Thessalonians 4:13–18). It was because of this extended period of time, the Church Age, that Yeshua did not complete the reading of Isaiah 61:2. Yeshua knew only the first part of the verse would be fulfilled in His first coming, the rest would be fulfilled when He returned, at His second coming.

Paul argues in Romans chapters 9–11, this extended period of time was necessary in order to extend salvation to the Gentiles. It was also necessary to further extend God's seventy years of judgment upon Israel for their continued unbelief. The seventy years of judgment in Babylon did not bring about "repentance" in the nation, it fulfilled the promise of

God of coming judgment and restoration.

The remnant of Jews who returned to Israel after the Babylonian captivity continued to be led astray by their leaders. God's judgment was again brought upon Israel as the Romans marched across the land. This judgment of God, as revealed to Daniel, would continue until the Messiah returned. Paul tells us in Romans 9–11 that during this time of Israel's exile and judgment by the nations, believing Gentiles (those grafted in by faith in the finish work of the Messiah) have the responsibility, even the priority, to see that the Gospel is brought to the Jewish people (see Romans 1:16). Their failure to do this will result in their own judgment by God, even as Israel's failure to bring the light of God to the Gentiles resulted in their judgment.

THE BROKEN COVENANT

Three additional questions need to be answered about events that will transpire during the final period of seven. Who makes the Covenant? With whom does he make the Covenant? Why is the Covenant broken?

Verse 27 states: "He will confirm a covenant with many for one 'seven' but in the middle of the 'seven' he will put an end to sacrifice and offering. And one who causes desolation will place abominations on a wing [of the temple] until the end that is decreed is poured out on him" (Daniel 9:27).

Grammatically, the "he" in verse 27 refers directly back to the leader (the ruler, or prince) who will come of verse 26. The reference to the leader (or prince) in verse 26 is a reference to Satan. He is the great deceiver. It was Satan who deceived Titus and the armies of Rome into seeking to destroy the Jewish people. Unsuccessful in this attempt, when Israel is again established as a nation (as she is in our day) Satan will once again deceive, control, and empower a world ruler who will seek to destroy the nation. The "He" of verse 27 is a direct reference to the Beast, or the antichrist — to the world ruler who will reign during the last period of seven, or the seven year period of the Tribulation.

The Tribulation, or the "seventieth seven" of Daniel's prophecy, will usher in the final apostasy of Israel. Israel rejects God and signs a covenant of peace with the enemy of peace, Satan, instead of accepting the New Covenant, and the Prince of Peace, the Messiah and LORD, Yeshua.

It is the signing of this covenant with the Beast, or antichrist, that will actually trigger the beginning of the Tribulation. Sin will have come full circle. Satan's attempt to destroy God's Word in the Garden of Eden will now be an attempt to destroy God's Word in the Tribulation. Through deception, unbelief, sin, and rebellion, Satan will attempt to destroy the promises of God, as well as the people unto whom the Messiah is to return. The signing of the covenant with the Beast will result in the outpouring of God's wrath upon Israel and the nations.

Israel will sign this covenant while being deceived by the Beast, or antichrist. The Beast will break the covenant three and one half years after Israel signs it. Israel does not break the covenant. Evidently, Israel will be pleased with the conditions offered in the covenant.

Satan made a similar offer of a covenant with the Messiah, Yeshua. He tempted Yeshua while He was in the wilderness, before He began His public ministry. One of the things Satan tempted Him with was the kingdoms of the World. We read: "Again, the devil took him to a very high mountain and showed him all the kingdoms of the world and their splendor. 'All this I will give you,' he said, 'if you will bow down and worship me.' Yeshua said to him, 'Away from me, Satan! For it is written: "Worship the LORD your God, and serve him only."' Then the devil left him, and angels came and attended him" (Matthew 4:8–11).

Perhaps Satan will use a similar temptation in enticing Israel to sign his covenant. Satan certainly has access to the Scriptures. He knows God's program for Israel as it is revealed in the Word of God. Perhaps he will offer Israel the very thing they have been seeking — a restored and rebuilt temple, the city of Jerusalem at peace with her surrounding neighbors, and restoration of the nation of Israel to a place of leadership among the nations of the world. Since Satan is the god of this age, and since the God of the universe has allowed Satan to exercise his demonic power within the restraints of His will, Satan can make such offers and, within the permissive will of God, he can fulfill the agreements which he makes.

Daniel is told that the Beast makes a covenant "with many" (9:27). The Hebrew here is more exacting. It says that he made the covenant with "the many." The use of the article makes the "many" specific. It means that the covenant is made with the leaders of Israel, in contrast to being made with the people of Israel. The reference is also a contrast between believers and non-believers. The acceptance of this covenant by the leaders of Israel reflects the culmination of their sin and disbelief. When the Messiah, Yeshua, came the first time, it was the leaders of Israel who rejected him; the common people accepted Him. Ironically, in the seventieth week of Daniel, the same thing will happen with the Beast (antichrist). The leaders will accept the Beast (antichrist) and his false prophet, while the people of Israel will reject him (see Revelation 13). Perhaps it will be the people's rejection of the Beast that will ultimately cause him to break his covenant and then make war with the people of Israel.

Although the purpose of the covenant in verse 27 is not stated, the correct understanding of the Hebrew words used gives insight into the meaning. The prophet is told that the ruler who will come will "confirm" a covenant with "the many." Many Bible commentators confuse the word "confirm" with the word "make." In doing so, they state that this ruler will "make" a covenant with Israel. This is not what Daniel is told; he is told that the ruler will "confirm" a covenant. The difference in meanings is significant. To "make" a covenant means a new type of covenant is created, while to "confirm" a covenant means to affirm the terms and conditions of an already existing covenant.

What covenants, made by God with Israel, could be utilized by Satan to his advantage, if the terms of the covenant were enforced? Certainly not the Mosaic Covenant, or the New Covenant. This leaves only the Abrahamic and Davidic Covenants. The Abrahamic Covenant gave the boundaries of the land of Israel and the promise that the land would be given to Israel through Isaac and Jacob. The Davidic Covenant promised a throne, a King, and (in effect) the temple in Jerusalem. Interestingly, these were the very same things promised by Cyrus and Artaxerxes in their decrees which began the "seventy sevens" revealed to Daniel.

Satan, masquerading as the "ruler who will come," will confirm the conditions of the Abrahamic and Davidic Covenants, so that Israel will once again be given control over the land and over the city of Jerusalem. This control will make it possible for the Jewish people to rebuild their temple and to re-institute the sacrificial system. Since Satan, under the sovereignty of God, has authority over the kingdoms of this world, he will deceive Israel and the nations into accepting such a covenant by presenting it as a condition for, and a prelude to, world peace. One can only imagine the power and prestige given to the leader who is able to bring about a peaceful solution to the Israeli/Arab conflict, thereby allowing Israel to rebuild the temple. Such an individual will be perceived as "a god on earth."

THE ABOMINATION OF DESOLATION

According to Daniel, the antichrist (Beast) will be such an individual. But his peace will be short-lived. Daniel is told that in the middle of the last period of seven, this individual, who has been so highly revered, will desecrate the temple. "He will confirm a covenant with many for one 'seven,' but in the middle of that 'seven' he will put an end to sacrifice and offering. And one who causes desolation will place abominations on a wing [of the temple] until the end that is decreed is poured out on him" (Daniel 9:27).

This was the verse in the book of Daniel that Yeshua referred to when His disciples questioned Him about His predictions of the coming destruction of the temple, and the city of Jerusalem. He said: "So when you see standing in the holy place 'the abomination that causes desolation,' spoken of through the prophet Daniel — let the reader understand..." (Matthew 24:15). Yeshua equated the cessation of the sacrifices and offerings in the middle of the final "seven" with the "abomination of desolation" spoken of in Daniel 9:27.

John was told, and he writes in the book of Revelation, that the temple which will stand during that final period of seven, along with the city of Jerusalem, will be trampled down by the Gentiles for a period of forty-two months, the equivalent of 1260 days of a biblical year, or three and one half biblical years.

Paul also tells us that the temple will be defiled. Although he does not call this the "abomination of desolation," his language is clear when he says that the defilement of the temple will be done by the man of sin, the son of perdition, who will sit in the temple of God, showing himself to be God. He states further that this individual will demand worship as if he were God (see 2 Thessalonians 2:3, 4). What Paul is describing is an "abomination of desolation" of the temple. He is picturing for his readers what Antiochus Epiphanes did when he erected a statue of Zeus in the Holy Place of the temple, commanding that the priests worship the statue and sacrifice pigs in its honor.

The Apostle Paul says the abomination of the temple by the man of sin will be far worse than the abomination during the days of Antiochus, and John is told that the abomination will be set up by the Beast (antichrist), who will demand worship. This Beast will be none other than an individual who is controlled by Satan himself (see Revelation 13).

The abomination is described as standing on the wing of the temple. For years this expression puzzled Bible scholars, but recent excavations of the Temple Mount have now revealed a fuller understanding of the architectural design of the temple. Scholars now believe that the wing of the temple was the place where the high priest would stand so he could be visible to all when pronouncing blessings upon the people. It is very likely that the wing of the temple was the place referred to as the Pinnacle of the temple, where Satan brought Yeshua and tempted him to throw himself down (see Matthew 4:5).

According to the writing of John in the book of Revelation, the false prophet, also empowered by Satan, will have an image of the Beast made that will appear on the wing of the temple. This image will be given breath by the false prophet, and all who pass by will be required to worship it (see Revelation 13:14–18). While the image stands on the wing of the temple, the Ruler (Beast) will dwell inside the temple (see Daniel 11:45; 2 Thessalonians 2:3, 4). Satan's desire to set his throne in the place of God's throne will be fulfilled.

The prophet Isaiah spoke of this desire of Lucifer (Satan), saying: "You said in your heart, 'I will ascend to heaven; I will raise my throne above the stars of God; I will sit enthroned on the mount of assembly, on the utmost heights of the sacred mountain'" (Isaiah 14:13).

During the last three and one half years of the last period of 'seven,' Satan (disguised as the Beast and the Ruler) will sit enthroned on the Mount of Assembly (the Temple Mount), on the utmost heights (the wing of the temple) of Mount Moriah, the Temple Mount. But, he will come to his end, and there will be no one to help him (see Daniel 11:45; Revelation 19:19, 20; Revelation 20:10).

The prophet Daniel was left to ponder the things revealed to him. He did not understand all that had been revealed to him, but he did know that his life, and the lives of the people of Israel, were held securely in the hands of a sovereign God — a just, righteous, and merciful God who knew the end from the beginning. He could be fully trusted to do what was right for Daniel, for the nation of Israel, and for the nations of the world.

Followers of Yeshua may not fully understand or comprehend all that God is doing in this world, or even in the circumstances of their own lives, but when they know God personally, through His Messiah (His Living Word), and through His Revelation (His written Word), they can experience the same assurance of faith. "...all things God works for the good of those who love him, who have been called according to his purpose" (Romans 8:28).

NOTES

Chapter 9. Revealing God's Divine Timetable

1 *Apocrypha*, Baruch 1:15–3:18.

2 Frederick A. Tatford, *The Climax of the Ages*, (Grand Rapids, MI: Zondervan Publishing House, 1953), p 143.

3 S.P. Tregelles, *Remarks on the Prophetic Visions in the Book of Daniel*, (London, England: Wertheimer, Lea and Co., 1883), pp 97–98.

4 [see] Charles L. Feinberg, *A Commentary on Daniel, the Kingdom of the* LORD, (Winona Lake, IN: B.M.H. Books, 1981), p 117.

◆

CHAPTER TEN

Talking With Divine Messengers

In the third year of Cyrus king of Persia, a revelation was given to Daniel (who was called Belteshazzar). Its message was true and it concerned a great war. The understanding of the message came to him in a vision....

On the twenty-fourth day of the first month, as I was standing on the bank of the great river, the Tigris, I looked up and there before me was a man dressed in linen, with a belt of the finest gold around his waist. His body was like chrysolite, his face like lightening, his eyes like flaming torches, his arms and legs like the gleam of burnished bronze, and his voice like the sound of a multitude....

He said, 'Daniel, you who are highly esteemed, consider carefully the words I am about to speak to you, and stand up, for I have now been sent to you....Do not be afraid, Daniel. Since the first day that you set your mind to gain understanding and to humble yourself before your God, your words were heard, and I have come in response to them. But the prince of the Persian kingdom resisted me twenty-one days. Then Michael, one of the chief princes, came to help me, because I was detained there with the king of Persia. Now I have come to explain to you what will happen to your people in the future, for the vision concerns a time yet to come.'

— Daniel 10:1, 4–6, 11–14

The earlier chapters of Daniel described his visions of things "that were" (seen previously). He now begins an introduction to the last two visions that were given to him — visions of things that "will be." These visions are more fully described in chapters eleven and twelve.

God is verifying to Daniel that what he has been told will certainly come to pass; He reaffirms to Daniel that He is Sovereign; He is Omnipotent. Life is not just a continuous series of circumstances, a game of chance. God is in control.

THE TIME AND PLACE

In this chapter Daniel is given a "behind the scenes" look at life. He sees, in part, why things happen as they do. He is given the assurance that God is fully trustworthy. In the visions which Daniel had already received, and in the visions he was yet to receive, God revealed exacting details of pre-written history, including the very actions and attitudes of both men and nations. These men and nations would "act out" God's sovereign program of redemption and judgment. The visions of Daniel affirmed to him that there is no contradiction between God's sovereignty and man's free will. Daniel recognized that in His omnipotence and omniscience, God takes into account every action and reaction of mankind, in all of creation. These visions caused Daniel to once again realize that prayer and repentance "grease the wheels of eternity" to accomplish the purposes of God — to His glory and for our good.

Daniel begins this chapter by informing his readers of the historical setting and period in which these new visions were given to him. He writes: "In the third year of Cyrus king of Persia, a revelation was given to Daniel (who was called Belteshazzar). Its message was true and it concerned a great war. The understanding of the message came to him in a vision" (Daniel 10:1).

The fact that Daniel saw and wrote about this vision during the reign of Cyrus has long perplexed Bible scholars. Daniel 1:21 states: "Daniel continued until the first year of Cyrus the king." But Daniel 10:1 states that Daniel was living, and received a vision during the third year of Cyrus' reign. Can these two visions be reconciled? The answer is that Daniel 1:21 implies that Daniel would continue until the commencement of a new kingdom which would be ruled by the Persian king, Cyrus (see Isaiah 44:28; 45:1). The verse does not necessarily imply that Daniel would die during the first year of the reign of Cyrus. It may also mean that Daniel would no longer be occupying the position of power and influence that he held under the Babylonian kings. A large number of influential Jews returned to Israel under Zerubbabel and Ezra, but Daniel evidently chose to remain in Babylon. The effect that this change in the Jewish population had upon Daniel's position in Persia is not known, but we do know many Jews were later persecuted under the Persians (see Esther).

Daniel is writing in the third person. He states: "...a revelation was given to Daniel (who was called Belteshazzar)..." (Dan. 10:1). This is evidence of the period of transition between the Babylonian and Persian empires. To the Jews who remained in Babylon, and to the Jews who returned to the land, the prophet was known by his Hebrew name, Daniel. But to the Babylonians, and now to the Persians who were ruling over the empire, he continued to be known by his Babylonian name, Belteshazzar — the name given him by King Nebuchadnezzar when he was first taken captive (Daniel 1:7). E. J. Young, in his commentary on Daniel, gives further insight when he states that he believes the reason Daniel used both names was "because the Babylonian empire is now overthrown and he would preserve his identity among the people. He thus attests that he is the same person who was carried into captivity over seventy years previously and that he is the one concerning whom the previous portions of the book relate."[1]

The elderly Daniel now writing, is the same man who had been taken captive over seventy years earlier. What a marvelous encouragement this verse is for believers who are now senior citizens. Society may brush aside such people, but God never does. He continues to work within us as long as there is breath in our bodies. God faithfully stands by His servants, and uses them to reveal His presence and His glory. Praise God, there are no age limits on His use of His servants. Retirement from serving, praising, and worshiping God is not within God's plan for His servants.

Having assured his readers that he is the same person who had received the earlier visions, Daniel continues by assuring them that the vision just revealed to him, and which he is about to describe, is absolutely true. The expression means that it will certainly happen! The perimeters of God's program have been fixed by Him; He will bring every detail of His program to fruition.

Daniel tells us that the vision he has just received concerns a "great war." This is the literal meaning of the Hebrew text. He also states that an understanding of the message was given to him in a vision (perhaps Daniel's understanding of the vision was enhanced by the panoramic view of the seventy 'sevens' that God had given him. This was significant to Daniel because it was in contrast to some of the visions which he, himself, said he did not understand.

The Jewish exiles who had left Babylon just two years earlier to rebuild the walls of the city of Jerusalem and the temple had already begun to experience the "times of distress" spoken of in Daniel 9:25. God had already revealed to Daniel that a long period of time would elapse before His Messiah would set up His Kingdom upon the earth. In the meantime, war had been determined until the time of the end. God now reveals to Daniel, in vision form, a detailed account of the years of conflict that would ultimately result in the destruction of the evil one, and usher in the Kingdom of God on earth.

Through the visions that were given to him, Daniel learned to see history from God's perspective rather than from his own perspective. He learned that in the midst of conflict, God remains faithful; He does not desert His people. Daniel learned that God is always faithful to His word. This is a lesson each follower of Messiah, Yeshua, needs to learn. It is easy to praise God when things are going well. It is easy to acknowledge that God is in control when things are going our way. But when conflicts and tribulations come (yes, even when a Holocaust comes) how easy it is to cry out, "God has forsaken us" while, in reality, He is just a prayer away!

FASTING AND PRAYER

Daniel received the message from the LORD, and he tells us he understood the message. He then took the action that typified his life — he began to fast and pray. He wrote: "At that time I, Daniel, mourned for three weeks. I ate no choice food; no meat or wine touched my lips; and I used no lotions at all until the three weeks were over" (Daniel 10:2–3).

Although Daniel does not state the reason that he fasted and prayed, he has revealed that he understood the vision. He knew some of his Jewish brethren were already back in the land of Israel; he knew some were even experiencing conflicts with the Samaritans and with others who lived in the land. He began praying and fasting on behalf of his kinsmen according to the flesh. The fact that Daniel was an old man did not negate his concern for the national welfare of his people, or for their personal salvation. Nor did it negate his concern for the majority of his Jewish brethren who were content to remain in Babylon, choosing the pagan lifestyle of Babylon rather than dedication to the God of Abraham, Isaac and Jacob. Many Jews were not interested in returning to the land of Israel. They had accepted the ways of the Babylonian and Persian societies, and had chosen the god of materialism. They had forgotten that they were part of the "Chosen People," a nation called out to be separate and holy unto God. They had forgotten that they were only strangers and foreigners in a distant land.

Sadly, many Christians today are like the Jews who chose to remain in Babylon; they have become so much a part of the society around them that there is very little difference between them and the non-believing societies in which they live.

Daniel was concerned for his people. He knew that their sinfulness and disobedience would ultimately reap punishment, and he fervently prayed that they would repent and return to God. He says he fasted for "three weeks." In the Hebrew it is: "three sevens (weeks) of days." Perhaps this was in reflection upon the seventy 'sevens,' that were divided into three distinct periods (the first period of seven 'sevens,' the second period of sixty-two 'sevens,' and the last period of one seven), and the fact that this extended period of God's judgment upon Israel had already begun.

Daniel abstained from eating meat and from drinking any wine during this three week period of mourning and fasting. These elements were symbols of enjoyment and festivity and, as such, he abstained from them. Further, he abstained from anointing himself with oil, or any other type of lotion. In the hot, arid countries of Babylon and the Middle East, it is common practice among the people to use some type of lubricant for their skin. Instead, Daniel chastened his soul, and with sincere humiliation he fasted and prayed.

His vision came while he was on the bank of the great river, Tigris. The Akkadian name for this great river was "Hiddekel" (see Genesis 2:14). The Tigris River and the Euphrates River are the two major rivers around which the ancient city of Babylon was built. Reading these verses, one can picture Daniel standing at the river's edge, weeping and praying. Perhaps he was the inspiration for the Psalmist, who wrote:

[By the rivers of Babylon] we sat and wept when we remembered Zion. There on the poplars we hung our harps, for there our captors asked us for songs, our tormentors demanded songs of joy; they said, 'Sing us one of the songs of Zion!'

How can we sing the songs of the LORD while in a foreign land? If I forget you, O Jerusalem, may my right hand forget its skill. May my tongue cling to the roof of my mouth if I do not remember you, if I do not consider Jerusalem my highest joy.

Remember, O LORD, what the Edomites did on the day Jerusalem fell. 'Tear it down,' they cried, 'tear it down to its foundations!' O Daughter of Babylon, doomed to destruction, happy is he who repays you for what you have done to us — he who seizes your infants and dashes them against the rocks (Psalm 137).

Daniel completed his fast on the twenty-fourth day of the first month, the month of Nisan. Nisan is the month in which Passover is celebrated, the festival of God's redemption of His people from Egypt and of His judgment upon the Egyptians. How appropriate, considering the vision Daniel was about to receive. He writes: "I looked up and there before me was a man dressed in linen, with a belt of the finest gold around his waist. His body was like chrysolite, his face like lightning, his eyes like flaming torches, his arms and legs like the gleam of burnished bronze, and his voice like the sound of a multitude" (Daniel 10:5–6).

WHO WAS THE DIVINE MESSENGER?

Whom did Daniel see? Whom was he describing? Most Bible commentators believe Daniel saw a theophany — that is an appearance of God. They say Daniel saw the pre-incarnate Messiah, and they equate this vision of Daniel with the appearances of the Angel of LORD (the pre-incarnate manifestation of the Messiah, the Son of God) of the Old Testament. They further equate this vision of Daniel with the vision of the risen and ascended Messiah, Yeshua, that John saw and which he describes in Revelation (see Revelation 1).

Other writers compare this vision of Daniel to the vision of Yeshua which the Apostle Paul had on the road to Damascus. Still others point to the Mount of Transfiguration, where Yeshua was glorified before the eyes of His disciples, Peter, James, and John.

While the description of the being that Daniel saw is similar in some ways to the appearances of the LORD, Yeshua, as He is revealed in Scripture, they are not altogether the same. The context and actions of Daniel indicate that he did not see a theophany, or an appearance of the Messiah, Yeshua. Evidence for this is seen in Daniel 10:13, which states: "But the prince of the Persian kingdom resisted me twenty-one days. Then Michael, one of the chief princes, came to help me, because I was detained there with the king of Persia."

Daniel 10:21 states: "But first I will tell you what is written in the Book of Truth. (No one supports me against them except Michael, your prince....)"

This angelic being was severely limited in his power and authority. The text states that he was detained by the king of Persia, and it further states that no one supported him but the archangel Michael. It appears that Michael is more powerful than he is. It is inconceivable that the LORD Yeshua, God's Messiah, His Son (God Himself) would be powerless against the forces of evil. Surely the Messiah would not have to call upon Michael for help and assistance. This is contrary to every concept taught in Scripture concerning God and the Son of God, the pre-incarnate Messiah. Scripture does teach that when the Son of God became flesh, He willingly limited His attributes of deity to those actions consistent with the will of His Father. However, before the incarnation, and after His ascension, He was clothed in the full glory of deity and could freely exercise all of the prerogatives of deity consistent with His attributes.

God is all-powerful. Whenever the pre-incarnate Son of God appears in the Old Testament, He is presented as being all-powerful. No one can delay the activity of God, or hinder the sovereign right of God to act.

When He opens a door no one can shut it. When He closes a door no one can open it. If it were possible for mankind to do so, or for the angelic world to do so, God would no longer be God.

Daniel recognized this as well, and he must have asked himself, "If, indeed, this angelic being is God coming in answer to my prayer, why has it taken so long?" In response to his inaudible question, Daniel was given a behind-the-scenes preview of what happens in spiritual conflict; he was given insight into how spiritual conflict affects both national and individual lives.

Who, then, is this angelic being, if he is not a pre-incarnate vision of the Messiah, the Son of God? To be consistent in His revelation to Daniel of pre-written history, God sent Daniel a very special angelic being. He did so because God wanted Daniel to know the type of spiritual warfare he and the nation of Israel were up against; God wanted Daniel to have an understanding of the type of beings, good and evil, who were making this conflict a reality.

Cherubim and Supernatural Beings

According to the Word of God, there is one class of created beings whose sole responsibility is to bring glory to God. These beings are called "Cherubim." The prophets Isaiah, Ezekiel, and the book of Revelation reveal that Cherubim and Seraphim surround the Throne of God. The Scriptures also reveal to us that God has created a certain order within the angelic hosts. Each created being has been assigned certain tasks and duties to perform. Evidently, there was a trial period for each created being which, if successfully completed, confirmed them in holiness. Once confirmed in holiness they remained pure and holy throughout eternity. If, however, they failed in the performance of their duties, and failed the test God assigned to them, they were confirmed in their wickedness.

The Scriptures make it clear that myriads of these created beings (supernatural beings) were confirmed in their holiness, but the Scriptures also reveal that myriads of these created beings failed and have been confirmed in their wickedness. One cherub whose duties and responsibilities were carried on from a position of authority, but who, because of sin, fell and was forever confirmed in his wickedness, was Lucifer — Satan. Interestingly, the description of this cherub uniquely matches the description given of the being Daniel saw. The prophet Ezekiel wrote:

> *Son of man, take up a lament concerning the king of Tyre and say to him: 'This is what the Sovereign* Lord *says: You were the model of perfection, full of wisdom and perfect in beauty. You were in Eden, the garden of God; every precious stone adorned you: ruby, topaz and emerald, chrysolite, onyx and jasper, sapphire, turquoise and beryl. Your settings and mountings were made of gold; on the day you were created they were prepared. You were anointed as a guardian cherub, for so I ordained you. You were on the holy mount of God; you walked among the fiery stones. You were blameless in your ways from the day you were created till wickedness was found in you' (Ezekiel 28:12–15).*

The prophet Ezekiel was addressing the King of Tyre, but in so doing he was describing him as if he were Satan himself. Satan was indwelling the King of Tyre, empowering him in his evil actions. The Word of God reveals that Satan was a guardian cherub, an anointed cherub, who sinned and rebelled against God. Ezekiel's description of Satan matches in every detail the description of the angelic being revealed to Daniel. The created being seen by Daniel was one of the guardian cherubim, an anointed cherub — one who had been confirmed in his holiness, who appeared like Satan did before he sinned and was confirmed in his wickedness.

Such an interpretation fits the facts given in the context of Daniel, chapter 10. According to the text, this special guardian cherub told Daniel he had been dispatched from the Throne of God as soon as Daniel began to pray. Daniel 10:12 states: "Then he continued, 'Do not be afraid, Daniel. Since the first day that you set your mind to gain understanding and to humble yourself before your God, your words were heard, and I have come in response to them'."

Verse 13 states: "But the prince of the Persian kingdom resisted me twenty-one days. Then Michael, one of the chief princes, came to help me, because I was detained there with the king of Persia."

It is clear that Satan will use unbelievers who occupy places of leadership to accomplish his purposes. One day, he will assume control of the world (as revealed to Daniel in his vision of the "seventieth" seven). The reference to the "Kings or rulers of Persia" speaks of Satan and his demonic host as they seek to destroy Israel and control the world.

This passage gives some unusual insight into the workings of the spirit world. First, it is clear that Satan is not all-powerful. He is a cherub and, although a cherub might have superhuman powers, he is not omnipotent, nor is he omnipresent. The spiritual conflict that Daniel was told about is restricted to certain nations at certain times in history.

Secondly, as Daniel reveals the vision of the struggle involving the king of Persia (Satan) and the cherub who was speaking with Daniel, it appears that the opponents were equal in their struggle and in their strength. Satan, being a cherub (though a fallen one), could not overcome another cherub, nor could this cherub overcome Satan by himself. Daniel was being told of a struggle between two equal forces.

Thirdly, Daniel was told that Michael was sent to assist the cherub who was detained, otherwise he would still be engaged in conflict. Michael appears to be a more powerful created being than the cherub, and he is therefore more powerful than Satan. In fact, Michael is the created being used by God to repel the forces of evil in the spiritual realm. The very name "Michael" means "who is like God." In the Tenach (Old Testament) Michael is called the "Great Prince" (see Daniel 12:1) and in the New Testament he is called "The Archangel" (see Jude 9).

SPIRITUAL WARFARE

It appears that within the spiritual world there exists a hierarchy of spiritual beings (see Ephesians 3:10; 1 Peter 3:22). This hierarchy also exists within the world of spiritual beings who have been confirmed in their wickedness, or the evil angels (see Ephesians 6:12). Just as God has assigned to each individual a guardian angel, so Satan assigns evil angels (demons) over individuals. And, as God assigns more powerful created beings over the nations, so Satan assigns more powerful evil created beings over the nations.

The struggle between good and evil in the spiritual realm enters into conflict whenever individuals seek to live lives that are holy and righteous, and whenever they are praying, worshipping, and communicating with God. Without the involvement of the obedient (the holy righteous) created beings on our behalf, nations and the individuals within those nations would fall under the darkness of the spiritual realm of

Satan. Light always repels darkness. However, if there is no light, darkness will always fill the void.

One might ask, "Why is Daniel told of this struggle?" "Why is it important for us to know these things?" "What is the practical application to me?" The answer is simply this: Daniel symbolized the nation of Israel that had been in captivity for seventy years. He was approaching the end of his life, and from his perspective he expected to die while still living in exile in Babylon; he was too old to return to the land. He did not expect to see the city of Jerusalem or the temple rebuilt. God was therefore reassuring this faithful prophet, through the visions of things yet to come, that although there would be continual struggle with evil, although people would be judged and chastened for their sin and unbelief, although Israel would once again be removed from their land, they would not cease being a nation. The program of God would be completed and God would keep His covenant promises which He had made with Israel.

Daniel was also being reassured that just as God would be faithful to His covenant with Israel, He would keep His covenant with Daniel. The prophet, Daniel, did die in exile, but his righteous life served to help repel the forces of evil and to give victory to the total program of God.

Daniel was further reassured that even if he died in exile, his body would not be left in exile forever, for he was told in verse 2 of chapter twelve that the righteous will be resurrected to everlasting life.

In his vision, Daniel was told that all of the satanic forces of the evil one would be hurled against Israel; he was told that the Gentile nations would form an alliance under Satan and that they would seek to eradicate the Jews from the pages of history. But God reminded Daniel, as He reminds us today, that the Jewish people will never cease to exist as a nation. God has placed Michael, the archangel, the most powerful of His created beings over the nation of Israel. Daniel was told that it will be Michael, who will stand up and protect the people of Israel when the covenant is broken, and when Satan will seek to destroy the Jewish people during the Great Tribulation.

This vision of the supernatural, of angelic hosts and spiritual warfare, was God's word of encouragement and hope to Daniel. God wanted Daniel to realize that he had not been forgotten. God wanted to reveal to Daniel that his faith, that had produced the fruits of righteousness in his life, was also being used by God to repel the forces of evil.

In like manner, God uses the faith and testimony of each believer today. Evil abounds in our world, and the voices of righteousness seem to go unheeded. But God reminds us through His Word that we should not be discouraged or weary in well doing. Through the reading and study of His Word, through an understanding of the visions He gave unto men like Daniel, God reveals to us that if believers could part the curtain that separates the natural world from the spiritual world, they would see, first hand, how their faith, and how righteousness in their lives, impacts the forces of evil. The forces of evil are repelled by faith and by the fruits of righteousness produced through the indwelling presence of God's Holy Spirit. We are more than conquerors through Yeshua, our Messiah and LORD!

NOTES
Chapter 10. Talking With Divine Messengers
[1]   Edward J. Young, *The Prophecy of Daniel*, (Grand Rapids, MI: Wm. B. Eerdmans Publishing Co., 1948).

♦

CHAPTER ELEVEN

Writing History Before It Happens

*(No one supports me against them except Michael, your prince. And in
the first year of Darius the Mede, I took my stand to support and protect him.)*

*Now then, I tell you the truth: Three more kings will appear in Persia,
and then a fourth, who will be far richer than all the others. When he
has gained power by his wealth, he will stir up everyone against the
kingdom of Greece.*

— Daniel 10:21b–11:2

The eleventh chapter of Daniel elaborates on the prophecies given in
chapter eight. Covering a great span of time starting with Cyrus, King of
Persia, and concluding with the final battle of Armageddon (the great
battle that will usher in the kingdom of the Messiah), this vision sets
forth a detailed account of the great Gentile empires of the world as,
through the centuries, they would seek to conquer and rule over Israel.

This prophecy came as the result of Daniel's prayer. It was delivered
by one of the guardian cherubim sent from the throne of God, who told
Daniel:

*Now then, I tell you the truth: Three more kings will appear in Persia,
and then a fourth, who will be far richer than all the others. When he*

has gained power by his wealth, he will stir up everyone against the kingdom of Greece. Then a mighty king will appear, who will rule with great power and do as he pleases. After he has appeared, his empire will be broken up and parceled out toward the four winds of heaven. It will not go to his descendants, nor will it have the power he exercised, because his empire will be uprooted and given to others (Daniel 11:2–4).

First the cherub assured Daniel that the vision he was about to reveal was the absolute truth. He then summarized in five short sentences the prophetic events enlarged upon in this chapter. The scope of this prophecy first involves three kings in Persia, concluding with a final fourth king who, the messenger said, would become very wealthy and powerful. The prophecy then occupies itself with the events of Greece, out of which comes an exceedingly powerful king whose kingdom, Daniel was told, would not be given to his descendants but would, instead, be divided and scattered toward the four winds of heaven after his death.

This prophecy and vision makes no mention of the Roman Empire. In the visions of Daniel, in chapters two and seven, the Roman empire was included along with Babylon, Medo-Persia, and Greece. But the prophecy set forth in chapter eleven makes no mention of Rome. Why would Rome not be mentioned here?

The answer is that Daniel, chapter eleven, reveals the background and the impetus for the rise of a ruthless king who would be empowered and controlled by Satan. This ruthless king would be the forerunner of the Beast — or the antichrist (also controlled by Satan), who will rule and reign during the Tribulation. In response to Daniel's prayer, God sent a messenger who delivered a vision which gave Daniel a preview of the hand of God at work on behalf of Israel and the Jewish people. But it was also a glimpse of the demonic powers that can control nations when sin is left unchecked. God showed Daniel what nations under demonic control will do to Israel prior to the establishment of a Messianic Kingdom.

The prototype of the antichrist was Antiochus Epiphanes, who came out of the Syrian-Greek Empire. The emphasis of the vision and prophecy of chapter eleven is upon this satanically controlled ruler; it therefore only details events leading up to the rise of power, and ultimate defeat of this ruler. The focus of the prophecy is on the times of the

Gentiles — from Antiochus to the antichrist.

Rome is not mentioned because the prototype of the antichrist, Antiochus, lived and died before Rome controlled Israel. Israel's rejection of God and His Law set into motion the events that allowed for Antiochus to gain control of Israel, and it was Israel's continued rejection of God and His revealed Word that eventually ushered in Rome's rule and the destruction of Jerusalem. Antiochus symbolized the prototype of the antichrist, while Rome symbolized the prototype of the Tribulation Empire.

Daniel was told that the precise length of the Medo-Persian Empire had been fixed by the sovereign God, who is always and ever in control of His creation. He was also told that the three kings who would come upon the scene of history (including the fourth king who would follow and who would be exceedingly wealthy) would certainly come to pass! The annals of history verify the literal historic fulfillment of this prophecy.

The prophecy was given during the reign of Cyrus (see Daniel 10:1). The kings who immediately followed Cyrus were Cambyses (Ahasuerus, cf. Ezra 4:6), Smerdis (Artaxerxes, Ezra 4:7), Hystaspes (Darius, cf. Ezra 4:24), and Xerxes (Ahasuerus, cf. Esther 1:1). These were the kings this prophecy had immediate reference to.

Xerxes (Ahasuerus), the last king of Persia, ascended the throne in 486 B.C., and died by the hand of an assassin in 465 B.C. He wanted Persia to be the military might of the world. His ambition was to make Persia invincible. The Greek historian, Herodotus (485–425 B.C.), tells us Xerxes amassed an army of 1,700,000 soldiers, excluding his naval forces. Aeschylus (525–456 B.C.) indicated that Xerxes had 1,200 ships in his navy.

When Xerxes reached the height of his career, thinking himself and his empire invincible (in precise fulfillment of the prophecy given to Daniel), he decided to attack Greece. But his advance on Greece was not without problems. He built a bridge over the Hellespont, and dug a canal near Athos. At the time, he had the full cooperation of the Phoenicians and the Egyptians. In fact, he used their engineers to build the bridge and the canal. But when a sudden storm destroyed the bridge, Xerxes, without any qualms, ordered that the heads of the engineers be cut off. He then had a new double bridge erected, over which his armies crossed on their way to Greece. When they reached Athens, he and his army sacked and burned the city. To every outward appearance, Xerxes did appear invincible; it seemed nothing could stop him.

THE PERSIAN EMPIRE

Daniel was told, however, that the days of Persia, like the days of Babylon, had been weighed in the scales of Divine justice and had been found lacking. He had been told that this fourth king, like those before him, would not succeed.

Just when Xerxes was about to conquer the world, to reach out and grasp the brass ring, his world came crashing down around him. The seemingly invincible Persian army suffered a humiliating and disastrous defeat at Salamis. The Phoenician and Egyptian fleets deserted him, and in 479 B.C. the Persians were defeated by the Greeks. Then again, in 466 B.C. the Greeks defeated the Persians. This time they forced the Persians to relinquish all of their territory outside of Asia Minor — territory that had been gained under the rule of Darius. Xerxes was forced to return home in ignominious defeat.

The book of Esther reveals a glimpse of Xerxes' life and moral character. He was a man who lived in luxury, who thought nothing of executing his own wife, the Queen, when she failed to do his bidding. Further, he thought nothing of signing an order to eradicate all Jews living in his empire. Esther reveals, however, that when Xerxes was confronted with the dilemma of killing the Jews or retaining his own honor, he chose to retain his honor. Perhaps it was to the moral character of Xerxes that Yeshua referred when He said, "What good is it for a man to gain the whole world, yet forfeit his soul?" (Mark 8:36).

The ultimate fate of Xerxes is not revealed to us in the Scriptures, but perhaps his encounter with the godly man, Mordecai, and his involvement with the loving and godly Queen Esther, brought him to a place of repentance. Perhaps even Xerxes found forgiveness by coming to faith in the God of Daniel. The book of Esther and the records of historians do reveal that Xerxes built up Persepolis and completed his palace at Apadana. He also continued to protect the Jews in his kingdom. Perhaps he did not forfeit his own soul!

The heavenly messenger goes on to tell Daniel of another warrior king who would come, saying: "Then a mighty king will appear, who will rule with great power and do as he pleases. After he has appeared, his empire will be broken up and parceled out toward the four winds of heaven. It will not go to his descendants, nor will it have the power he exercised, because his empire will be uprooted and given to others" (Daniel 11:3–4).

KINGS OF THE NORTH AND SOUTH

As far as Daniel and the people of Israel were concerned, the end of Xerxes meant the end of the Persian empire as well. No other kings are mentioned, and the prophecy here leaps over hundreds of years, to the Grecian Empire and to Alexander the Great.

Alexander the Great attacked the Persian empire, and then went on to conquer the then-known world. The emphasis of the prophecy given to Daniel in chapter eleven, verses 5 and 6, is not to add more detail concerning Alexander the Great, but to reveal to Daniel things that would transpire to the empire *after* Alexander the Great. Primary consideration is given to the land of Israel. The prophet was told not only what would happen to the land of Israel, but to Syria and to Egypt as well. Syria and Egypt are the countries spoken of in the references to the "king of the North" and the "king of the South." Syria lies to the north of Israel, while Egypt lies to the south. Daniel is told:

> *The king of the South will become strong, but one of his commanders will become even stronger than he and will rule his own kingdom with great power. After some years, they will become allies. The daughter of the king of the South will go to the king of the North to make an alliance, but she will not retain her power, and he and his power will not last. In those days she will be handed over, together with her royal escort and her father and the one who supported her* (Daniel 11:5, 6).

Alexander the Great's empire was divided among his four generals (Ptolemy, Lysimachus, Seleucus Nicator, and Cassander) after his death. As time progressed, and as new kings arose, there were further divisions of the once-great Grecian Empire. When Antigonus was defeated at Ipsus in 301 B.C., Ptolemy Soter (the son of Lagus) obtained the rulership of

Egypt. He appropriated unto himself the name "king of the South" (Negev). As a result of an earlier division, Seleucus became ruler of Babylonia, and as time went on he also obtained Cappadocia, part of Phrygia, Upper Syria, Mesopotamia and the valley of the Euphrates. He was the founder of the royal house of the Seleucidae, the "kings of the north." The references, then, to the "king of the North" and the "king of the South" are not to be understood as a references to a single king, but to the line of kings who ruled over the northern and southern empires, i.e. Syria and Egypt.

When reading Daniel, chapter 11, one must be careful to examine the context of the prophecy, the use of the personal pronouns, and the history of the period in determining exactly which king of the North, and which king of the South is being spoken of. For example, the kings referred to in verse six, are not the same kings referred to in verse five. The king of the North was Antiochus II Theos, while the king of the South was Ptolemy II Philadelphus. These two kings, as the prophecy indicates, were at constant war with one another. They finally settled their differences and made peace through a matrimonial alliance, exactly as the prophecy said they would.

When Antiochus came into power he was already married to a woman named Laodice. He also had two sons, Seleucus Callinicus and Antiochus. Yet, for the sake of peace with Egypt, and for an enormous amount of money, he agreed to divorce Laodice and to disinherit his children. The money was to come from the dowry which Ptolemy of Egypt promised to pay Antiochus as soon as he was free to marry Ptolemy's daughter, Bernice. That marriage took place, and a peace treaty was made between the king of the North and the king of the South.

The peace didn't last long. Ptolemy, ruler of Egypt and the father of Bernice, died only a few years after Bernice and Antiochus were married. After his father-in-law's death, Antiochus, in typical fashion of his character and behavior, repudiated Bernice and proceeded to remarry Laodice and to re-instate his two sons by that marriage. His downfall was that he failed to reckon with "a woman scorned." Laodice nursed great hatred for Antiochus, as well as for Bernice, and soon after they had remarried, Laodice poisoned Antiochus and then arranged for the murder of Bernice and her infant son. Just as the prophecy of Daniel had predicted, all who had been involved in this unholy alliance between the king of the North and the king of the South, perished.

Once again the Word of God is shown to be accurate in its prophetic truths. Another truth is also evident: sin begets sin and righteousness begets righteousness. Within these prophecies God revealed that unconfessed sin generates more sin. Additionally, sin (even though it may be confessed and forgiven) can produces consequences that extend to future generations. It is God's desire that believers in every age understand His revealed Truth, and that they walk in that Truth. Believers, today, are under even greater responsibility to live lives that are holy and righteous, for they have the indwelling presence of the Holy Spirit, who enables them to do what is right. The failure of believers to live holy lives produces consequences that weaken the testimony and the power of God in this world.

God's Truth was not revealed to the prophets of old so mankind could enjoy the intellectual exercise of trying to discern the future, or to set dates for some cataclysmic event. His Truth was revealed in prophetic form, and through historic events, so that individuals living at the time of the events (or individuals reading the historical accounts of the events) would recognize the accuracy of God's Word, and be encouraged by knowing that He is in control of every circumstance of life.

Having revealed to Daniel the vision of the struggle between the king of the North and the king of the South, the messenger continued speaking, adding detail to the vision, revealing how this struggle will eventually engulf the land of Israel; it will ultimately usher in the antichrist. Daniel 11:7–10 states:

One from her family line will arise to take her place. He will attack the forces of the king of the North and enter his fortress; he will fight against them and be victorious. He will also seize their gods, their metal images and their valuable articles of silver and gold and carry them off to Egypt. For some years he will leave the king of the North alone. Then the king of the North will invade the realm of the king of the South but will retreat to his own country. His sons will prepare for war and assemble a great army, which will sweep on like an irresistible flood and carry the battle as far as his fortress.

When Antiochus was poisoned, Laodice's son, Seleucus II Callinicus, ascended the throne. Immediately, he was faced with the consequences of the murderous actions of his mother. When Ptolemy III Euergetes, ruler in Egypt and the brother of Bernice, heard that his sister, Bernice, had been murdered by Laodice, he was furious. He was further enraged to learn that Laodice's son now sat on the throne of Syria. He sought immediate revenge! To avenge his sister's death, Ptolemy III Euergetes attacked Syria and captured the fortress of Seleucia. He quickly put Laodice to death and subjugated the country. He then proceeded to capture all of the Selucian Empire, which included almost the whole of Asia that was beyond the Euphrates river, leaving Seleucus Callinicus almost a vassal king.

The prophetic language is precise. Daniel 11:8 reveals that he (the king of the South) would "seize their gods, their metal images and their valuable articles of silver and gold and carry them off to Egypt."

When Ptolemy returned to Egypt he took with him 4,000 talents of gold, 40 talents of silver, and 250 molten images and idolatrous vessels. Returning with the gold and silver is understandable — this is the booty and plunder, the spoils of war.

But why does the prophecy indicate that he would take their "gods?" The capture of a nation's gods indicated that the nation's national and divine power had passed into the hands of the victor (see Isaiah 46:1; Jeremiah 48:7; 49:3). The capture of a nation's gods was the worst defeat a nation could suffer. This truth is revealed in the book of 1 Samuel, where the utter defeat of the nation of Israel was felt when the Philistines captured the Ark of the Covenant (see 1 Samuel 4:1–22).

When Seleucus Callinicus died, he was succeeded by his son, Seleucus III Ceraunus (227–224 B.C.), who only reigned two years before his death. Seleucus III Ceraunus was succeeded by his brother, Antiochus III (224–187 B.C.), who was also called "the Great." This is why, in verse 10, there is a change in pronouns from the plural to the singular. After the death of his brother, Antiochus III, who was only 15 years old, was left alone to carry on the war against the king of the South.

As the prophet had been told, both sons assembled great armies in their attempts to erase the insult of the Egyptian invasion, and to avenge the defeat of their father. It was especially galling to them to see the

191

Egyptians controlling the fortress of Seleucia, which was only sixteen miles from their capital city of Antioch.

Finally, after 27 years, Antiochus III (the Great) was successful in capturing the fortress of Seleucia from the Egyptians. His attack was so successful, in fact, that he was able to gain back much of the Syrian territory, as far south as Gaza, that was being held by the Egyptians. The result of this surprising victory by the king of the North (Antiochus III the Great) enraged the king of Egypt, who by that time was Ptolemy IV Philopater.

Daniel the prophet was told: "Then the king of the South will march out in a rage and fight against the king of the North, who will raise a large army, but it will be defeated" (Daniel 11:11).

Ptolemy left Egypt and marched into Syria with an army of 70,000 men, 5,000 horses, and seventy three elephants. Antiochus III, on the other hand, had amassed an army of 62,000 men, 6000 horses, and 102 elephants. The two great armies met at Raphia (south-west of Gaza). Unaware of the words that had been given to the prophet Daniel, Antiochus III attacked the Egyptians, certain of a swift victory and sweet revenge. But Daniel had been told Antiochus' defeat was certain.

To Antiochus' surprise and horror, the battle with the Egyptians was a complete debacle. He lost over 10,000 soldiers, and an additional 4,000 men were taken prisoner. The Syrian army was completely routed; Antiochus lost all of the territory he had gained earlier. Cities throughout Syria, as well as Israel, proclaimed their loyalty to the King of the South, Ptolemy of Egypt. Ptolemy was jubilant!

The messenger's words to Daniel went further: "When the army is carried off, the king of the South will be filled with pride and will slaughter many thousands, yet he will not remain triumphant" (Daniel 11:12).

Daniel was told that the heart of the king of the South would be filled with pride, leading him to slaughter many thousands, but he would not remain triumphant. This is exactly what happened to Ptolemy IV Philopater, king of Egypt. After his victory he became puffed up with pride. Thinking himself to be a god who could do no wrong, he returned to his life of licentiousness, paying no attention to his subjects. In fact, he made their lives more difficult by increasing their taxes and by demanding more from them in order to maintain his lavish lifestyle.

Josephus wrote that when Ptolemy IV went up to Jerusalem, he demanded that the priests let him enter the temple; he wanted to enter the Holy of Holies. But legend says he fell down speechless before he could enter. Upon his return to Alexandria, Egypt, in revenge for what had happened, he initiated a persecution of the Jews. Historians tell us that over 40,000 Jews were killed because they refused to convert to idolatry. By the time he finished his pogrom, out of the thousands of Jews living in Alexandria, only three hundred retained their civil rights. As the prophet Daniel declared, he caused tens of thousands to fall.

In Daniel 11:13 we read: "For the king of the North will muster another army, larger than the first; and after several years, he will advance with a huge army fully equipped."

Ptolemy IV Philopator died in 205 B.C. His only heir was an infant son named Ptolemy V Epiphanes. Here was the opportunity Antiochus had been waiting for. Nearly thirteen years had elapsed since his ignominious defeat at the hands of Ptolemy Philopator. He wanted his revenge, and he wanted to re-instate his family honor. During the thirteen intervening years since his defeat, Antiochus had been able to conquer the lands to the east of his empire —Persia, Bactria, and India — and his great victories over those countries gave him the title of Antiochus the "Great." In 203 B.C., using the great wealth he had gained from his many conquests, Antiochus financed another war against Egypt. His wealth enabled him to procure an army larger than the one he'd had at Raphia. Secular history confirms every statement and detail revealed to Daniel in this chapter.

The prophet was told: "In those times many will rise against the king of the South. The violent men among your own people will rebel in fulfillment of the vision, but without success" (Daniel 11:14).

In fulfillment of this prophecy, but unaware that he was the subject of it, Antiochus was able to persuade King Philip V of Macedon to join him in his invasion of Egypt. They agreed to divide the land between them. There was also an uprising in Egypt against the young king, Ptolemy V Epiphanes.

THE ZEALOTS

The messenger then uses an unusual expression. He tells the prophet, "the violent men among your own people will rebel in fulfillment of the vision, but without success."

The literal meaning of these words is, "the violent ones among your people will lift themselves up in order to fulfill the vision, but they will stumble." The word translated "violent ones" is from the Hebrew word "pahreetz." It literally means "to break through," or "to burst open." In common usage it was used to describe a burglar or a robber. It is used in this way in Jeremiah 7:11; Ezekiel 7:22; 18:10. While it cannot be proved conclusively, this seems to be a reference to those who were later called "zealots."

Long before the zealots became an organized "political party" in Israel, certain individuals among the Jews who lived in Israel chose to rebel against the oppression which was forcibly imposed upon the Jewish people. Throughout this period of time, and up to the time of the fall of Masada, zealots were actively revolting against the Gentile nations that ruled over Israel. Although these zealots had some victories, they were eventually defeated.

In many instances (as in the case here) their revolts and fighting were used of God to fulfill His prophetic word. The "violent ones" in this verse should not be understood to be "murders," "gangsters," or "robbers." Rather, the "violent ones" refers to religious Jews who believed they needed to fight in order to survive. The term is used in contrast to the "pious" Jews who remained pacifists regardless of what their rulers did. Were it not for the modern day "zealots," many more Jewish people would have perished in the concentration camps of Europe. With God's help, it is the modern day zealot, the Israeli, who is making Israel a reality.

Daniel was told that it would be during this period of struggle between the king of the North and the king of the South, and while Israel is being used as the battleground for this armed struggle, that attempts would be made by the Jews to re-establish their own independence. The messenger told Daniel that the Jews would seize opportunities to once again rise as a nation, but each attempt would end in failure. Their final attempt to establish their identity as a nation would result in the Tribulation and the rise of the antichrist.

The revolt of the Jews during the days of Antiochus the Great, ended in defeat. Jews who had participated "stumbled." They "fell." When

Antiochus returned to Israel after his victorious campaign against Egypt in 198 B.C., he sought out and slew Jews who had not helped him, or who had favored the Egyptian rule over his own.

The vision continues and in verse 15, Daniel is told: "Then the king of the North will come and build up siege ramps and will capture a fortified city. The forces of the South will be powerless to resist; even their best troops will not have the strength to stand."

The fulfillment of this verse came when Antiochus the Great routed the forces of the Egyptians at Mount Panium in 198 B.C. Ten thousand Egyptian soldiers fled in fear of their lives to the fortified city of Sidon. Sensing victory, Antiochus and his forces built huge earthen siege ramps against the walls of the city. This is exactly what Daniel was told would happen. Eventually, famine brought about the surrender of the city of Sidon. The Egyptian General, Scopas, and his army, along with three other select Egyptian Generals (Eropus, Memocles and Damoxenus) who had been sent by the king of the South to help Scopas defeat the Syrians, were captured and forced to surrender. Antiochus then repossessed all of Coelesyria, Phoenicia and Israel.

The unfolding of the vision continues in verse sixteen:

The invader will do as he pleases; no one will be able to stand against him. He will establish himself in the Beautiful Land and will have the power to destroy it (Daniel 11:16).

The reference to the "Beautiful Land" is a reference to the land of Israel. Once Antiochus had defeated the Egyptians, he returned to Israel. He allowed the Jews who had helped him to worship at the temple. He gave them relief from the heavy taxes he had imposed. But those Jews who had helped the Egyptians, or who had revolted against him, were killed or imprisoned.

The decrees of Antiochus allowing the Jews some freedom were short lived however. The prophecy stated, "He will establish himself in the Beautiful Land and will have the power to destroy it." This is what Antiochus did. He turned Israel into a launching pad, where he and his troops could further harass the Egyptians. Israel became a bloody battlefield, and the continual warfare resulted in the "Beautiful Land" becoming a desolate wilderness. Likewise, the people once again began to suffer from the heavy taxation of continued war.

The messenger then tells Daniel:

He will determine to come with the might of his entire kingdom and will make an alliance with the king of the South. And he will give him a daughter in marriage in order to overthrow the kingdom, but his plans will not succeed or help him (Daniel 11:17).

Using Israel as his base of operations, Antiochus determined that he would conquer all of Egypt. In revenge for what Egypt had done to his father and brother, he planned to literally destroy it. However, his plan for an armed invasion of Egypt was thwarted when Rome, which was beginning to ascend in power, threatened to intervene and assist Egypt, should Antiochus carry out his threat of invasion. Antiochus was already entangled in conflict with Rome, and could not take the chance of a Rome-Egyptian alliance against him. Therefore, in fulfillment of the prophecy given to Daniel, Antiochus decided to secure through a treaty what he could not accomplish through military action. He made a treaty with Egypt, the terms of which included giving his daughter, Cleopatra, who was then only a child (this is the way prophecy uses the expression "daughter of women"), in marriage to the young Ptolemy V Epiphanes, the Egyptian prince who was thirteen years of age.

The words of the prophecy literally came true when Cleopatra refused to help her father, Antiochus, siding with her husband instead. Antiochus was infuriated because he was rendered helpless in his attempt to conquer and destroy Egypt. In his anger, and in his attempt to establish himself as the world leader, Antiochus turned his attack against Pergamum and Greece. He amassed a fleet of 300 ships and began to ravage the Mediterranean coast. He captured the islands of Rhodes, Samos, Eubaea, Colophon, and many others.

Rome could no longer ignore such rampages and it was decided that they would destroy Antiochus. The Roman consul, Acilius, met and defeated Antiochus at the pass of Thermopylae, forcing him to leave Greece. In 190 B.C., determine to drive Antiochus out of all of Asia Minor, Rome sent Lucius Cornelius Scipio to meet Antiochus' army of 80,000 men at

Magnesia, near Smyrna. The armies of Rome defeated Antiochus and forced him to renounce all claims to any territory in Europe or in Asia Minor west of Taurus. They also made him submit to conditions of peace that totally humiliated him. As a part of that humiliation, and also as a means of keeping Antiochus from making further trouble in the region, the Roman army took his younger son (also named Antiochus) to Rome as a hostage.

This was what God told Daniel would happen. "Then he will turn his attention to the coast lands and will take many of them, but a commander will put an end to his insolence and will turn his insolence back upon him. After this, he will turn back toward the fortresses of his own country but will stumble and fall, to be seen no more" (Daniel 11:18–9).

The "coast lands" were the islands of Greece. The "commander" was the Roman consul, Acilius. In ignominious defeat, Antiochus returned to his homeland. His last attempt to rebuild his empire and to rebuild his fortresses had failed because the heavy taxation and fines imposed upon him by Rome did not leave him enough resources to rebuild. In a desperate attempt to secure the needed money, he and some of his men plundered the temple of Jupiter Belus at Elymais. Ironically, in the midst of their attempted robbery of the temple, they were surprised by some Persian soldiers and in the ensuing struggle Antiochus the Great was slain. The prophecy given to Daniel, "but he will stumble and fall and be found no more," was thus fulfilled.

MINUTE DETAILS

Some may question why it was necessary for God to include such minute detail in giving this prophecy to Daniel. Daniel, chapter eleven, is really the only place within Scripture where one can document verse after verse of prophecy being historically fulfilled in every detail.

Our God — the God of Daniel — the LORD of all creation — is a God of minute detail! He is interested in, and involved in every detail of His creation. In revealing these prophecies in such detail, God made it clear to Daniel, and to people of every generation, that He is Sovereign over all. He is in control. Nothing can escape His knowledge, nor can anything take place apart from His Sovereign Will.

The book of Proverbs states: "The eyes of the LORD are everywhere, keeping watch on the wicked and the good" (Proverbs 15:3). And centuries after Daniel received the prophecies of Daniel, chapter eleven, Yeshua shared similar words with His disciples. He said:

> *Therefore I tell you, do not worry about your life, what you will eat or drink; or about your body, what you will wear. Is not life more important than food, and the body more important than clothes? Look at the birds of the air; they do not sow or reap or store away in barns, and yet your heavenly Father feeds them. Are you not much more valuable than they? Who of you by worrying can add a single hour to his life?*
>
> *And why do you worry about clothes? See how the lilies of the field grow. They do not labor or spin. Yet I tell you that not even Solomon in all his splendor was dressed like one of these. If that is how God clothes the grass of the field, which is here today and tomorrow is thrown into the fire, will he not much more clothe you, O you of little faith? So do not worry, saying, 'What shall we eat?' or 'What shall we drink?' or 'What shall we wear?' For the pagans run after all these things, and your heavenly Father knows that you need them. But seek first his kingdom and his righteousness, and all these things will be given to you as well. Therefore do not worry about tomorrow, for tomorrow will worry about itself. Each day has enough trouble of its own (Matthew 6:25–34).*

Detailed prophecy, and its detailed fulfillment, should bring peace to the heart of every believer. If God orders the events of nations in such detail, He can certainly order the events of our lives. With such a wonderful, Sovereign LORD ruling in our lives, why should believers be anxious?

Having given Daniel this detailed account of the struggles and the death of Antiochus the Great, the messenger continued by revealing events that would take place after the death of Antiochus the Great — events that would subsequently set the stage of world history for the coming Beast, or the antichrist. Daniel is told: "His successor will send out a tax collector to maintain the royal splendor. In a few years, however, he will be destroyed, yet not in anger or in battle" (Daniel 11:20).

The successor to Antiochus III the Great was his son Seleucus Philopater (187–176 B.C.), mentioned in our study of Daniel, chapter eight. In temperament, Seleucus Philopator was very different from his father. He was laid back and easy going, not at all interested in being a forceful conqueror or leader. Instead, he only wanted peace and serenity for his empire. He was satisfied with the status-quo. His most vexing problem was the 1,000 talents a year in taxation which the Romans had levied upon his Syrian empire. In order to meet this tax burden, Seleucus kept increasing the taxation of his subjects, including the Jews in Israel.

Seleucus Philopator hired Heliodorus to be his tax collector (or "exactor"). In fulfillment of the prophecy given in verse 20, Seleucus sent Heliodorus throughout his empire to collect the taxes from the people. These trips by Heliodorus were a source of constant irritation to the inhabitants of Palestine. While he was on one of his tax-collection trips, Heliodorus attempted to plunder the temple treasury in Jerusalem, but his venture failed. Perhaps sensing that his own days were numbered for failing in his attempt to raid the temple treasury, Heliodorus administered poison to the king, and Seleucus died after a short, unexciting reign.

Daniel was told, "...In a few years, however, he will be destroyed, yet not in anger or in battle" (verse 20), and the prophecy had been literally fulfilled. Seleucus had reigned for only twelve years before he was poisoned by his own tax-collector.

The death of Seleucus Philopator paved the way for the fulfillment of the next prophecy given to Daniel. He was told: "He will be succeeded by a contemptible person who has not been given the honor of royalty. He will invade the kingdom when its people feel secure, and he will seize it through intrigue" (Daniel 11:21).

ANTIOCHUS EPIPHANES

The contemptible person spoken of here is none other than Antiochus Epiphanes. Antiochus, who had no right to the throne, was able to seize it by overthrowing Heliodorus (the tax-collector who had poisoned Seleucus Philopator) and putting him to death. Antiochus' older brother, Demetrius, the rightful heir to the throne, was being held as a hostage in Rome, so Antiochus claimed the throne for himself. He invaded the kingdom when its people felt secure; he literally seized the throne through intrigue.

A detailed portrait of this wicked and treacherous king, Antiochus

Epiphanes, is disclosed in Daniel 11:21–35. Because of his wicked actions, his treatment of the Jewish people, and his utter contempt and defilement of the temple in Jerusalem, Antiochus Epiphanes is referred to as the proto-type of the Beast, or the antichrist, spoken of in the New Testament. Some commentators refer to him as the "Antichrist of the Old Testament."

In chapter eight of Daniel he was called the "little horn" (see Daniel 8:9–12). He was a man who opposed both the people of God and the worship of God. He wanted his people to worship him as God. This is why he took the title "Epiphanes," meaning "the illustrious," or the "magnificent" one. However, after the people had been subjected to a taste of his cruel leadership, they soon changed his title and among themselves, they referred to him as "Antiochus Epimanes," meaning the "madman."

Daniel was told that once Antiochus assumed power he would quickly move to increase his empire: "Then an overwhelming army will be swept away before him; both it and a prince of the covenant will be destroyed" (Daniel 11:22).

This verse raises some interesting questions. What army could this be referring to? Who is the prince of the covenant who will be destroyed?

Suggested answers to these questions have been offered by various commentators. Some have stated that the "overwhelming army" is a reference to Antiochus' enemies who were utterly defeated by Eumenes and Attalus. Other commentators have suggested that the phrase "overwhelming army" is a reference to the supporters of Demetrius, the rightful heir to the throne, whom Antiochus defeated. But the view most commentators support, and the view which is most logical, is the suggestion that the "overwhelming army" is a reference to the great and mighty army of Egypt that Antiochus defeated shortly after coming into power.

Who is the "prince of the covenant"? Some commentators have suggested that this is a reference to the high priest of Israel, Onias III. However, shortly after Antiochus came into power, he had Onias III replaced by Onias' brother, Jason. Another reason this suggestion does not seem likely is that verses 23–25 indicate that a covenant (treaty) with the prince (or king) of the South (Egypt) would be made. Historically, Antiochus made such a treaty with Ptolemy Philometor, king of Egypt. It would therefore appear that he (Antiochus) is the "prince of the covenant" spoken of. In his commentary on Daniel, Frederick A. Tatford wrote:

Feigning friendship for Ptolemy, the Macchiavellian Antiochus made a treaty with the youthful monarch. His deceitful character was at once manifested. Ignoring the terms of the treaty, but with profuse protestations of friendliness, Antiochus immediately began to scheme to overreach his royal ally. With a very small army, he proceeded up the Nile as far as Memphis, which he invested, and although his army was so small, it was sufficient to build up his strength and power.

Still under the pretence of friendship for Ptolemy, Antiochus unexpectedly further invaded Galilee and Lower Egypt and captured Pelusium and the most fertile districts. He accomplished what his predecessors had never been able to do and virtually made himself master of Egypt. The plundered provinces yielded rich booty and, with a munificence unknown to earlier Syrian monarchs, he distributed his gains with lavish prodigality among his followers (see, e.g., 1 Macc. 3:31). Adam Clarke says that 'he spent much in public shows, and bestowed largess among the people.... He would sometimes go into the streets and throw about a handful of money, crying out, 'Let him take it, to whom Fortune sends it,' hoping by means such as these to purchase popularity and the allegiance of his subjects.[1]

This is exactly what the messenger had told Daniel Antiochus would do when he came into power. Daniel was told: "After coming to an agreement with him, he will act deceitfully, and with only a few people he will rise to power. When the richest provinces feel secure, he will invade them and will achieve what neither his fathers nor his forefathers did. He will distribute plunder, loot and wealth among his followers. He will plot the overthrow of fortresses — but only for a time" (Daniel 11:23–24).

Within the permissive will of God, and in fulfillment of His prophetic program, Antiochus came into power and was able to accomplish these great feats. But while Antiochus thought his victories and power limitless, Daniel had been told that his time and his power were to be determined by the Sovereign Will of God. Daniel was told that Antiochus, like all rulers under the heavens, both good and bad, could only exercise power and authority within the predetermined plan of God.

Further detail and insight into Antiochus' victories in Egypt were then revealed to Daniel. In verses 25 through 28, the personal pronoun "he" is a reference to Antiochus, while the phrases "king of the South" and "two kings" are references to Antiochus and Philometor who sat together at the table, plotting their scheme to overthrow Ptolemy Physcon (Euergetes, the brother of Philometor), who had been made king of Egypt in Philometor's place. Daniel was told these amazing prophetic words:

With a large army he will stir up his strength and courage against the king of the South. The king of the South will wage war with a large and very powerful army, but he will not be able to stand because of the plots devised against him. Those who eat from the king's provisions will try to destroy him; his army will be swept away, and many will fall in battle. The two kings, with their hearts bent on evil, will sit at the same table and lie to each other, but to no avail, because an end will still come at the appointed time. The king of the North will return to his own country with great wealth, but his heart will be set against the holy covenant. He will take action against it and then return to his own country (Daniel 11:25–28).

The actual details of the battle between Antiochus and the king of the South (Egypt), as well as Antiochus' subsequent return to Israel and Syria, were given in Daniel, chapter eight. However, in this passage God again gives Daniel (and believers of all ages) a reminder that He is always in control. For every trial in life, an end will come at the appointed time. When the circumstances of our lives seem confusing, when there is seemingly no hope, the child of God should always remember that God has fixed a time when the end of all such struggles will cease. He is faithful to His word. His promises cannot fail.

Such words of comfort and promise meant much to Daniel who was then told that Antiochus would turn his heart against "the holy covenant." The phrase "the holy covenant" is a reference to the temple in Jerusalem. God tells Daniel that within His permissive will, the newly rebuilt temple would be defiled. This time the aggressor would be the

Syrian king, Antiochus.

On his return from Egypt, Antiochus carried with him large quantities of plunder and loot which he had taken from the Egyptians (in fulfillment of the words spoken to Daniel). As he neared Israel, he heard reports of the revolt of the Jews and of their attempts to create an independent state. Jason, the high-priest whom Antiochus had earlier deposed from the high priesthood, had raised an army of over 1,000 mercenaries, and was trying to capture Jerusalem from Menelaus, the high-priest whom Antiochus had placed in control of the temple. Antiochus was furious! By the time he reached Jerusalem, his wrath was burning! He attacked Jerusalem with the fury of a powerful hurricane. He massacred 40,000 Jews and sold another 40,000 as slaves. Jason fled to the country of the Ammonites.[2]

Antiochus restored Menelaus as the high priest and then, with ceremonial pomp and circumstance, he raided the temple. He invaded the Holy of Holies and robbed the temple of the golden altar and the gold and silver vessels, taking over 1,800 talents of gold and silver. He further defiled the temple by sacrificing pigs on the altar, after which he boiled the pigs' flesh in water and sprinkled the broth on and around the whole temple.[3]

Rage continued to burn within Antiochus; he was determined to capture all of Egypt and make it a captive nation to his expanding empire. Daniel had been told this would happen: "At the appointed time he will invade the South again, but this time the outcome will be different from what it was before. Ships of the western coastlands will oppose him, and he will lose heart. Then he will turn back and vent his fury against the holy covenant. He will return and show favor to those who forsake the holy covenant" (Daniel 11:29–30).

The power God extended to the Gentile rulers, whom He raised up to chastise the Jewish people because of their sin and disbelief, always seemed to increase the corruption of their already-evil natures. They were never satisfied; they were always driven for more. Someone has said that power corrupts, and total power corrupts totally. So it was with Antiochus. He was determined to capture all of Egypt, and he was equally determined to destroy anyone who stood in his way. He failed, however, to reckon with the Sovereign God who had given him his place of authority. Instead of acknowledging God, and giving thanks for the place God had given him in the scheme of things, Antiochus detested God. He lifted himself up as though he was God. God's judgment of such pride and rebellion in the heart of man is swift and sure. God had already declared: "...this time the outcome will be different from what it was before" (verse 29).

Through the messenger, God had revealed to Daniel that He would raise up a nation that would assist Egypt in its defeat of Antiochus. In Daniel 11:30 we read: "Ships of the western coastlands will oppose him, and he will lose heart. Then he will turn back and vent his fury against the holy covenant."

The Hebrew uses the word "Kittim" as the name for this nation, while the NIV translates the word "western coastlands." The earliest use of the word "kittim" is a reference to one of the four sons of Javan (see Genesis 10:4). It was used in reference to a city on Cyprus, a city the Phoenicians called "KTY" or "Kitti." Later in Jewish history the term "kittim" took on the meaning of the entire island of Cyprus, including the Mediterranean people in general.

Josephus uses the term "Kittim" in this way. He wrote: "...it is now called Cyprus: and from that it is that all islands, and the greatest part of the sea-coasts, are name Cethim [Chittim] by the Hebrews: and one city there is in Cyprus that has been able to preserve its denomination; it is called Citius by those who use the language of the Greeks, and has not, by the use of that dialect, escaped the name of Cethim [Chittim]."[4]

Still later in history the term "Chittim" was used of Greece. It is used this way in I Maccabees 8:5 where we read: "Beside this, how they had discomfited in battle Philip, and Perseus, king of the Citims, (Chittim) with others that lifted up themselves against them, and had overcome them."

Other Jewish literature, including the Dead Sea Scrolls, identifies "Chittim" with Rome, and then with the final nations which will come against Israel in the latter days. W. H. Brownlee wrote:

The most conclusive proof for the Roman identification is 4QpNah, [one of the Dead Sea Scrolls] which after noting the failure of '[Deme]trius, king of Greece...to enter Jerusalem' states that God had never given the city 'into the power of the kings of Greece from the time of Antiochus until the rulers of the Kittim arose.' The clear chronological distinction placing the rise of the 'rulers of the Kittim' after the time of the 'kings of Greece' (Syria) points conclusively to the Romans as the Kittim. Yet after 44 B.C., when Caesar became a virtual king, one could speak of 'the king of the Kittim.' [5]

Within Jewish literature the term "kittim" can be used of Rome as a nation, or of symbolic "Rome" (the forces of evil which will come against Israel in the End of Days). Viewed this way, there is an interesting parallel to the use of the term "kittim," as given in the prophecy to Daniel, and the use of the term "kittim," as used by Balaam in his prophecy. Balaam prophesied: "…Ah, who can live when God does this? Ships will come from the shores of Kittim; they will subdue Asshur and Eber, but they too will come to ruin" (see Numbers 24:23, 24).

This was a prophecy concerning the Philistine invasion of Israel, but it seems to have a double meaning in reference to things that will happen to Israel during the Tribulation Empire. At that time, Israel will be invaded by the western nations (symbolized by Rome) but they will come to ruin. The reference, then, to "Kittim" or to "ships of the western coastlands" in Daniel 11:30, is a reference to the nation of Rome. However, it is also a reference to the final days when the Beast (or the antichrist) comes into power, since the next sequence of events told to Daniel concern Antiochus' defilement of the temple — which makes him the prototype of the Beast (antichrist) who is more fully described in verses 36–45.

In verse 30, the word "Kittim" is meant as a reference to Rome. Rome was the nation that intervened and literally stopped Antiochus' invasion of Egypt. It was evidently this frustration over not being able to conquer Egypt, and anger over Rome's ability to stop him cold in his tracks, that made Antiochus once again turn his wrath upon Israel and the Jewish people.

The actions and reactions of Antiochus are not unlike the actions and reactions of the Beast (antichrist) during the Tribulation period. According to the Book of Revelation, Satan will be cast out of heaven during the middle of the Tribulation Period. Stripped of the privileges he may previously have had within the permissive will of God, and knowing that his time is short, the Bible tells us Satan will immediately seek to destroy Israel and the Jewish people. John wrote:

And there was war in heaven. Michael and his angels fought against the dragon, and the dragon and his angels fought back. But he was not strong enough, and they lost their place in heaven. The great dragon was hurled down — that ancient serpent called the devil, or Satan, who leads the whole world astray. He was hurled to the earth, and his angels with him.

Then I heard a loud voice in heaven say: 'Now have come the salvation and the power and the kingdom of our God, and the authority of his Christ. For the accuser of our brothers, who accuses them before our God day and night, has been hurled down. They overcame him by the blood of the Lamb and by the word of their testimony; they did not love their lives so much as to shrink from death. Therefore rejoice, you heavens and you who dwell in them! But woe to the earth and the sea, because the devil has gone down to you! He is filled with fury, because he knows that his time is short.'

When the dragon saw that he had been hurled to the earth, he pursued the woman who had given birth to the male child. The woman was given the two wings of a great eagle, so that she might fly to the place prepared for her in the desert, where she would be taken care of for a time, times and half a time, out of the serpent's reach.

Then from his mouth the serpent spewed water like a river, to overtake the woman and sweep her away with the torrent. But the earth helped the woman by opening its mouth and swallowing the river that the dragon had spewed out of his mouth. Then the dragon was enraged at the woman and went off to make war against the rest of her offspring— those who obey God's commandments and hold to the testimony of Yeshua (Revelation 12:7–17)

History often repeats itself. The wrathful actions of Antiochus toward the Jewish people and toward the temple of God will be duplicated by the Beast during the Tribulation Period, but God declared that neither would be totally successful. Evil will never triumph because the Sovereign God of the universe is in control of all history.

THE TEMPLE DEFILED

Daniel is then told about the desecration of the temple by Antiochus: "His armed forces will rise up to desecrate the temple fortress and will abolish the daily sacrifice. Then they will set up the abomination that causes desolation. With flattery he will corrupt those who have violated the covenant, but the people who know their God will firmly resist him" (Daniel 11:31–32).

Daniel was told that Antiochus would use flattery to persuade some of the Jews to follow him — but Daniel was also told that others would firmly resist him. The mention of the Jews who would resist Antiochus is a reference to the Maccabees. The Maccabees successfully stood up against Antiochus. As the victors, they cleansed the temple and reinstated temple worship. It was through the Maccabees that the Hasmonean Kingdom was established — a kingdom that lasted until the time of Herod and the birth and death of the Messiah, Yeshua.

Those "who violated the covenant" is a reference to the Hellenized Jews who had been influenced by Antiochus to give up their Jewish faith in favor of the pagan Greek Hellenized culture. It is also a reference to the on-going and continuing struggle that all believers face as they live within the pagan societies and cultures of the world. Each day they must choose to either serve God, or succumb to the social/religious mores and beliefs of the societies in which they live. The temptation to follow the world system is very alluring, but the Scriptures make it clear that the child of God should not conform his life to this world system. He should, instead, seek to live a godly and holy life. Daniel was told, "...the people who know their God will firmly resist him [the evil one]" (Daniel 11:32). James says the same thing: "...Resist the devil, and he will flee from you" (James 4:7).

God's promise is not that life will always be easy, or that His children will never suffer persecution, hatred, or death. His promise to faithful followers of His Word is that, in every situation and circumstance within their lives, He will be with them. He will never leave them, nor forsake them.

This prophet Daniel is told: "Those who are wise will instruct many, though for a time they will fall by the sword or be burned or captured or plundered. When they fall, they will receive a little help, and many who are not sincere will join them. Some of the wise will stumble, so that they may be refined, purified and made spotless until the time of the end, for it will still come at the appointed time" (Daniel 11:33–35). Commenting on these verses Frederick Tatford wrote:

Tribulation and persecution have always been a Divine means of testing reality and of purging away the dross and this was particularly exemplified during the period described by the prophecy. Some of the faithful and pious teachers of the people suffered martyrdom and, confronted by such a possibility, the people immediately fell into two classes. The unreal and insincere, realizing the potential danger, dropped away. The faithful, becoming forcibly aware of the price they might personally be compelled to pay, proved the reality of their profession: the rest only confirmed their character and purged it of all but that which was true. How frequently in life are trials and difficulties Divinely permitted for the express purpose of proving the believer's faith. It is only by the fire that the gold is refined and purified: it is only by suffering that character is perfected. Leupold points out that the words translated 'refine' and 'cleanse' are literally 'smelt' and 'sift'. Just as metals are smelted to remove the useless materials in the form of slag, so will these teachers be purified in the fires of affliction. Similarly, just as sifting removes the undesirable chaff and leaves behind the pure grain, so will these saints lose the unworthy chaff in the time of trial. But all such testings are for only a specific period —'it is yet for the time appointed.' There is a limit to every trial and God in His goodness never lays upon His people a testing which is too great to bear.[6]

Daniel is told that the struggle between good and evil, this testing and trying of believers, will continue until the time of the end, and that this "time of the end" will certainly come in its appointed time (see verse 35b). Interestingly, this is the same truth that Yeshua told his disciples. The disciples wanted to know when the temple would be destroyed and when the end of age would come (that is, this appointed time for the end). In response to their questions, Yeshua told them there would be warfare — nation against nation, kingdom against kingdom. He further told them there would be famines and earthquakes. He said people would be deceived, and that the increase of wickedness would cause the love of many to grow cold. Some will be persecuted and others will be put to death (see Matthew 24:3-13).

Yeshua did not tell his disciples that these things were signs of His imminent return. Instead, He was emphasizing to His disciples, as God had emphasized to Daniel, that such things are the natural consequence of the evil and wicked age in which we live. In fact, Yeshua told His disciple that all of these would happen, but the appointed end would not come as a result of these events (see Matthew 24:6).

He went on to explain to His disciples that the "appointed end" would come when specific events prophesied by the prophet Daniel have taken place. He said they should watch for two things. First, the "gospel of the kingdom" will be preached in the whole world as a testimony to all nations; second, the temple in Jerusalem will be defiled by the "abomination of Desolation" (see Matthew 24:14, 15).

The proclamation of the "Gospel of the Kingdom" is the "Good News" of the death, burial, and resurrection of the Messiah, Yeshua — but it is also the sure promise of His coming Kingdom. It is the evidence that even in the days of intense tribulation and persecution, there will be individuals who are wise and are instructing many in the ways of God. Even in those terrible and awesome days, there will still be individuals who know God and who will firmly resist the evil one.

Yeshua then directed the attention of His disciples to the "Abomination of Desolation" that will stand in the temple. He said that this would be the sure sign of the appointed "time of the end," and He directed their attention back to the prophet Daniel. The prophecy of the Abomination of Desolation was first made in Daniel, chapter eight. It was amplified in Daniel 9:27, and it is once again stressed in Daniel, chapter eleven — especially in verses 36–44. He is told: "The king will do as he pleases. He will exalt and magnify himself above every god and will say unheard-of things against the God of gods. He will be successful until the time of wrath is completed, for what has been determined must take place" (Daniel 11:36).

THE REIGN OF THE BEAST

Here the subject of the prophecy changes. Daniel is no longer being told about the activities of Antiochus Epiphanes. Instead, he is told details of the coming reign of the Beast (antichrist) who will rule over Israel and the nations of the world. This is clear from the language that is used to describe the king being spoken of. It cannot be a reference to Antiochus Epiphanes, for within the context of the last mention of him (in verses 29-32), he was not able to do as he pleased. Instead, he was stopped in his attempt to conquer all of Egypt.

Daniel 11:36 describes a king who will do as he pleases. He is called the "willful king" because he will do his own will, with no regard to the will of God. He will speak blasphemous, monstrous, unheard of things about the God of Abraham, Isaac, and Jacob. This king will exalt himself. This is the same language that is used of Satan in Isaiah 14:12-17. This willful king will be none other than the Beast (antichrist)—the one who will be empowered by Satan. He will rule during the time of the end (i.e. the Tribulation Period, or the Seventy 'Sevens' of Daniel).

Paul gives a similar description of this willful king: "He will oppose and will exalt himself over everything that is called God or is worshiped, so that he sets himself up in God's temple, proclaiming himself to be God" (2 Thessalonians 2:4).

Note the similarity in Daniel 11:45: "He will pitch his royal tents between the seas at the beautiful holy mountain. Yet he will come to his end, and no one will help him."

The reference here to his "royal tents" or "royal pavilion" is a reference to his seat of authority. The phrase "between the seas at the beautiful holy mountain" is a euphemism for the land of Israel and the Temple Mount at Jerusalem. "Between the seas" means the Mediterranean Sea and the Dead Sea; the city of Jerusalem is situated between these two seas, in the hills of Judea. The "holy mountain" is the Temple Mount — Mount Moriah.

The Beast, the willful king, will make a covenant with Israel. It is the signing of this covenant that will inaugurate the last period of seven years which Daniel was told must come upon the nation of Israel to finish God's program of judgment and redemption (see Daniel 9). The willful king will break the covenant after three and one-half years (or in the middle of the Tribulation Period) and it will be at this time that he will defile the temple by setting up the Abomination of Desolation (Daniel 9:27). He will then turn his wrath upon Israel and the Jewish people, because he knows his time is short.

Daniel is given an interesting description of this willful king: "He will show no regard for the gods of his fathers or for the one desired by women, nor will he regard any god, but will exalt himself above them all. Instead of them, he will honor a god of fortresses; a god unknown to his fathers he will honor with gold and silver, with precious stones and costly gifts. He will attack the mightiest fortresses with the help of a foreign god and will greatly honor those who acknowledge him. He will make them rulers over many people and will distribute the land at a price" (Daniel 11:37–39).

The phrase, "He will show no regard for the gods of his fathers ..." has puzzled and caused difficulty for both translators and commentators. What does the phrase mean?

Some state that this verse should be translated, "He will show no regard for the God of his fathers." If this is true, it would seem that the one spoken about would have to be Jewish by descent. There are many Bible commentators who state that the Beast, or the antichrist, will be a Jew. They use this verse as a proof text. In his commentary on Daniel, one very fine Jewish Christian scholar states: "This expression, 'The God of his fathers', is the usual one in the Old Testament for the God of Abraham, Isaac, and Jacob; the God of the patriarchs; the God of Israel. This is the name of God that is used in the prayer book of the Jews to this very day."[7] He thus concludes that the Beast (antichrist) will be Jewish by descent.

However, further examination of the Hebrew phrase "gods of his fathers" that appears in Daniel 11:37 reveals that this phrase is distinctly different from all other appearances of a similar phrase which is used five times in the Scriptures and in all the Jewish prayer-books. In all other references in the Scriptures (2 Kings 21:22; 2 Chronicles 21:10; 28:25; 30:19; 33:12), as well as in all other references in the Jewish prayer books, the phrase "God of his fathers" is preceded by the unpronounceable name for God, the sacred Tetragrammaton "yod, heh, vav, heh" that is translated "Jehovah" or "LORD." In the Jewish prayer books it is pronounced "Adonai." The absence of the name LORD before "God of his fathers" in Daniel 11:37 is most striking. It is a singular occurrence. Therefore, based upon the context, it would be best to translate this as "gods of his fathers." Based on this translation, it does not necessarily follow that the Beast (antichrist) comes from Jewish descent. This is also in keeping with the context, as the prototype for the Beast (antichrist), Antiochus Epiphanes, was of Syrian-Greek descent, not Jewish descent.

The belief that the Beast (antichrist) will not be of Jewish descent is further supported by John's vision of the Beast recorded in the Revelation. He said:

And the dragon stood on the shore of the sea. And I saw a beast coming out of the sea. He had ten horns and seven heads, with ten crowns on his horns, and on each head a blasphemous name. The beast I saw resembled a leopard, but had feet like those of a bear and a mouth like that of a lion. The dragon gave the beast his power and his throne and great authority. One of the heads of the beast seemed to have had a fatal wound, but the fatal wound had been healed. The whole world was astonished and followed the beast. Men worshiped the dragon because he had given authority to the beast, and they also worshiped the beast and asked, 'Who is like the beast? Who can make war against him?'

The beast was given a mouth to utter proud words and blasphemies and to exercise his authority for forty-two months. He opened his mouth to blaspheme God, and to slander his name and his dwelling place and those who live in heaven. He was given power to make war against the saints and to conquer them. And he was given authority over every tribe, people, language and nation. All inhabitants of the earth will worship the beast — all whose names have not been written in the book of life belonging to the Lamb that was slain from the creation of the world (Revelation 13:1–8).

John describes the beast (dragon, Satan, antichrist) as coming up out of the sea. The definition and the symbolism of what is meant by the word "sea" is given to us in Revelation 17:15 where John is told: "Then the angel said to me, "The waters you saw, where the prostitute sits, are peoples, multitudes, nations and languages." John was told that the sea, or waters, that he saw in his vision, represented the Gentile nations of the world. The Beast who comes up out of the sea, comes up out of the sea of nations, and is therefore from Gentile background, not Jewish.

Some may argue, "How can this be?" "How will Israel accept a false Messiah if he is not Jewish?" The answer is, "They won't." Such confusion is generated by an improper understanding of the word "antichrist." The word "antichrist" is never used to refer to a false Messiah, a substitution for the Messiah, or to refer to a false Christ. Rather, the word always means "anti" or "against" — against Messiah. Further, within Scriptures, the word "antichrist" is never used in reference to a world ruler.

The word "antichrist" only occurs five times within the Scriptures, and it only appears in the writings of John. The five passages where this word occurs are: 1 John 2:18, where it is used both in the singular and plural form; John 2:22; John 4:3; and 2 John, verse 7. Examination of John's usage of the word "antichrist," reveals that in each one of these references the word is used to mean an "evil or malevolent spirit" which blinds the heart of man to the fact that Yeshua, God's Messiah, was God manifest in the flesh.

Satan continually attempts to get man to reject God and His Messiah; he continually attempts to get man to replace faith in God with faith in themselves. John tells us that even during the time when he was living, there were many antichrists. John did not use the word "antichrist" to refer to one individual, or to one particular world ruler. Rather, he used it to indicate the increasing numbers of people who refused to believe in and accept Yeshua as God's Messiah, God manifest in the flesh, in whom the fullness of the Godhead dwelt bodily.

The usage of the word "antichrist" to indicate a single individual, or a world ruler, did not come about until the writings of the early church fathers when the term was applied to heretical teachers, to the leaders of the Roman Empire, and even to the Popes. The usage of the word finally took on the popular connotation of one world leader who would arise at the end of days.

The Scriptures refer to this final world ruler as the Beast (Revelation 11:7); the man of sin and the son of perdition (2 Thessalonians 2:8); the Lawless one (2 Thessalonians 2:8); the Devil, or Serpent [dragon] (Revelation 12:9); the Beast out of the Sea (Revelation 13:1); the willful king

(Daniel 11:36); the little horn (Daniel 7:8); the prince that would come (Daniel 9:26). Scriptures never refer to the final world ruler as the antichrist.

According to the Scriptures, this final world ruler will be a dictator; he will be an individual who is totally energized by Satan. His foremost desire and burning ambition will be to *be* God — not to be anti-Christ, or against Messiah. The chief desire of this world ruler will be to have the whole world worship him as God.

To achieve his ultimate goal, this world ruler (Beast) will have a false prophet who will deceive the world into worshipping him [the Beast] (see Revelation 13:11–18). The Scriptures do not particularize, but perhaps the false prophet will be of Jewish descent, for John tells us that he will come up out of the earth (see Revelation 13:11). In prophecy, the phrase "the earth" is often a reference to the land of Israel. This would also be in keeping with Jewish tradition which stresses looking for the prophet Elijah to come before the dreadful Day of the LORD. At every Passover table, even in our days, a place is set for Elijah and the youngest child of the family is sent to the door to see if Elijah has come to announce the coming of Messiah.

It should not surprise Christians that the Beast, or final world ruler, will come out of the Gentile nations. The prototype of the Beast was a Syrian-Greek. Additionally, the Tribulation Period will be the final days of the "Times of the Gentiles." This period of time will be Satan's last chance to use the nations in his attempt to destroy the nation of Israel — to defeat the program of God and institute his own program in its place.

Daniel was told that this willful king would not regard the gods of his fathers, nor would he have a natural desire for women. Instead, he will honor the god of forces. The fact that this ruler will have no desire for women is a reference to his perverse nature and character. He will have no use for family or family values. His sole concern will be to gratify himself; his only interest will be in things that can help him accomplish his own purposes. He will be consumed by his own selfishness and by his desire for power.

Daniel's vision of the willful king bears a striking resemblance to the portrait of Satan as painted by Isaiah in chapter 14:12–17, and the picture of the Beast who bestows favor on all who will worship him and who will receive his mark in their foreheads that we read about in Revelation, chapter thirteen. Those who refuse to worship him will be persecuted or killed. But those who choose to worship him do so at a terrible price — the forfeiture of their own soul.

Christians have long speculated about how such a world dictator will gain control of the world. No one knows but God! Such a world ruler can only come upon the scene of history at God's appointed time of the end. The Word of God to Daniel is sure. It will surely come to pass! Daniel was told: "...Yet he will come to his end, and no one will help him" (Daniel 11:45b).

THE DESTRUCTION OF THE BEAST

A quick preview of the end time events which will bring about the final fall of Satan and the Beast (the lawless king) was then given to Daniel. We read:

At the time of the end the king of the South will engage him in battle, and the king of the North will storm out against him with chariots and cavalry and a great fleet of ships. He will invade many countries and sweep through them like a flood. He will also invade the Beautiful Land. Many countries will fall, but Edom, Moab and the leaders of Ammon will be delivered from his hand. He will extend his power over many countries; Egypt will not escape. He will gain control of the treasures of gold and silver and all the riches of Egypt, with the Libyans and Nubians in submission. But reports from the east and the north will alarm him, and he will set out in a great rage to destroy and annihilate many. He will pitch his royal tents between the seas at the beautiful holy mountain. Yet he will come to his end, and no one will help him (Daniel 11:40–45).

Within these verses we have a glimpse of the illustrious career of this willful king as he seeks to control the Middle East. Additionally, these verses give a direct reference to the armies that will comprise the final and climactic battle of Armageddon.

Reviewing the chronological events of the end time, it appears there will come a northern invasion of Israel by Gog and Magog (Ezekiel 38,

39). This confederacy of nations will invade Israel at some time after the rapture of the Church. Ezekiel makes it clear that this invasion will take place in the "latter days," or the "latter years" — a reference to the Tribulation period (see Ezekiel 38:8, 16). But the invasion will not be successful. Instead, the confederacy of nations will be almost completely destroyed upon the mountains of Israel (see Ezekiel 39).

Victory for Israel will come as a result of the direct intervention of God, who will pour out His judgment upon the armies of Gog and Magog. But amazingly, because of the world-wide deception in those days, God will not receive the glory or the credit for Israel's miraculous victory. Instead, the Beast, the willful king with whom Israel is united in a covenant relationship, will receive the credit. As a result of this great victory, and as a tribute to the fulfillment of the covenant he has established, the willful king will make plans to move his world headquarters to Jerusalem. Israel will discover, to their dismay, that their covenant of peace is, in reality, a covenant of death.

The prophet Isaiah spoke these alarming words: "Therefore hear the word of the LORD, you scoffers who rule this people in Jerusalem. You boast, "We have entered into a covenant with death, with the grave we have made an agreement. When an overwhelming scourge sweeps by, it cannot touch us, for we have made a lie our refuge and falsehood our hiding place" (Isaiah 28:14, 15).

Daniel was told that after the Beast confirms the covenant with Israel, the king of the South and the king of the North will engage him in battle. One of the provisions of the covenant which Israel will sign with the Beast, is that he will protect them against all of their enemies. A key reason for Israel's acceptance of the terms of this covenant will be that it will offer an unparalleled opportunity for world peace. It would appear that the covenant will not stop the invading armies from entering Jerusalem. Instead, it seems that the covenant will simply guarantee the intervention of the willful king and his armies into Israel, and eventually into Jerusalem.

With the signing of this covenant, Israel ushers in the Tribulation. In that day, Israel, like the other nations of the world, will be deceived by Satan. In the past, Israel sought to establish and to maintain peace within her borders by seeking alliances with the nations, rather than through dependency upon God.

Daniel 11:40 states: "At the time of the end the king of the South will engage him in battle, and the king of the North will storm out against him with chariots and cavalry and a great fleet of ships. He will invade many countries and sweep through them like a flood."

The way the personal pronouns are used should be carefully studied. In the phrase, "...the king of the South will engage him in battle,..." the "him" is a reference to the willful king referred to in verse 36. Daniel is told that the king of the North will storm out against him. The reference to "him" is a reference to the willful king of verse 36. In the latter portion of verse 40 the pronoun used changes to "he." This should be understood as a reference to the willful king of verse 36.

Daniel is told that the willful King, the Beast, the one who will be empowered by Satan, will gain complete victory over all of the countries of the Middle East. The only exceptions will be the countries of Edom, Moab, and Ammon. The reason Edom, Moab, and Ammon are not conquered is not given, but perhaps it has to do with the geographical and topological features of the Middle East. The countries to the east of the Jordan River were not involved when battles took place between the north and the south. On the other hand, it may have to do with the origins of the willful king, and his religious beliefs. It may be that this great political ruler will come from one of the Muslim countries.

The battle with the king of the North and the king of the South will bring the armies of the Beast, and the Beast himself, into Israel (or into the Beautiful land). Once in the land, the Beast will capture Jerusalem and set up his world headquarters there (see verse 45). He will establish Jerusalem as his seat of authority and worship, and Jerusalem will become the symbolic Babylon, as seen by the prophet John and recorded in Revelation, chapters 17–18.

The Beast's victories will be short-lived. The great alliance of nations, formed through his persuasion, will soon turn against him. Daniel was told, "But reports from the east and the north will alarm him,..." (see Dan. 11:44).

John describes an enormous demonic army of 200,000,000 who will move across the Euphrates River toward Israel. Seeing that, the Beast will realize he has no one to help him. He will realize the hopelessness of the situation, and will therefore turn all of his wrath on Israel and the Jewish people — his last attempt to destroy the people unto whom the Messiah, the Prince, will return. The events of those climactic days will be so grave that it will appear that the nation of Israel is without hope. But the Sovereign God, the faithful God of Daniel, gives these words of encouragement, "yet he (the Beast) will come to his end, and no one will help him" (Dan. 11:45).

The God of Israel, the God of Daniel, the God and Father of our LORD, Yeshua, *our* great God, is faithful to His word! He can be fully trusted to do all that He has said. "How blessed is he whose help is the God of Jacob, Whose hope is in the LORD his God" (Psalm 146:5).

NOTES

Chapter 11. Writing History Before It Happens

1   F. A. Tatford, *The Climax of the Ages*, p 194.
2   *Apocrypha*, 2 Maccabees 5:5–14.
3   *Apocrypha*, 1 Maccabees 1:21–28; 2 Maccabees 5:15–21.
4   *Works of Josephus*, p 31.
5   William H. Brownlee, *The International Standard Bible Encyclopedia*, Vol. III, (Grand Rapids, MI: Wm. B. Eerdmans Publishing Co., 1988) p 46.
6   Tatford, *Climax of the Ages*, p 201.
7   C. L. Feinberg, *A Commentary On Daniel*, p 174–175.

♦

Chapter Twelve
Waiting to Go Home

Then I, Daniel, looked, and there before me stood two others, one on this bank of the river and one on the opposite bank. One of them said to the man clothed in linen, who was above the waters of the river, 'How long will it be before these astonishing things are fulfilled?'

The man clothed in linen, who was above the waters of the river, lifted his right hand and his left hand toward heaven, and I heard him swear by him who lives forever, saying, 'It will be for a time, times and half a time. When the power of the holy people has been finally broken, all these things will be completed.'

I heard, but I did not understand. So I asked, 'My Lord, what will the outcome of all this be?'

He replied, 'Go your way, Daniel, because the words are closed up and sealed until the time of the end. Many will be purified, made spotless and refined, but the wicked will continue to be wicked. None of the wicked will understand, but those who are wise will understand.

— Daniel 12:5–10

THE GREAT PRINCE MICHAEL

In the original text there were no chapter or verse divisions. While the modern translations of the Bible include a chapter break and head-

219

ings, the text of chapter twelve is, in reality, a continuation in thought and action with the events of the "time of the end" as foretold in chapter 11:36–45. Daniel is told:

> *At that time Michael, the great prince who protects your people, will arise. There will be a time of distress such as has not happened from the beginning of nations until then. But at that time your people — everyone whose name is found written in the book — will be delivered. Multitudes who sleep in the dust of the earth will awake: some to everlasting life, others to shame and everlasting contempt. Those who are wise will shine like the brightness of the heavens, and those who lead many to righteousness, like the stars for ever and ever (Daniel 12:1–3).*

Daniel is told of the events that will take place in the final days of the Tribulation Period. He hears that the world ruler, the Beast (who is none other than Satan incarnate) will set his throne (his world headquarters) in Jerusalem. From Jerusalem, he will establish his one world government, and vast commercial and economic control over all of the nations. He will turn Jerusalem into a commercial, political, satanically religious city, making it "harlot Babylon" as described by John in Revelation 17–18. In his contempt for God, he will defile the temple, setting himself up to be god.

Some who read the prophecy of Daniel 12:1–3 shake their heads and wonder how these things could possibly happen, never giving thought to the fact that the tragic events which will take place in Jerusalem during the Tribulation, happen to countless individuals even in our days when they allow Satan and his world system to rule in their individual lives. One aspect of the Tribulation is that it will completely unmask Satan for who and what he is. Satan's final attempt to establish his throne in Jerusalem, to make himself God, will end in his destruction. So it is with individuals who make this world system their God. During this life they may gain the whole world, but in the process they lose their own soul.

Daniel is told how the destruction of the Beast will come about, and how the Jewish people will be saved from total annihilation. He is told: "...There will be a time of distress such as has not happened from the beginnings of nations until then" (verse 1). What makes this such a great time of distress? Two things.

First, it is the time of the outpouring of God's wrath upon the inhabitants of the earth. It is the fulfillment of the promise made to Daniel, the fulfillment of the final period of seven — the Tribulation — the time of Jacob's Trouble. Nothing in all of world history will compare with the awesome catastrophic judgments of that time!

Second, it is the time when Satan will be forever exiled from heaven. In the book of Revelation John told of that awesome time. He said: "And there was war in heaven. Michael and his angels fought against the dragon, and the dragon and his angels fought back. But he was not strong enough, and they lost their place in heaven. The great dragon was hurled down — that ancient serpent called the devil, or Satan, who leads the whole world astray. He was hurled to the earth, and his angels with him" (Revelation 12:7–9).

During the Tribulation, there will not only be war on earth, but there will be a great war going on in heaven as well. Satan will be cast out of heaven and hurled down to the earth. The reference to "the earth" is a direct reference to Israel. Once Satan has been cast out of heaven he will indwell the Beast, the willful king, who has made his headquarters in Jerusalem. In his anger and rage, he will turn his wrath upon Israel and upon all who refuse to bow down and worship him. Were it not for the mercy of God, and His intervention, no one would be able to escape the wrath of the Beast in those terrible days.

God encouraged Daniel by telling him that at this horrific time, Michael, the great archangel, the great prince who protects Israel, will come to their aid once again. It was Michael who overcame Satan (as he worked through the prince of Persia); Michael's intervention enabled Daniel to receive the answer to his prayer. In the time of the end, Michael and his angels will once again do battle with Satan. They will be victorious over Satan and will cast him out heaven. As Satan's fury is unleashed on the people of Israel during the Tribulation, it will be Michael who will enter into supernatural battle, offsetting the demonic hordes of Satan and giving protection to the people of Israel, lest they perish in the Great Tribulation.

God's Book of Names

Daniel is told, "...everyone whose name is found written in the book — will be delivered" (verse 1b). Notice that not all Israel will be delivered, only those whose names are recorded in God's Book of Life. This means that being born Jewish will not automatically ensure that an individual's name will be recorded in God's book. This raises the question, "What will be required to have one's name recorded in God's Book of Life?"

The Scriptures make it clear that during the Tribulation, just as in our day, faith in God's Son, Yeshua, will be the only way one's name will be recorded in God's Book of Life. Only by acceptance of Yeshua's death, burial, and resurrection can any individual find salvation. There is no other way. Yeshua said of Himself: ["I am the way] and the truth and the life. No one comes to the Father except through me" (John 14:6).

If the Jews will not be saved unless their names have been recorded in God's Book of Life, it follows that the same will be true of Gentiles. Hence, the necessity for bringing the Gospel to all nations, to the Jews first and also to the Gentile. This is why Yeshua gave His disciples the "Great Commission." He commanded them to bring the Gospel to everyone, making disciples of all nations (including Israel). And in the Olivet Discourse, Yeshua emphasized that the end would not come until the "...gospel of the kingdom [is] preached in the whole world as a testimony to all nations, and then the end will come" (Matthew 24:14). During the Tribulation the Gospel will continue to be preached, and both Jews and Gentiles will continue to be saved on the basis of the Gospel message.

The question may be raised, "Since Daniel is told it will be individuals whose names are written in God's book who will be delivered, and since all believers today have their names written in God's book, doesn't this verse indicate that all believers will go though the Tribulation and be delivered out of it?" Such questions are not applicable to this passage of Scripture. Daniel has been addressing Israel. He is being told about Israel's future. Throughout all of the prophecies and visions within the book of Daniel, there is no mention of the Church. God's revelation to Daniel regarding Israel's future was simply an unfolding and continuation of Israel's history as it would transpire following the seventy year captivity. Daniel was shown Israel, present and future, as if the Church Age did not exist.

The reference to individuals who are delivered, then, is to individuals who have placed their faith in the finished work of Yeshua and have become "believers" during the Tribulation. Some will be saved because of the testimony and ministry of the 144,000 (Revelation 7, 14). Others will be saved through the testimony of the Two Witnesses (Revelation 11). Being delivered is not a reference to the Rapture, or to the Church going through the Tribulation. God is simply emphasizing to Daniel that even during the horror of the days of the Tribulation, He will be faithful and will keep His promises to those who desire to live by faith in His Messiah. He will not allow them to be deceived by the plots and ploys of Satan, even though Satan will be ruling during the Tribulation. True believers will always be delivered from God's wrath in whatever age they live.

This is what Yeshua taught in the parables of the Kingdom and in other parables found in Matthew 13, 24, and 25. At the time of the end, after the Great Tribulation, the LORD Yeshua will appear in power and great glory. He will then separate the sheep from the goats, the wheat from the chaff, the righteous from the unrighteous. Those who are righteous will enter into His kingdom and will rule and reign with Him during the one thousand year kingdom that He will establish on the earth. But the unrighteous will enter into condemnation, awaiting their final judgment day at the Great White Throne.

A DAY OF RESURRECTION

Daniel is told of a coming resurrection day: "Multitudes who sleep in the dust of the earth will awake: some to everlasting life, others to shame and everlasting contempt" (verse 2). The wording of this verse bears careful consideration. By contrasting those who will be raised to everlasting life, and others who will be raised to everlasting contempt, the implication is that there will be a first resurrection and a second resurrection. Those who awake "to everlasting life" are resurrected before those who awake to "shame and everlasting contempt." This is the first time such a two-fold resurrection is mentioned within the Scriptures. Daniel is also told that this is a physical resurrection, not a spiritual one. This is emphasized by the use of the word "sleep."

Throughout the Scriptures, when the word "sleep" is used in reference to the dead, it always refers to the body. Sleep is an activity of the body, not of the soul (see Matthew 9:18–25; Mark 5:35–42). The Bible never speaks of "soul-sleeping." The body may "sleep" in death, but the soul does not. Death, for the believer, is to be absent from the body and to be present with the LORD. The soul/spirit of the believer will be with the

LORD while he awaits the resurrection of his body. Death for the unbeliever means that his soul/spirit is held in a place of torment while it awaits the resurrection of the body and the final Great White Throne Judgment.

Until the time of death (or the time when our Messiah will return for His own) believers and non-believers, like the wheat and the tares, live side by side. In revealing these two distinct resurrections, the Scriptures disclose that at the moment of death believers are forever separated from non-believers. Each individual has only his or her lifetime in which to respond to God's revelation. Believers have a great responsibility to share the Gospel with non-believers, knowing that after death each will go a separate way. Each will experience a different resurrection. The believer will experience a resurrection like that of the Messiah, Yeshua. He is the first-fruits of the resurrection for the believer (see 1 Corinthians 15:20–23; Philippians 3:20, 21). But the non-believer will experience a resurrection solely for the purpose of standing before the Great White Throne Judgment. The non-believer will be judged for those things which were done in the body (Revelation 20:11–15). Since the non-believer has no sin-bearer, he will be raised in the image and likeness of his own corruptible body. The believer, who has received Yeshua as sin bearer, will be raised in the image and likeness of Him.

Commenting on this passage, Dr. Charles Lee Feinberg wrote:

Notice that this passage does not state how much time will elapse between the first and the second resurrection. Luke 20:35 speaks of 'those who are considered worthy to attain to…the resurrection from [out of] the dead.' This terminology means that there is to be a resurrection at which some are raised and some are not. This expression is used of Christ and the saints, but never of the unsaved.

First Corinthians 15:20–28 relates the resurrection of the dead directly to the kingdom rule of Christ on earth. Moreover, the resurrection is explicitly said to occur in different stages. Immediate succession is not taught in First Corinthians, because so much time has already elapsed between Christ, 'the first fruits of those who are asleep' (1 Corinthians 15:20), and the company that will rise at His coming (1 Corinthians 15:23). The end-resurrection will occur only when Christ has delivered up the kingdom to His Father. In other words, the thousand-year-long kingdom age elapses between the first resurrection of believers and the second resurrection, that of unbelievers. Revelation 20:4–6 also speaks of a first and a second resurrection, with the entire kingdom age of one thousand years intervening. Some in Israel in that day will be raised in the resurrection of the godly, while others will be reserved to experience the resurrection of the wicked, who will undergo the wrath of God.[1]

THE WISE MAN

A promise was given to Daniel, and to all who are wise in seeking to win souls. He was told, "Those who are wise will shine like the brightness of the heavens, and those who lead many to righteousness like the stars for ever and ever" (verse 3). The writer of Proverbs expressed it in this way: "The fruit of the righteous is a tree of life, and he who wins souls is wise" (Proverbs 11:30). The Scriptures also promise a special soul-winners' crown to all who win others to the Messiah (see 1 Thessalonians 2:19, 20).

The placement of this promise within the context of this prophecy should also be noted. It comes after the prophet Daniel has been told of the time of the end, after he has been told of the resurrection of some to everlasting life and others to everlasting damnation. It is placed at a strategic place in the prophecy in order to emphasize the fact that righteousness can only be found when there are righteous people living to tell of the truth of God. This was the emphasis and purpose of Daniel's entire life. He lived as a stranger in a strange land. He had been removed from the place where his God dwelt, yet he faithfully served his God. He did not waver in his commitment to God. Through the witness of Daniel's righteous life, many people living in the great pagan Babylonian Empire came to faith in the living God. This is what God desires from each one of His children. It is His desire that each believer be an extension of His righteousness and holiness. God wants each believer to be "wise in winning souls" (Jews and Gentiles) to the God of Abraham, Isaac and Jacob, through faith in the Messiah, Yeshua.

SEAL THE SCROLL

Daniel is told a very strange thing in chapter twelve, verse 4: "But you, Daniel, close up and seal the words of the scroll until the time of the end. Many will go here and there to increase knowledge."

This is one of the many verses within the book of Daniel that is often taken out of context, and given a variety of interpretations. Some state that this verse is a reference to automobiles, to airplanes, to rapid transit, or other means of swift transportation and communication. Others have used this verse to purport that the end will come when knowledge has increased. An examination of the text and the context shows, however, that this verse does not teach any of those things.

The messenger gave Daniel an order — "...close up and seal the words of the scroll until the time of the end." These words stand in stark contrast to the words of the Spirit of God to John on the Isle of Patmos: "Then he told me, "Do not seal up the words of the prophecy of this book, because the time is near" (Revelation 22:10).

Daniel was told to close and seal up the words of the prophecy, while John was instructed *not* to seal up the words of the prophecy. This was done because the book of Revelation concludes the total revelation of God's program. It includes God's program for the Jews, for the Gentiles, and for the Church of God. No further revelation is needed. God's program of redemption and judgment had been completely revealed for the understanding of any and all who were willing to examine the evidence and allow the Spirit of God to direct their minds and hearts. Also, the New Testament always pictures the believer as living in the "end of the age."

Since Pentecost, believers have always lived in the "closing days of the age." Yeshua could return at any time. There are no signs for the Rapture. Believers are to live their lives daily expecting the coming of the Messiah. This is why the Rapture is called the "Blessed, or Purifying hope" of the believer. When God sounds the trumpet, the believer's hope will be made complete. God will then bring a swift and final conclusion to His program on earth. Only God's patience and love for man has delayed this judgment (see 2 Peter 3:9). It is God's desire that believers share His love and concern for all mankind, and participate with Him in His program of reaching lost souls for eternity. Thus, from a New Testament perspective, the believer is living in the "end times."

For Daniel, however, the events revealed were to be unfolding over a long period of time. Certain prophetic events were yet in the distant future when they were spoken of to Daniel, yet they had to be fulfilled before the end could come. One of those events was the death, burial, and resurrection of the Messiah. Daniel was told to seal up the words until the time of the end.

Amazingly this was literally fulfilled. Although Daniel was recognized as prophet, the Jewish scribes never placed his book with the writings of the other prophets. Instead, his book was sealed and hidden among the section of the Torah called the Ketuvim (writings). Rather than being cataloged with the writings of the prophets, it is listed in the Jewish Scriptures among the other poetical writings. For all intents and purpose, it was sealed. As if that was not enough, in later Jewish history a curse was placed upon anyone who dared to study the book of Daniel, or who used the book of Daniel to calculate the coming of the Messiah. The end result has been that, of all of the books that make up the Jewish Bible (the Tenach), very few commentaries on the book of Daniel have been written by Jewish scholars.

Daniel was told that the revelation that had been given to him was to be closed (or sealed) "until the end of time." The implication of this verse is that it would be "unsealed" at the time of the end. This means that as the world approaches the Tribulation, and as the stage of history is set for the coming of the Messiah, there will be a renewed interest in studying the prophecies within the book of Daniel. The reference "many will go here and there to increase knowledge" is a direct reference to the study of the book of Daniel and to the study of prophecy itself. In the Hebrew text the definite article "the" is used, thus specifying "the knowledge" will increase. That is, the knowledge of the prophecy of Daniel. Year by year, both the study of history and the study of archaeology verify the Scriptures and shed greater light on the understanding of Daniel's prophecy, confirming it's truth.

Today there has been increasing interest in the study of the book of Daniel, both by Jewish and by Christian scholars. There has also been a great interest in the study of Daniel among some Hasidic Jews who, for the first time since the seventeenth century, now boldly state that mankind is living in the days of Redemption — the days preceding the coming of the Messiah. Some Hasidic Jews have gone so far as to proclaim the Hasidic rabbi of Brooklyn, Menachem Schneerson, the Messiah.

The messenger indicated to Daniel that as the end of days draws near,

227

there will be increasing interest in the study of the prophecies of Daniel. It may be the study of the book of Daniel that God will use during the Tribulation to speak to the hearts of many Jewish people concerning the person and work of the LORD, Yeshua.

The prophecies of Daniel give conclusive evidence —evidence backed by historical records — to the fact that the Messiah has come and was cut off (died) for the sins of His people. Further, the book of Daniel gives the promise that Israel will be delivered from the wrath of the Beast, and extends the promise of everlasting life to all who seek God's righteousness, by faith in God's Messiah.

EXILED BUT NOT FORGOTTEN

In chapter twelve, verses 5 through 7, Daniel's attention has been drawn back to the Tigris River, and he sees two other heavenly messengers. He wrote:

Then I, Daniel, looked, and there before me stood two others, one on this bank of the river and one on the opposite bank. One of them said to the man clothed in linen, who was above the waters of the river, 'How long will it be before these astonishing things are fulfilled?'

The man clothed in linen, who was above the waters of the river, lifted his right hand and his left hand toward heaven, and I heard him swear by him who lives forever, saying, 'It will be for a time, times and half a time. When the power of the holy people has been finally broken, all these things will be completed.'

Following his three week period of mourning, Daniel went out to the great river, the Tigris (see Daniel 10:2–4). There he received his vision of the first heavenly messenger (verse 4), after which he received the great revelation of the end of time. How long it took to reveal all of this to Daniel is not known, but at some point during the revelation of the prophecy of the end times, two other heavenly messengers joined Daniel. They, too, were listening to the revelation and were most curious. The New Testament reveals that angels are most desirous of knowing and understanding the plan and program of God (see 1 Peter 1:10–12).

These visions of Daniel are a continuation of his visions told of in earlier verses. In chapter ten we are told that Daniel was confronted by a man dressed in linen (see 10:5). This man, who first spoke to Daniel, was identified as a guardian cherub. (Since the other two did not know the details of the events being revealed to Daniel, it would appear that they were likely of a lesser rank among the supernatural beings created by God to worship and assist Him.) The man in linen was not a theophany or a christophany (appearance of God or an appearance of the Messiah). This is evidenced by the fact that when he is asked the question regarding the time of these events, he lifts his hands and swears by God, Himself — the one who lives forever. Had this been an appearance of the Messiah, or a manifestation of God, he would have spoken authoritatively. He would not have needed to swear by the One who lives forever.

The appearance of these cherubim and angels to Daniel was in direct answer to his prayers. They were sent by God to give comfort to Daniel, to assure him that his prayers were being heard, and to let him know that though they were in exile, the people of God had not been forgotten or forsaken. God wanted to assure Daniel that his faith and his desire to live a righteous life had not gone unnoticed by God.

As Daniel watched the heavenly visitors, he heard one of them ask: "How long will it be before these astonishing things are fulfilled?" The answer to the question is immediately forthcoming. One can almost hear it echoing over the waters of the Tigris River. "It will be for a time, times and half a time" (verse 7). This is the same expression that was used in Daniel 7:25, and the same expression that is used of Israel in Revelation 12:14. It means three and one half years. It represents the last three and one half years of the Tribulation, the time during which the Beast establishes the Abomination of Desolation in the Holy Place (thus the breaking of the covenant with Israel) until he is destroyed in the final battle of Armageddon.

The man in linen continues by adding these words: "When the power of the holy people has been finally broken, all these things will be completed" (verse 7b). This is a reference to the satanic and demonic power that Satan has wielded over the Jewish people since the beginning of the period called the "times of the Gentiles" — a power he will continue to exercise until the end of the "times of the Gentiles."

From the time God called Jacob (Israel) out of Egypt, until the final day of the Battle of Armageddon, Satan has exercised his influence and power over the leaders and inhabitants of the nations in his attempt to destroy Israel and the Jewish people. Satan has used every means possible to keep Jerusalem (the place where God chose to place His Name) from being the City of Peace. Instead of enjoying peace, the history of Jerusalem is one of warfare and hatred. The words of Yeshua ring startlingly true: "They will fall by the sword and will be taken as prisoners to all the nations. Jerusalem will be trampled on by the Gentiles until the times of the Gentiles are fulfilled" (Luke 21:24).

The promise of God is, that when Satan's power over the holy people has been broken, the Messiah will return and Jerusalem will be rebuilt. It will then be the city where God dwells (see Ezekiel 48:35).

Daniel heard the answer given to the heavenly messengers, but he did not understand it so he asked:

> "My LORD, what will the outcome of all this be?" He replied, "Go your way, Daniel, because the words are closed up and sealed until the time of the end. Many will be purified, made spotless and refined, but the wicked will continue to be wicked. None of the wicked will understand, but those who are wise will understand" (Daniel 12:8–10).

Daniel wanted to grasp the total scope of this revelation of prophecy, but it's meaning eluded him. The messenger knew Daniel's understanding was limited by his humanity; it would never be possible for him to comprehend the meaning of the events spoken of, for they had not yet transpired. Daniel is therefore told, "Go your way, Daniel, because the words are closed up and sealed until the time of the end."

In His sovereignty, all dates, all times, all seasons are fixed and known only to God. Only He knows when the last person will accept Messiah, and so usher in the Rapture. Only He knows when the heart of a man like Pharaoh of old, will become so hardened that he will not, and cannot, repent. Men, on the other hand — even men like Daniel — can never measure eternity, and can never fully understand the mysteries of God. As mortals, men must exercise faith in the eternal God, and place this trust and hope in Him when they are unable to see the full picture.

Daniel was told that he understood as much as was humanly possible for him to know. God had revealed unto him everything necessary to enable him to live a righteous and holy life.

So it is with mankind today. Through His Word, God has revealed everything we need to know concerning Himself. He has revealed His love and His desire to have fellowship with His creation. He has revealed how man can know Him, through faith in the finished work of His Son, Yeshua. His Word makes it clear that He longs for us to live lives that glorify Him.

Further, God has revealed in His Word a broad outline of future events and He has warned us that our failure to accept His Word will result in judgment. His ultimate judgement will extend both to disobedient individuals and to the nations in which they live. Conversely, His Word reveals that a response of obedience to His revelation can stay God's hand of judgment. How individuals live their lives in relationship to God has a direct bearing upon how God will bless, or withhold blessing, from the nation in which they live.

Daniel was told that many would be purified, but many would remain wicked. The wicked would not understand, but the wise will give themselves to understanding. In effect, Daniel was given a principle for holy living. The individual who desires to study the Word of God and to live in obedience to God's commands will grow in wisdom. That growth in wisdom will produce a greater desire to live a holy life. As the lifestyle becomes more holy, and the individual grows closer to God, there is less and less desire for the things of the world.

On the other hand, individuals who hear God's Word but choose to ignore its message, choosing to remain in their wickedness, become more wicked and grow further and further from God. Because of their refusal to heed His revelation, the wicked will ultimately face the eternal judgment of God. Daniel understood that the visions and revelation of God had not been given to him just for the purpose of his own edification, or to satisfy his curiosity about the future. He understood that these things had been revealed so that he, and all who would hear his words, would want to be purified, and then to warn the wicked of impending judgment.

SOME EXTRA DAYS

Finally, to emphasize that His Word is true, and to stress that these prophecies will surely come to pass and men must know that they will be responsible to heed the truth, the subject reverts to an earlier vision and prophecy that was given to Daniel. It is a specific prophecy that relates to a specific event which Daniel was told would certainly happen. The messenger said: "From the time that the daily sacrifice is abolished and the abomination that causes desolation is set up, there will be 1290 days. Blessed is the one who waits for and reaches the end of the 1335 days" (Daniel 12:11–12).

These verses have caused a great deal of confusion. Why are they included here, and what do they mean? Why was Daniel told that from the time that the daily sacrifice is abolished, and the Abomination of Desolation is set up, is 1290 days and the one who reaches the end of 1335 days is blessed? In all other references in Scripture the length of time given from the time of the Abomination of Desolation to the end is 1260 days. Why is this prophecy different? What is meant by the 1335 days?

There are no genuinely satisfactory answers to these questions. Some Bible scholars state that the reference to the 1290 days and the 1335 days is a reference to Antiochus Epiphanes. They try to show that the length of time Antiochus defiled the temple was 1290 days, and that it was an additional forty-five days (or 1335 days) until the death of Antiochus. His death, in turn, brought to an end the calamities he had inflicted upon the Jewish people. However, there is nothing in the context to suggest that the subject (the end of time and the Tribulation) has now switched back to the days of Antiochus Epiphanes. Additionally, Daniel had already been told that the length of time the temple would be defiled in Antiochus' day would be "2300 evenings and mornings" (see Daniel 8:14). The 2300 evenings and mornings represented the daily sacrifice which was done twice a day. The actual time Antiochus would defile the temple was 1150 days, a little over three years. This was actually fulfilled.

Most scholars agree that the extension of time mentioned in Daniel 12:11–12 is a reference to the Tribulation. Where, however, does it fit into the program that God has already revealed? One possible scenario exists. In the book of Revelation, John states that after the seventh seal was broken, and before the trumpet judgments begin, there is silence in heaven for about one half hour (see Revelation 8:1).

The seal judgments are opened during the first three and one half years of the Tribulation, and the trumpet and bowl judgments are completed during the last half of the three and one half year period. Why the pause of one half hour in the middle of the Tribulation? Several events must transpire in the middle of the Tribulation in order to complete the last half. One of these events is the breaking of the covenant with Israel and the establishment of the Abomination of Desolation. Another event is the great war which will be waged in heaven, culminating with Satan being cast down to the earth. A third event is the sealing of the 144,000 Jews from the tribes of Israel. And a fourth event is the raising up of the two witnesses.

The seven year Tribulation is presented as two three-and-one-half year segments. If the two segments include a pause, or a period of time in the middle approximating one half hour, this could explain the extra days given in the prophecy of Daniel.

The phrase "there was silence in heaven for about an half an hour" could very well be a reference back to Daniel, and to the period of time mentioned — an extra thirty to seventy-five days. If this is the case, the prophet is being told that these are specific lengths of times, and the one who reaches the end of the 1335 days will be blessed because he will not only see the Messiah coming in the clouds of glory, but will have also entered into the Messianic Kingdom of our LORD.

Some Bible scholars feel the extra thirty days, or the extra seventy-five days, should be added to end of the Tribulation. A few state that extra time is needed for the LORD to purge out of his kingdom those who have committed sin (see Matthew 13:41). Others feel the extra days are needed to begin the celebration of Sukkot (tabernacles) of which the prophet Zechariah spoke (see Zechariah 14:16–21).

Perhaps the extra days are added to give to Daniel the reassurance that there will be those who do survive the 1260 days of the Great Tribulation and become citizens of the great Millennial Kingdom of our LORD.

DANIEL'S FATE FORETOLD

Concluding His revelation, God lovingly reveals to Daniel his own fate. He is told: "As for you, go your way till the end. You will rest, and then at the end of the days you will rise to receive your allotted inheritance" (Daniel 12:13).

Daniel was given the assurance not only of resurrection, but of an eternal reward. In that great day when the trumpet of the LORD will sound, Daniel, along with all other saints throughout the ages, will be raised. His body will be raised from the dust of the earth and he will receive his allotted inheritance. This same promise is given to all who have placed their faith and trust in the LORD, Yeshua. They will never be forgotten. They will never be forsaken. The faithful God who keeps covenant with His people will never leave them nor forsake them.

The young man, Daniel, who chose to forsake the world system and live a life that was separated unto God, has now grown old. He has grown in grace and holiness, and the messenger does not leave him without giving him God's promise that nothing will ever separate him from the God whom he loves. In death, he would be separated for a time from his physical body, from his beloved land, Israel, and from the temple in Jerusalem, but he would never be separated from his LORD. And at the end of days, he had God's promise that he would once again stand in Jerusalem, on the holy mount, to eternally worship the living God whom he had chosen to serve.

God, who did not spare His own Son, offers every man, woman, and child who has placed faith in His Son, Yeshua, the same promise He extended to Daniel:

Who shall separate us from the love of [Messiah]? Shall trouble or hardship or persecution or famine or nakedness or danger or sword?

No, in all these things we are more than conquerors through him who loved us. For I am convinced that neither death nor life, neither angels nor demons, neither the present nor the future, nor any powers, neither height nor depth nor anything else in all creation, will be able to separate us from the love of God that is in Christ [Yeshua] our LORD (Romans 8:35, 37–39).

NOTES
Chapter 12. Waiting To Go Home
[1] C. L. Feinberg, *Commentary on Daniel*, p 183.

Chronological Table

I. NATIONAL ISRAEL

1025–1010 B.C.	Saul
1010–971 B.C.	David
971–931 B.C.	Solomon

After Solomon's death national Israel was divided.
10 Tribes in the Northern Kingdom — called ISRAEL.
2 Tribes in the Southern Kingdom — called JUDAH.

II. DIVIDED KINGDOM
931–586 B.C.

ISRAEL	JUDAH	ASSYRIA
931–910 Jeroboam	931–913 Rehoboam	883–859 Ashurnasirpal
910–909 Nadab	913–911 Abijah	
909–886 Baasha	911–870 Asa	
886–885 Elah		
885 Zimri (7 days)		
885–880 Tibni		
880–874 Omri		
874–853 Ahab	870–848 Jehoshaphat	859–824 Shalmanesser III
853–852 Ahaziah	848–841 Jehoram	
852–841 Jehoram	841 Ahaziah	
841-814 Jehu	841–835 Athaliah	823–810 Shamsi-Adad V
814–798 Jehoaz	835–796 Joash	810–805 Samimuramat
798–782 Jehoash	796–767 Amaziah	805–782 Adadnirari III

782–753 Jeroboam II	767–740 Uzziah-Azaria	781–772 Shalmaneser IV
753–752 Zachariah	(co-regent from 791)	772–755 Ashurdan III
752–Shallum (1 mo.)		754–745 Ashurnirari V
752–742 Menahem		745–727 Tiglathpileser III
742–740 Pekahia	740–735 Jotham	
740–732 Pekah	(co-regent from 750)	
732–722 Hoshea	731–715 Ahaz	727–722 Shalmaneser V
722 Samaria cap-	715–686 Hezekiah	722–705 Sargon II
tured by Assyrians	686–642 Manasseh	705–681 Sennacherib
	642–640 Amon	681–669 Esarhaddon
	640–609 Josiah	696–627 Ashurbanipal II
	609 Pharaoh Necho,	627–620 Ashuretililani
	king of Egypt, defeated	625 Assyrians captured
	Josiah, king of Judah, at	by Babylonians
	Megiddo (2 Chron. 35:	620–612 Sinshariskun
	20–24) ; subsequently	614 Fall of Assur
	placed Jehoiakim on	612–610 Ashuruballit II
	the throne instead of	612 Fall of Nineveh
	Jehoahaz, Josiah's other	609 End of Assyrian Empire
	son (2 Chron. 36:4).	
	In the same year, Necho	
	defeated Nabopolassar,	
	king of Babylon.	

JUDAH, continued

606   In this year, the 20th year of Nabopolassar, king of Babylon, and the 3rd year of Jehoiakim, king of Judah, Jerusalem was taken by Nebuchadnezzar (2 Chron. 36:6, 7; Dan. 1:1, 2) and the seventy years of captivity commenced (Jer. 25:11). Daniel taken captive.

605   Nebuchadnezzar defeated Pharaoh-Necho at Carchemish. He also ascended to the throne of Babylon in the same year, which was the 4th year of Jehoiakim (Jer. 25:1).

597   Jehoiachin succeeded his father as king of Judah. Jerusalem was taken a second time by Nebuchadnezzar, Jehoiachin was carried away captive and Zedekiah became king (2 Kings 24:8–17). Ezekiel exiled and Jeremiah exiled.

593   Astyages became king of Media.

589   Jerusalem was besieged for the third time by Nebuchadnezzar (2 Kings 25:1, 2).

588   The tenth year of Zedekiah and the eighteenth year of Nebuchadnezzar (Jer. 32:1).

586   Jerusalem was taken and destroyed (2 Kings 25:4–21).

III. 586 B.C. BEGINNING THE TIMES OF THE GENTILES
(To Conclude with the return of the Messiah)

586   Jerusalem was taken and destroyed (2 King 25:4–21).

561   Nebuchadnezzar was succeeded by Evil-Merodach (2 Kings 25:27).

559   Cyrus became king of Persia and Neriglissar king of Babylon.

555   Nabonidus succeeded Neriglissar as king of Babylon.

549   Cyrus conquered Media.

541   Belshazzar became regent during the lifetime of his father, Nabonidus.

538   Cyrus took Babylon and Darius the Mede became ruler (Dan. 5:31). Cyrus permits the Jews to rebuild Jerusalem.

536   Cyrus succeeded Darius. This year marked the end of the seventy years of captivity which commenced in 606 B.C. (see above), and Cyrus issued a decree authorizing the Jews to return to Jerusalem and to rebuild the temple (Ezra 1:1–4).

529   Cambyses succeeded Cyrus.

521   Darius I, Hystaspes, became king of Persia.

485   Xerxes I (the Ahasuerus of the Book of Esther) became king of Persia.

465   Artaxerxes I succeeded Xerxes.

445   Twentieth year of Artaxerxes. Daniel's seventy "weeks" commenced (Dan. 9:24–27). A decree was issued for the restoration of Jerusalem (Neh. 2:1–9).

336   Alexander the Great became king of Macedon.

323   Death of Alexander

312   The era of the Seleucidae commenced. Seleucus I became king of Syria.

283   Ptolemy II, Philadelphus, became king of Egypt.

280   Antiochus I became king of Syria.

261   Antiochus II became king of Syria.

247   Ptolemy III, Euergetes, became king of Egypt.

246   Seleucus II became king of Syria.

226   Seleucus III became king of Syria.

223	Antiochus III, the Great, became king of Syria.
222	Ptolemy IV, Philopator, became king of Egypt.
205	Ptolemy V, Epiphanes, became king of Syria.
187	Seleucus IV became king of Syria.
181	Ptolemy VI, Philometor, became king of Egypt.
176	Antiochus IV, Epiphanes, became king of Syria.
170	Jerusalem was captured by Antiochus Epiphanes.
168	The Jewish revolt was crushed and the temple was defiled by Antiochus Epiphanes.
165	Jerusalem was liberated by Judas Maccabaeus, the temple cleansed and the Feast of Dedication instituted.
164	Antiochus V became king of Syria.
162	Demetrius I became king of Syria.
151	Alexander Balas became king of Syria.
146	Demetrius II became king of Syria, and Ptolemy Physcon became king of Egypt. In the same year, Greece was conquered by Mummius and became a Roman province.
65	Syria became a Roman province.
63	Jerusalem was captured by Pompey.
4	So far as can be determined, this was the actual date of our Lord's birth.

C.E.

33	The crucifixion of Christ took place (483 prophetic years of 360 days after 445 B.C.).
70	Jerusalem was captured by Titus.

Maps of the Ancient World

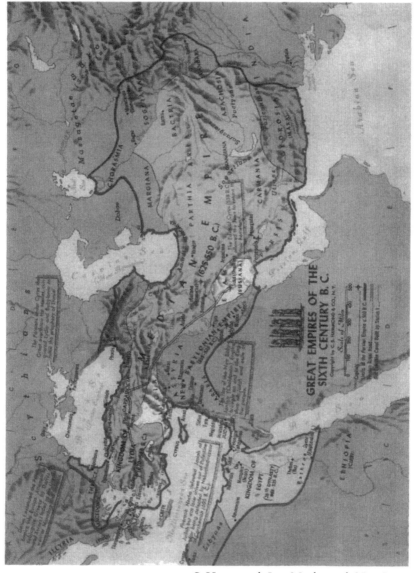

© Hammond, Inc. Maplewood, New Jersey

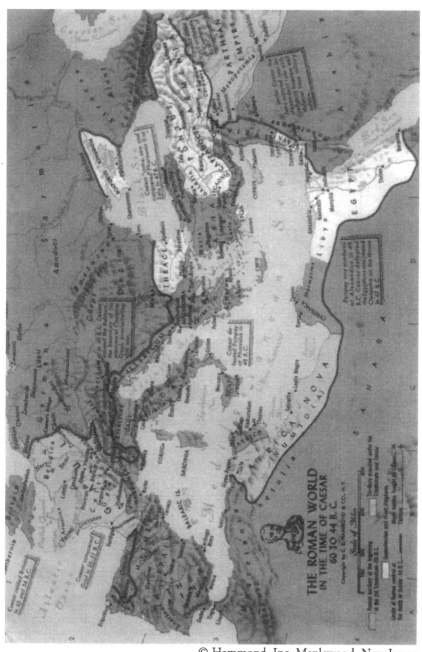

© Hammond, Inc. Maplewood, New Jersey

A Prophetic Time Line

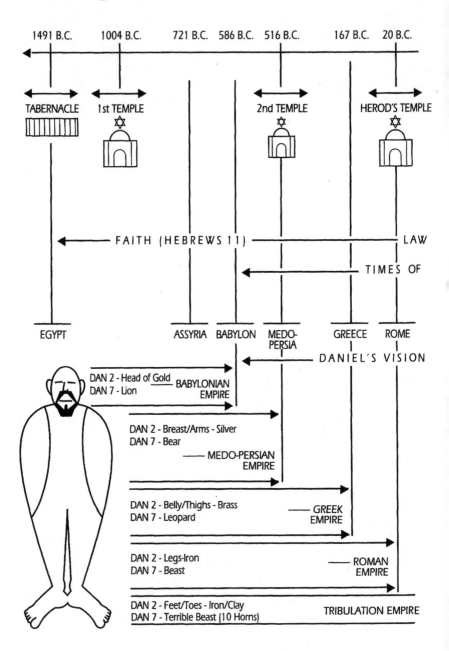

1491 B.C.	1004 B.C.	721 B.C.	586 B.C.	516 B.C.	167 B.C.	20 B.C.

TABERNACLE 　1st TEMPLE 　2nd TEMPLE 　HEROD'S TEMPLE

FAITH (HEBREWS 11) ────────── LAW

TIMES OF

EGYPT 　ASSYRIA 　BABYLON 　MEDO-PERSIA 　GREECE 　ROME

DANIEL'S VISION

DAN 2 - Head of Gold 　BABYLONIAN
DAN 7 - Lion 　EMPIRE

DAN 2 - Breast/Arms - Silver
DAN 7 - Bear

MEDO-PERSIAN
EMPIRE

DAN 2 - Belly/Thighs - Brass
DAN 7 - Leopard

GREEK
EMPIRE

DAN 2 - Legs-Iron
DAN 7 - Beast

ROMAN
EMPIRE

DAN 2 - Feet/Toes - Iron/Clay
DAN 7 - Terrible Beast (10 Horns) 　TRIBULATION EMPIRE

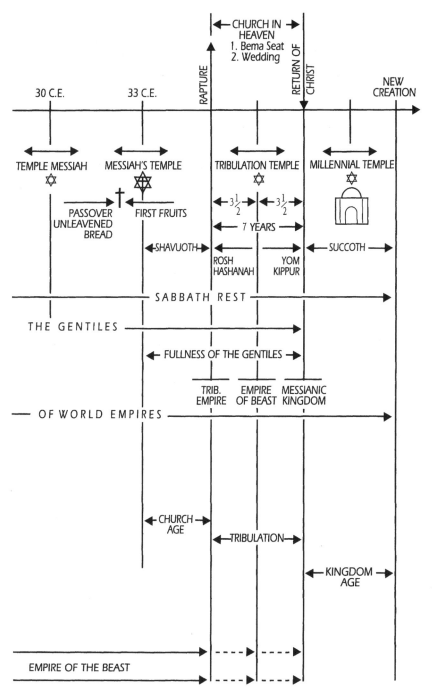

Prepared by: Rev. Harold A. Sevener ©1975

243

Selected Bibliography

Anderson, Sir Robert. *The Coming Prince*, 9th. ed. London: Hodder and Stoughton, 1909.

—. *Daniel in the Critics' Den.* London: James Nisbet and Co., Limited, 1902.

Anderson, Robert A. *Signs and Wonders: A Commentary on the Book of Daniel.* International Theological Commentary. Grand Rapids, MI: William B. Eerdmans, 1984.

Andrews, Samuel J. *Christianity and Anti-Christianity in Their Final Conflict* (Revised and Popular Edition). Chicago, IL: Bible Institute Colportage Association, 1898.

Apocrypha: American Bible Society, Printed in Great Britain: Eyre & Spottiswoode, n.d.

Archer, Gleason L. *The Aramaic of the 'Genesis Apocryphon' Compared with the Aramaic of Daniel.* In New Perspectives on the Old Testament, edited by J. Barton Payne. Waco, TX: Word, 1970.

—. *Daniel* (vol. 7) *The Expositor's Bible Commentary.* Grand Rapids, MI: Zondervan Publishing House, 1985.

—. *Translation, Jerome's Commentary on Daniel.* Grand Rapids, MI: Baker Book House, 1958.

Auberlen, Carl August. *The Prophecies of Daniel and the Revelations of St. John* (translated by Adolph Saphir). Andover: Draper, 1857.

Baldwin, Joyce G. *Daniel: An Introduction and Commentary.* Downers Grove, IL: InterVarsity Press, 1978.

Barnes, Albert. *Notes, Critical, Illustrative, and Practical, on the Book of Daniel.* New York: The World Publishing House, 1877.

Bevan, A. A. *A Short Commentary on the Book of Daniel.* Cambridge, England: Cambridge University Press, 1892.

Boutflower, Charles. *In and Around the Book of Daniel.* Grand Rapids, MI: Zondervan Publishing House, 1963.

Boyer, James L. *Chart of the Period Between the Testaments.* Winona Lake, IN: BMH Books, 1962.

Brooks, Keith L. *The Certain End as Seen by the Prophet Daniel.* Los Angeles, CA: American Prophetic League, 1942.

Brownlee, W. H. Kittim. *The International Standard Bible Encyclopedia.* Grand Rapids, MI: Wm. B. Eerdmans, 1979.

Calvin, John. *Calvin's Commentaries—Daniel Vol. 2.* Grand Rapids, MI: Wm. B. Eerdmans Publishing Company, 1948.

Charles, R. H. *A Critical and Exegetical Commentary on the Book of Daniel.* Oxford, England: Clarendon Press, 1929.

Collins, J. J. *Daniel, with an Introduction to Apocalyptic Literature. The Forms of Old Testament Literature*, Vol. 20. Grand Rapids, MI: Wm. B. Eerdmans, 1984.

Culver, Robert D. *Daniel and the Latter Days.* Westwood, NJ: Fleming H. Revell Co., 1954.

Curtis, E. L. *Daniel. Hastings Dictionary of the Bible.* New York: Charles Scribner's Sons, 1908.

Dean, H. *Old Testament Commentary, Daniel* (Edited by Ellicott). New York: E.P. Dutton, n.d.

Desprez, Philip S. *Daniel, or the Apocalypse of the Old Testament.* London, Edinburgh: Williams and Norgate, 1865.

Dougherty, Raymond P. *Nabonidus and Belshazzar.* New Haven, CT: Yale University Press, 1929.

Dressler, Harold H. P. *The Identification of the Ugaritic DNIL With the Daniel of Ezekiel.* Vetus Testamentum 29 (1979).

Driver, S. R. *The Book of Daniel.* London: Cambridge University Press, 1936.

Emerson, Wallace. *Unlocking the Mysteries of Daniel.* Orange, CA: Promise Publishing Co, 1988.

Farrar, F. W. *The Book of Daniel in the Expositor's Bible.* Vol. 4. New York: George H. Doran Company. W. Robertson Nicoll, ed., n.d.

Fausset, A. R. *The Book of Daniel, Critical and Experimental Commentary.* Vol. IV. Grand Rapids, MI: Wm. B. Eerdmans Publishing Co., reprinted 1948.

Feinberg, Charles Lee. *A Commentary on Daniel.* Winona Lake, IN: BMH Books, 1981.

Ferguson, Sinclair B. *Daniel. The Communicator's Commentary,* Lloyd J. Ogilvie, ed. Waco, TX: Word Books, 1988.

Folsom, Nathaniel S. *Critical and Historical Interpretation of the Prophecies of Daniel.* Boston, MA: Crocker and Brewster, 1842.

Gaebelein, A. C. *The Prophet Daniel,* 14th ed. New York: Our Hope Publishing Co, 1911.

Ginsberg, H. Louis. *Studies in Daniel.* New York: Jewish Theological Seminary of America, 1948.

Goldwurm, Rabbi Hersh. *Daniel/A New Translation with a Commentary Anthologized from Talmudic, Midrashic and Rabbinic Sources.* Artscroll Tanach Series. Brooklyn, New York: Mesorah Publications Ltd., 1980.

Gordon, Sam. *Heaven Rules. Understanding the Dreams of Daniel the Prophet from Babylon.* Belfast, Ireland: Ambassador Productions Ltd., 1991.

Harrison, R. K. *Daniel. The International Standard Bible Encyclopedia.* Grand Rapids, MI: Wm. B. Eerdmans Publishing Co., 1979

Hartman, Louis F. and Alexander A. Di Lella. *The Book of Daniel.* Anchor Bible, no. 23. Garden City, New York: Doubleday and Co., 1978.

Harton, George H. *An Interpretation of Daniel 11:36–45.* Grace Theological Journal 4, no. 2 (Fall 1983).

Hengstenberg, E. W. *Dissertations on the Genuineness of Daniel.* (Translated by B.P. Pratten). Edinburgh, Scotland: T.& T. Clark, 1849.

Howlett, Duncan. *The Essenes and Christianity.* New York: Harper and Row Brothers, 1957.

Ironside, H. A. *Lectures on Daniel the Prophet.* New York: Loizeaux Brothers Inc., 17th ed., 1960.

Irving, Edward. *Babylon and Infidelities Foredoomed of God: a Discourse on the Prophecies of Daniel and the Apocalypse* (2 vols.). Glasgow, Scotland: Chalmers and Collins, 1826.

Jeffery, A. Daniel. *The Interpreter's Bible.* Vol. VI. Edited by George A. Buttrick. New York: Abington Press, 1956.

Josephus, Flavius. *The Works of Flavius Josephus.* Translated by William

Whiston. Grand Rapids, MI: Associated Publishers and Authors, Inc., n.d.

—. *Josephus the Jewish War*. Gaalya Cornfeld, General Editor. Benjamin Mazar, Paul L. Maier, Consulting Editors. Grand Rapids, MI: Zondervan Publishing House, 1982.

Keil, C. F. and Delitzsch, F. *Biblical Commentary on the Book of Daniel*. Biblical Commentary on the Old Testament. Grand Rapids, MI: Wm. B. Eerdmans Publishing Company, 1955.

Kelly, William. *Notes on the Book of Daniel*, 7th ed. New York: Loizeaux Brothers Inc., 1943.

Lacoque, A. *The Book of Daniel*. Translated by David Pellauer. Atlanta, GA: John Knox Press, 1979.

Lang, G. H. *The Histories and Prophecies of Daniel*. Miami Springs, FL: Conley and Schoettle Publishing Co. Inc., 1985.

Larkin, Clarence. *The Book of Daniel*. Philadelphia, PA: Rev. Clarence Larkin Est, 2802 N. Park Ave., 1929, 1949.

Lattey, C. *The Book of Daniel*. Dublin, Ireland: Browne and Nolan, 1948.

Laurence, Richard, (translator). *The Book of Enoch the Prophet*. London, England: Kegan Paul, Trench & Co., 1883.

Leupold, H. C. *Exposition of Daniel*. Grand Rapids, MI: Baker Book House, 1969.

Litch, J. *A Complete Harmony of Daniel and the Apocalypse*. Philadelphia, PA: Claxton, Remsen, and Hoffelfinger, 1873.

Mauro, Philip. *The Seventy Weeks and the Great Tribulation*. Boston, MA: Hamilton Bros., 1923.

McClain, Alva J. *Daniel's Prophecy of the Seventy Weeks*. Grand Rapids, MI: Zondervan Publishing House, 1969.

McDowell, Josh. *Daniel in the Critics' Den*. San Bernadino, CA: Campus Crusade for Christ, 1979.

Mickelson, A. Berkeley. *Daniel and Revelation: Riddles or Realities?* Nashville, TN: Thomas Nelson, 1984.

Millard, A. R. *Daniel 1–6 and History*. The Evangelical Quarterly, 49, no. 2 (April–June), 1977.

Montgomery, James A. *A Critical and Exegetical Commentary on the Book of Daniel*. New York: Charles Scribner and Sons, 1927.

Newell, Philip R. *Daniel, the Man Greatly Beloved and His Prophecies*. Chicago, IL: Moody Press, 1951.

Olyott, Stuart. *Dare to Stand Alone.* Welwyn Commentary Series. Welwyn: Evangelical Press, 1982.

Pettingill, William L. *Simple Studies in Daniel.* Findlay, OH: Fundamental Truth Publishers, n.d.

Philip, James. *By the Rivers of Babylon: Studies in the Book of Daniel.* Aberdeen, Scotland: Didasko Press, 1971.

Poythress, V. S. "Hermeneutical Factors in Determining the Beginning of the Seventy Weeks (Dan. 9:25)." Trinity Journal 6 n.s. (1985): 131–149.

Price, Walter K. *In The Final Days.* Chicago, IL: Moody Press, 1977.

Prince, J. Dyneley. *A Critical Commentary on the Book of Daniel.* New York: Lemcke & Buechner, 1899.

Pusey, E. B. *Daniel the Prophet.* New York: Funk and Wagnalls, 1885.

Robinson, T. *A Homiletic Commentary on the Book of Daniel.The Preacher's Complete Homiletic Commentary on the Old Testament.* New York: Funk and Wagnalls Company, n.d.

Rowe, Robert D. *Is Daniel's 'Son of Man' Messianic?* In *Christ the Lord,* edited by Harold H. Rowden. Downer's Grove, IL: InterVarsity Press, 1982.

Rowley, H. H. *Darius the Mede and the Four World Empires of the Book of Daniel:* A Historical Study of Contemporary Theories. Cardiff: University of Wales Press Board, 1935.

—. *The Relevance of an Apocalyptic: A Study of Jewish and Christian Apocalypses from Daniel to Revelation.* London, England: Lutterworth Press, 1950.

Rushdoony, R. J. *Thy Kingdom Come: Studies in Daniel and Revelation.* Philadelphia, PA: Presbyterian and Reformed Publishing Co., 1971.

Slotki, Judah J. *Daniel, Ezra, Nehemiah, with Hebrew Text and English Translation.* Soncino Books of the Bible: A. Cohen. Gen. Ed. London, England: The Soncino Press, Ltd., 1962.

Smith, R. Payne. *Daniel, an Exposition of the Historical Portion of the Writings of the Prophet Daniel.* New York: Cranston and Curts, n.d.

Stevens, W. C. *The Book of Daniel,* rev. ed. Los Angeles, CA: Bible House of L.A., 1943.

Stuart, Moses. *A Commentary on the Book of Daniel.* Boston, MA: Crocker and Brewster, 1850.

Tanner, Joseph. *Daniel and the Revelation, a Study of the Historical and Futurist Interpretation.* London, England: Hodder and Stoughton, 1898.

Tatford, Frederick A. *The Climax of the Ages, Studies in the Prophecy of Daniel.* Grand Rapids, MI: Zondervan Publishing House, 1964.

Taylor, William M. *Daniel the Beloved.* New York: Harper, 1878.

The Holy Bible. New International Version. New York International Bible Society. Grand Rapids, MI: Zondervan Publishing House, 1978.

Thiele, Edwin R. *The Mysterious Numbers of the Hebrew Kings.* Rev. ed. Grand Rapids, MI: Zondervan Publishing House, 1983.

Thompson, J. E. H. *Daniel, The Pulpit Commentary.* Chicago, IL: Wilcox and Follett Co., 1900.

Thurman, William C. *The Sealed Book of Daniel Opened.* Philadelphia, PA: John Goodyear, 1864.

Tregelles, S. P. *Remarks on the Prophetic Visions in the Book of Daniel.* London, England: Wertheimer, Lea and Co., Publishers, 1883.

Veldkamp, H. *Dreams and Dictators: On the Book of Daniel.* Translated by T. Plantinga. St. Catherines, Ontario, Canada: Paideia, 1979.

Wallace, Ronald S. *The Lord is King: The Message of Daniel.* Downers Grove, IL: Intervarsity Press, 1979.

Walvoord, John F. *A Commentary on Daniel.* Grand Rapids, MI: Wm. B. Eerdmans, 1949.

—. *Daniel: The Key to Prophetic Revelation.* Chicago, IL: Moody Press, 1971.

West, Nathaniel. *Daniel's Great Prophecy, etc..* New York: The Hope of Israel Movement, 1898.

Whitcomb, John C. *Darius the Mede.* Grand Rapids, MI: Wm. B. Eerdmans, 1959.

—. *Daniel.* Chicago, IL: The Moody Press, 1985.

—. *Daniel's Great Seventy-Week Prophecy: An Exegetical Insight.* Grace Theological Journal 2, no. 2. Fall, 1981.

Wilson, Robert D. *The Aramaic of Daniel in Biblical and Theological Studies by Members of the Faculty of Princeton Theological Seminary.* New York: Charles Scribner's Sons, 1912.

—. *Daniel. International Standard Bible Encyclopedia.* Vol II. edited by James Orr. Grand Rapids, MI: Wm. B. Eerdmans Publishing Co., reprinted, 1946.

—. *Studies in the Book of Daniel: A Discussion of the Historical Questions.* New York: G.P. Putnams's Sons, 1917.

—. *Studies in the Book of Daniel: Second Series*. New York: Fleming H. Revell Co., 1938.

Wiseman, D. J., ed. *Notes on Some Problems in the Book of Daniel*. London: Tyndale Press, 1965.

Wood, Leon. *A Commentary on Daniel*. Grand Rapids, MI: Zondervan Publishing Company, 1973.

—. *Daniel: A Study Guide*. Grand Rapids, MI: Zondervan Publishing House, 1975.

Wright, Charles H. H. *Daniel and His Prophecies*. London, England: Williams and Norgate, 1906.

Yamauchi, Edwin Y. *The Archaeological Background of Daniel*. Bibliotheca Sacra 137, no. 545 (January-March), 1981.

Young, Edward J. *The Prophecy of Daniel*. Grand Rapids, MI: Wm. B. Eerdmans, 1949.

Zocler, Otto, and Strong, James. *Lange's Commentary, the Book of Daniel*. New York: Charles Scribner's Sons, 1915.